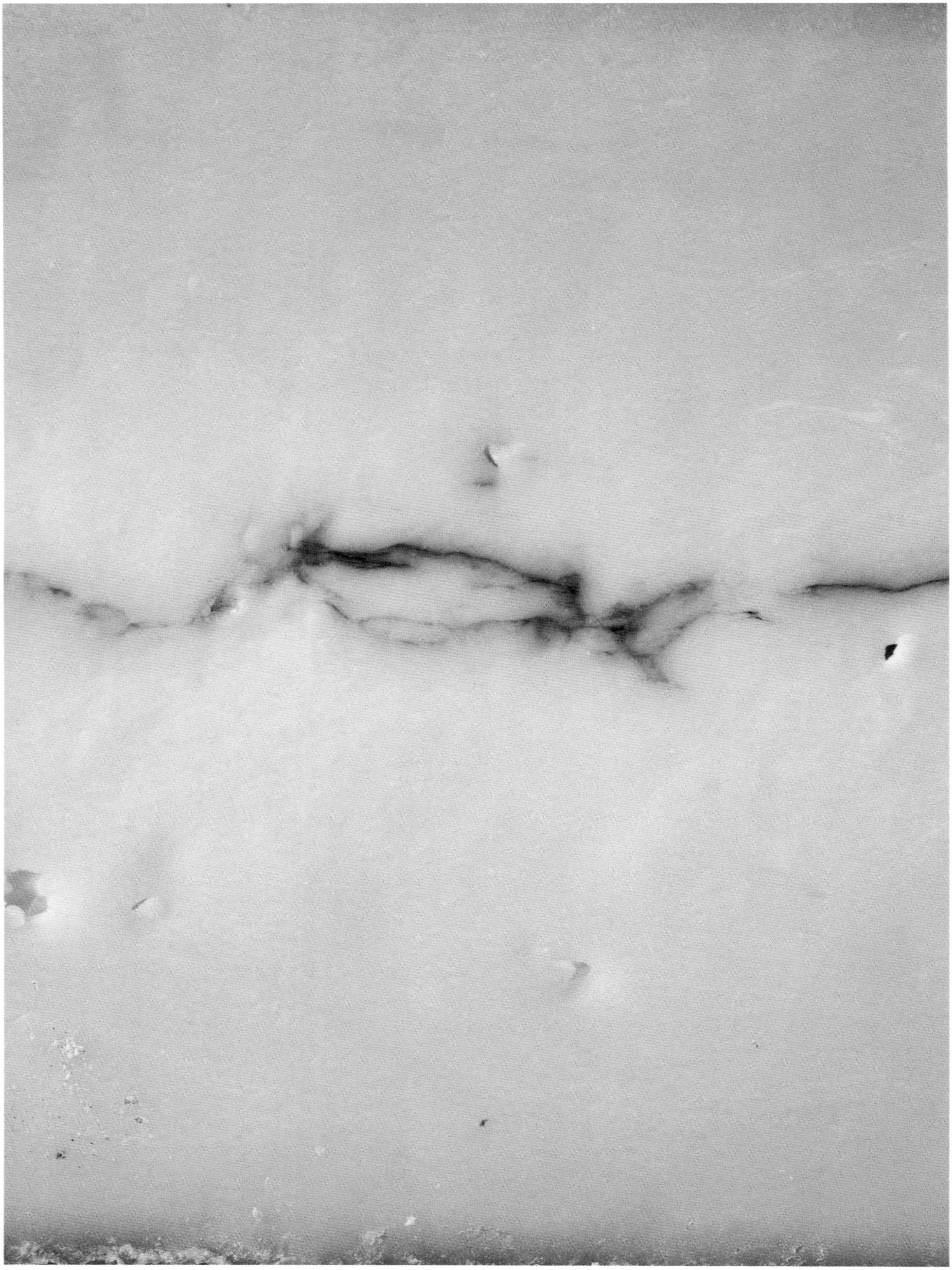

JAMES MARTIN

Cheese

100 ULTIMATE RECIPES FOR CHEESE LOVERS

PHOTOGRAPHY BY DAN JONES

quadrille

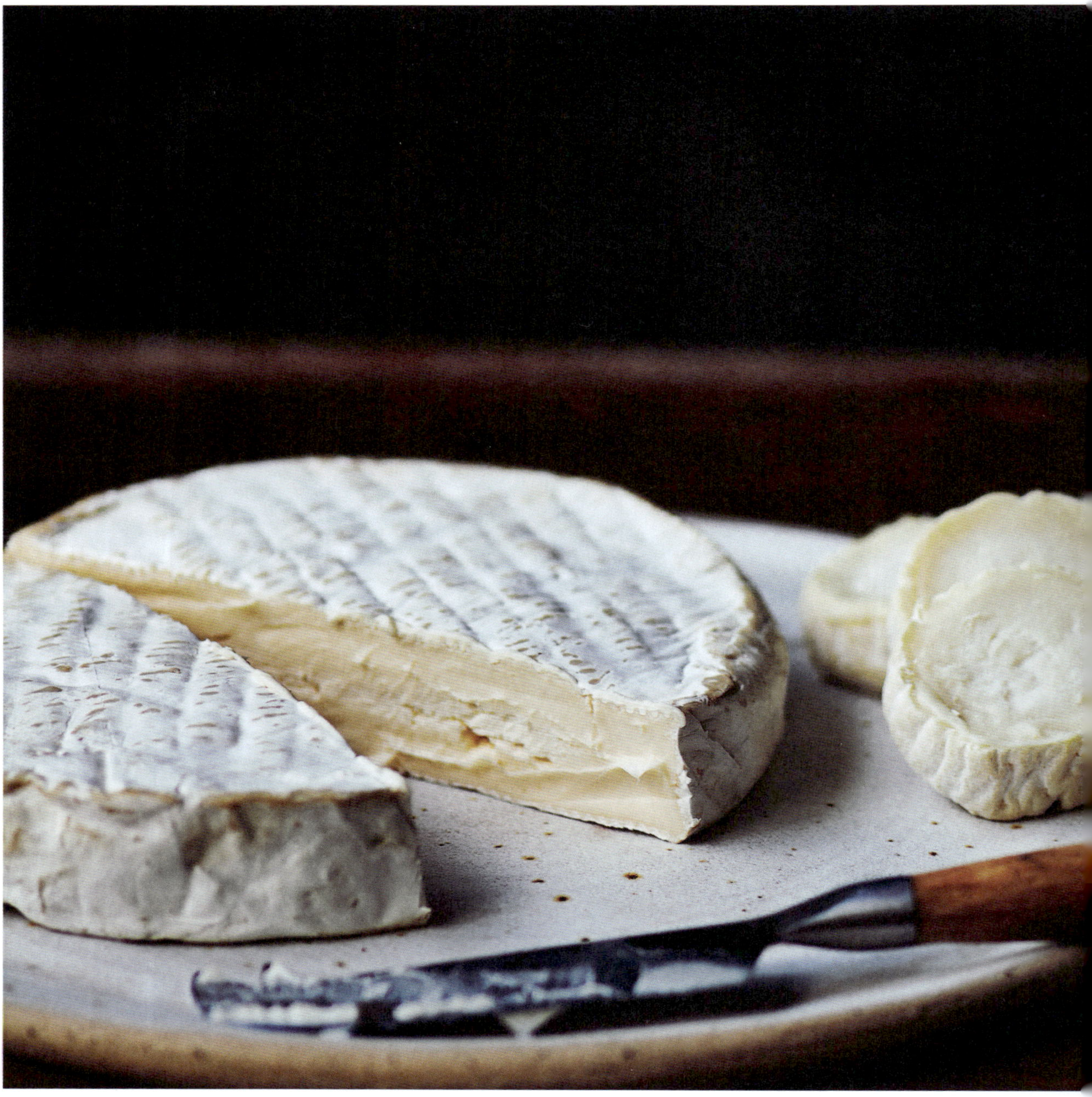

CONTENTS

INTRODUCTION 6
SMALL PLATES AND SNACKS 14
MAINS 102
ON THE SIDE 182
SWEET 198
INDEX 217
ACONWLEDGEMENTS 222

INTRODUCTION

Cheese is an everyday kitchen hero. You probably have at least one type in your fridge right now, whether it's a nugget of Cheddar, a block of Parmesan for grating over your pasta or half a tub of creamy mascarpone. Found at every mealtime, from cheesy waffles for breakfast to a classic Welsh rarebit for lunch, mac and cheese for a comforting dinner, and even cheesecakes and sweet bakes to round off the day for dessert, it's an ever-present, incredibly varied and supremely versatile ingredient.

By most estimates there are nearly 2,000 types of cheese to be found across the globe and there is an almost infinite variety of flavours and textures. Made from cow's, goat's, sheep's and even buffalo's milk in the case of some types of mozzarella, the different methods of production result in a product that can be hard or soft, creamy or tangy and even almost bitter in the case of some blue cheeses. (For more on types of cheese, see pages 12–13.) While we might think of cheese as more of a key ingredient in European cooking, particularly the cuisines of France, Italy and Spain, it still features in recipes from further afield. For example, paneer has a starring role in Indian curries – often paired with spinach for sag paneer or bathed in a buttery sauce as in my recipe, which I've shared later in this book.

With so many different varieties, the culinary usages for cheese are almost limitless. From the everyday to the extraordinary, cheese recipes range from the simple to the cordon bleu. Cheese can be the star of the show, as in the case of salads showcasing luscious balls of burrata or a slab of feta atop a Greek salad, or the final flourish as a grating of Parmesan lifts a bowl of risotto or pasta to the next level, while a cheesy lid or toast is the crowning glory on a bowl of French onion soup. And, of course, there's the ultimate showcase for the best cheese you can lay your hands on – the cheeseboard. The perfect way to round off a meal or to enjoy as a deliciously simple lunch, pick a selection of cheeses and enjoy them with complementary accompaniments like crackers, pickled onions and figs. For inspiration, see my Best-ever Cheeseboard (page 18).

And don't make the mistake of thinking cheese is confined to the savoury. Mascarpone is a vital part of a classic tiramisu, while no New York cheesecake is complete without a good portion of full-fat cream cheese to make its signature creamy filling. Even blue cheese makes an appearance, the mild and sweet Dolcelatte creating the perfect sauce to partner succulent poached pears.

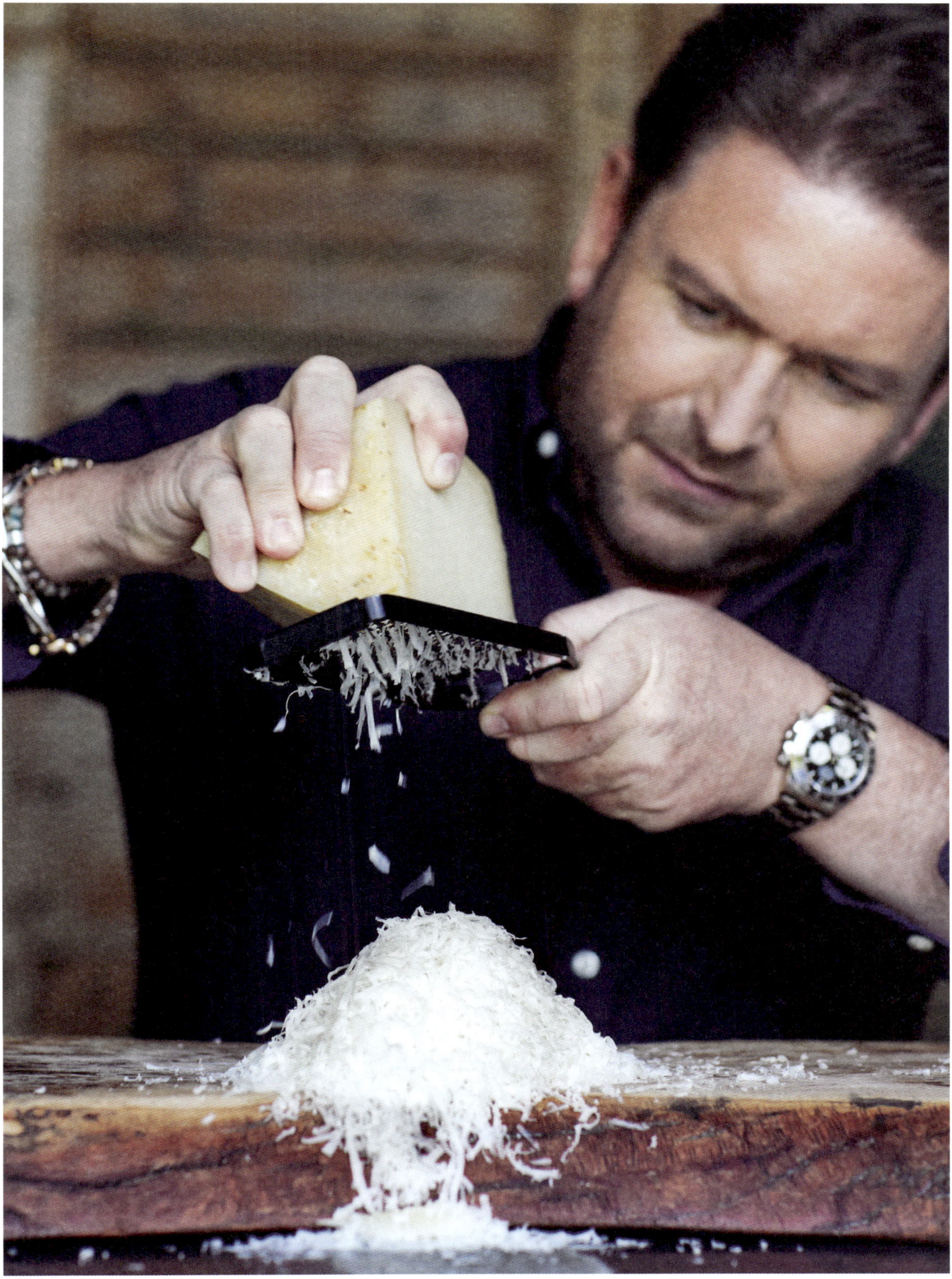

My own love affair with cheese started with my grandma's Cheddar scones. She would make them by hand, loaded with grated cheese, and I would eat them straight out of the oven, split and thickly buttered. They were totally delicious and as light as a feather. Another early memory was eating cheese and Yorkshire Brack with my grandfather for supper – don't knock it until you've tried it!

Once I started working in the restaurant world, my eyes were opened up to the pleasures of cheeses from all over Europe. I've been lucky enough to visit some of these producers while filming my adventures. A particular stand out was a visit to an old French army barracks on the Swiss-France border that housed 90,000 Comté cheeses – it was off the charts! Another memorable trip was to a family-run farm making Manchego, set in the most beautiful location surrounded by nut and apricot trees. They had nine dogs, all of which enjoyed the cheese too!

Perhaps the country that first springs to mind when thinking about cheese is France. Whether it's a crusty baguette with a wedge of Brie or that ultimate cheesy mashed potato dish, Aligot, made with Tomme d'Auvergne or Tomme de l'Aubrac, the use of cheese in French cuisine goes from the simple to the sublime. If you fancy mastering the rise of a double-baked cheese soufflé or the ease of oven-baking Camembert in its box, either solo or studded with bacon and rosemary, you'll find recipes inspired by the French love affair with cheese scattered throughout the pages of this book.

In a recent journey across Spain, I sampled tapas plates featuring slices of Manchego, alone or alongside membrillo or some locally produced ham, or used to fill another ever-present favourite – croquetas. See my Spanish Salad and croquetas recipes for ways to enjoy one of Spain's most famous culinary exports.
Italy offers a vast array of cheeses, from creamy burrata and mozzarella, to nutty Taleggio, hard varieties like Parmigiano Reggiano and Pecorino Romano and blues such as Dolcelatte and Gorgonzola. The ways of using cheese are as varied as the types on offer – stir it through and use to adorn risotto, roll it into gnocchi, stuff it into ravioli or cannelloni or tear over to top a classic Margherita pizza.

But you don't need to leave these shores to find truly great cheese and some of my favourite varieties are produced right here in the UK. While perhaps our most famous exports are Cheddar and Stilton, we also boast Tunworth – a soft, creamy cheese to rival the very best French Camembert – and you can even find the UK's own buffalo's milk mozzarella made by Laverstoke Park Farm in Hampshire.

I have attended and worked at the International Cheese & Dairy Awards (ICDA) for the last ten years and even been a judge. It's such a treat to try and taste new cheeses from independent producers alongside those from world-class manufacturers. Working on the Saturday show (ITV's James Martin's Saturday Morning), I've been lucky enough to be able to feature some incredible cheese producers from this country – small artisan makers who work incredibly hard and are so passionate about their cheeses. I have to mention Sonia and Mario from Yorkshire Pecorino who make the most delicious Italian-style cheeses, but in West Yorkshire. Giel from Cornish Gouda in Looe saved his family's farm aged 17 when they were going to close down as milk prices were so poor; Giel learned how to make Gouda cheese and they have gone from strength to strength selling stunning cheeses. Doddington's in Berwick, Northumberland produce a fabulous cheese washed in Newcastle Brown Ale and, finally, Greg at Sharpham's cheese, who I've worked with for many years, offers a fabulous variety of cheeses – some of which you'll spot throughout this book.

From well-loved classics to cheesy new twists, salads to soups, pies to pasta, or coating a rack of lamb to filling a crusty cob, I hope these recipes inspire you to try new cheeses, as well as finding new and exciting ways to enjoy much-loved favourites.

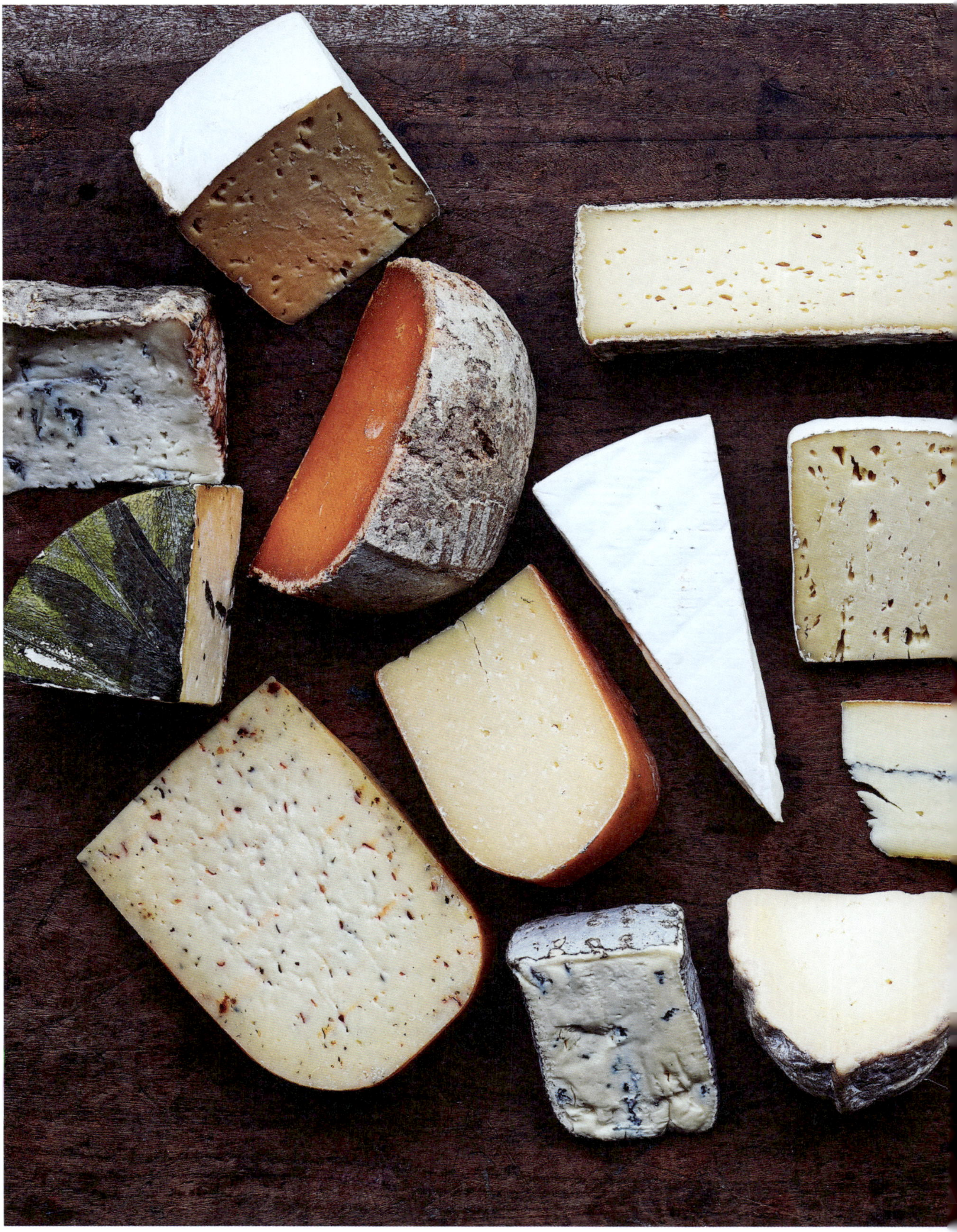

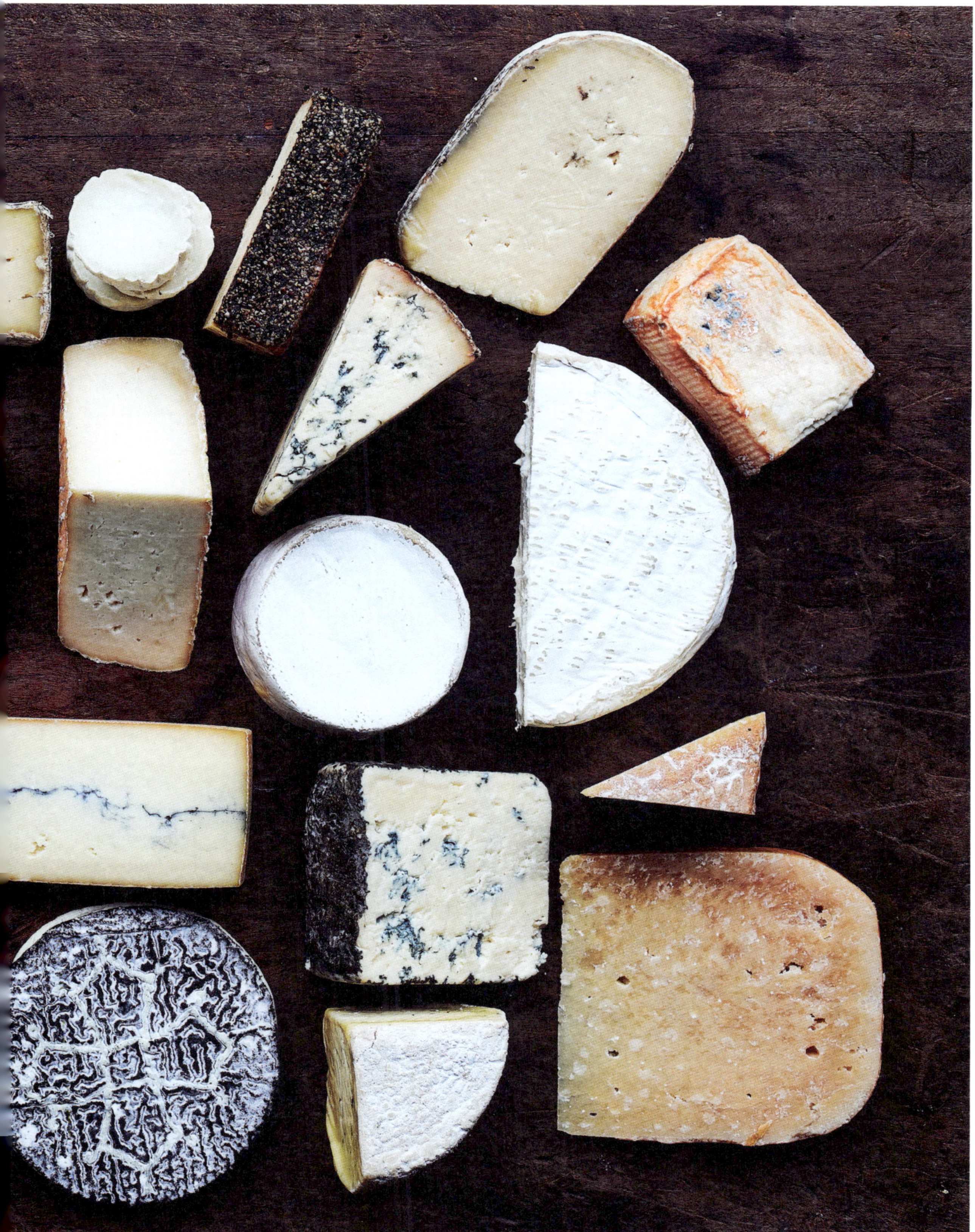

CHEESE VARIETIES

The cheeses I've used in this book fall into four broad categories: hard, soft, blue, and goat's and sheep's cheese. Most can be enjoyed both raw and cooked, although a few, such as halloumi, do need to be cooked, or are more enjoyable that way, like paneer. I've suggested substitutes if you don't have a certain cheese to hand – when switching bear in mind both the flavour and texture of the cheese.

HARD
Parmesan – Italian cheese made from cow's milk and aged for at least 10 months. Parmigiano Reggiano is Parmesan that has been aged for at least a year and up to three years. Most often used to top pasta and risotto, or for cheese sauces.
Substitute – Grana Padano or Pecorino Romano.

Grana Padano – originating from northern Italy and similar to Parmesan but with less strict regulations governing its production.
Substitute – Parmesan or Pecorino Romano.

Cheddar – the UK's most popular cheese, made from cow's milk and ranging in flavour from mild to sharp and tangy.
Substitute – Red Leicester is moister but with a milder flavour. Try Parmesan for cheese sauces.

Red Leicester – another popular English cow's milk cheese with a distinctive reddish orange colour.
Substitute – Cheddar.

Wensleydale – crumbly, slightly sweet English cheese made from cow's milk.
Substitute – Cheshire or Caerphilly, which are similar in both texture and taste.

Gruyère – hard cow's milk cheese with a nutty flavour produced near La Gruyère in Switzerland and in the alpine Comté and Savoie regions of eastern France.
Substitute – Comté or Emmental.

Comté – French alpine cow's milk cheese.
Substitute – Gruyère is the best replacement, but you could also try Emmental or Fontina.

Gouda – distinctive Dutch semi-hard cheese made from cow's milk.
Substitute – Emmental or Edam.

Tomme – semi-hard cheese produced mainly in the French Alps and Switzerland from cow's, ewe's or goat's milk.
Substitute – it can be hard to find a good replacement – firm mozzarella is often used, or Cantal, a French cheese.

Provolone – Italian semi-hard cow's milk cheese, often in a distictive pear, sausage or cone shape.
Substitute – another mild white cheese such as mozzarella or Manchego.

SOFT
Ricotta – a creamy cheese made from sheep's, cow's, goat's or water buffalo's milk and used for both sweet and savoury dishes.
Substitute – mascarpone, full-fat cream cheese. For savoury dishes, try goat's or sheep's curd.

Mascarpone – mild and creamy Italian cheese found in pastas, risotto and puddings.
Substitute – ricotta or full-fat cream cheese. You could also try goat's or sheep's curd for some savoury dishes, but these will impart a stronger flavour.

Mozzarella – made from cow's or buffalo's milk, the most common fresh version is used raw in salads or to finish off pizzas and other oven-bakes. There's also a firm version, which can be grated.

Substitute – burrata is similar to the fresh type, but wetter in texture and more luscious in flavour, so a better substitute in salads than bakes.

Burrata – a creamier version of fresh mozzarella, filled with soft curds and cream (straciatella).
Substitute – mozzarella, although it won't give you quite the same luxurious creaminess.

Brie – soft cow's milk cheese with a white rind.
Substitute – Camembert or Tunworth both provide a similar texture and flavour profile.

Camembert – moist and creamy French cheese made from cow's milk with a white rind.
Substitute – Brie or Tunworth.

Tunworth – an English soft cheese, with a wrinkled white rind.
Substitute – Camembert or Brie.

Paneer – Indian cow's or buffalo's milk cheese.
Substitute – halloumi has a similar texture and flavour.

Taleggio – semi-soft Italian cheese often melted into or onto dishes, or used in bakes.
Substitute – Camembert or Brie are similar in texture but with arguably stronger flavours. Fontina also works well.

Cream cheese – I always use full-fat cream cheese for both flavour and texture. If you're heating the cream cheese, the fat content ensures that it doesn't split.
Substitute – ricotta or mascarpone.

BLUE
Stilton – semi-soft crumbly English cheese, most often with blue-green veins (although a white version is also available).
Substitute – Gorgonzola is similar.

Dolcelatte – creamy, soft Italian blue cheese made from cow's milk.
Substitute – Gorgonzola dolce, though it has a less firm texture and a stronger flavour.

Gorgonzola – another Italian blue cow's milk cheese that comes in two varieties: dolce (sweet) and piccante (spicy). The first is soft, buttery and creamy, while piccante is firmer and crumblier.
Substitute – Stilton or Dolcelatte where you would use dolce and Roquefort for piccante.

GOAT'S AND SHEEP'S
Goat's cheese – goat's milk cheese can be soft and creamy, sometimes coated in ash or with a rind, or a hard cheese.
Substitute – ricotta, feta or mascarpone would all work instead of soft goat's cheese; try Pecorino Romano in place of hard.

Feta – one of Greece's most famous exports, made from sheep's or a mixture of sheep's and goat's milk.
Substitute – halloumi, although this will need to be cooked if used to top salads.

Halloumi – Cypriot cheese made from a mixture of goat's and sheep's milk, although it does sometimes include cow's milk. It has a high melting point so holds its texture well and is great grilled or turned into fries (see page 69).
Substitute – paneer has a similar texture though isn't quite as firm.

Pecorino Romano – an Italian cheese similar in texture to Parmesan but made from sheep's milk.
Substitute – Parmesan, Grana Padano or Manchego.

Manchego – semi-soft cheese made in the La Mancha region of Spain from the milk of Manchega sheep.
Substitute – Pecorino Romano or Parmesan.

SMALL PLATES AND SNACKS

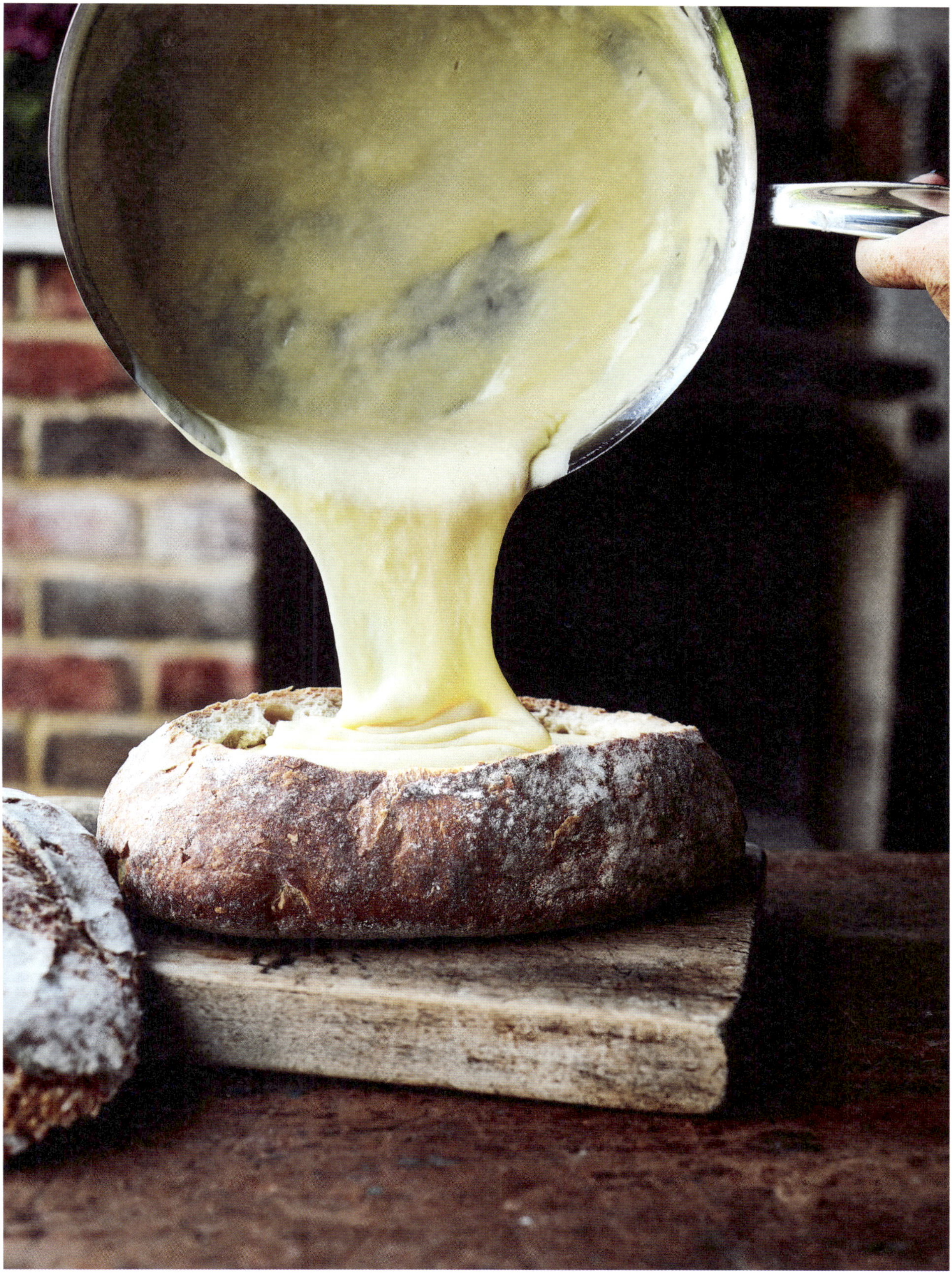

BAKED CAMEMBERT WITH BACON, PEAR CHUTNEY AND WALNUT SALAD
\
SERVES 4

2 Camemberts, in wooden boxes
8 slices of streaky bacon
a few sprigs of rosemary

FOR THE CHUTNEY
50g caster sugar
1 shallot, diced
2 garlic cloves, grated
2 pears, peeled and diced
50g sultanas
2cm piece of fresh ginger, grated
25ml white wine vinegar
sea salt and freshly ground black pepper

FOR THE DRESSING
50ml walnut oil
1 tablespoon white wine vinegar
1 teaspoon Dijon mustard
1 teaspoon water

TO SERVE
50g salad leaves
50g croutons
25g walnut halves

One of the simplest ways to enjoy Camember is to stud it with rosemary and bacon and bake it in its box. The result is molten deliciousness, which works perfectly alongside a simple salad, and a homemade chutney to cut through the creamy richness.

Preheat the oven to 220°C (200°C fan)/425°F/gas 7.

To make the chutney, heat a non-stick pan over a medium heat and, when hot, add the sugar. Do not stir but carefully swirl in the pan until the sugar is brown and caramelised. This should take about 3–4 minutes. Once the sugar has caramelised, add the remaining ingredients and bring to the boil. Remove from the heat and leave to cool completely.

Take the Camemberts out of their wrapping, and discard the paper. Cut the top off both cheeses, pop the bacon and rosemary on top and place the cheeses back into the wooden boxes (lids off). Transfer to a baking tray and bake for 12–14 minutes until the cheeses are hot and bubbling and the bacon is crisp.

For the dressing, whisk all the ingredients together in a bowl. Put the salad leaves, croutons and walnuts in a bowl, spoon over the dressing and toss together.

To serve, pop the cheeses onto a plate or board with the chutney and salad.

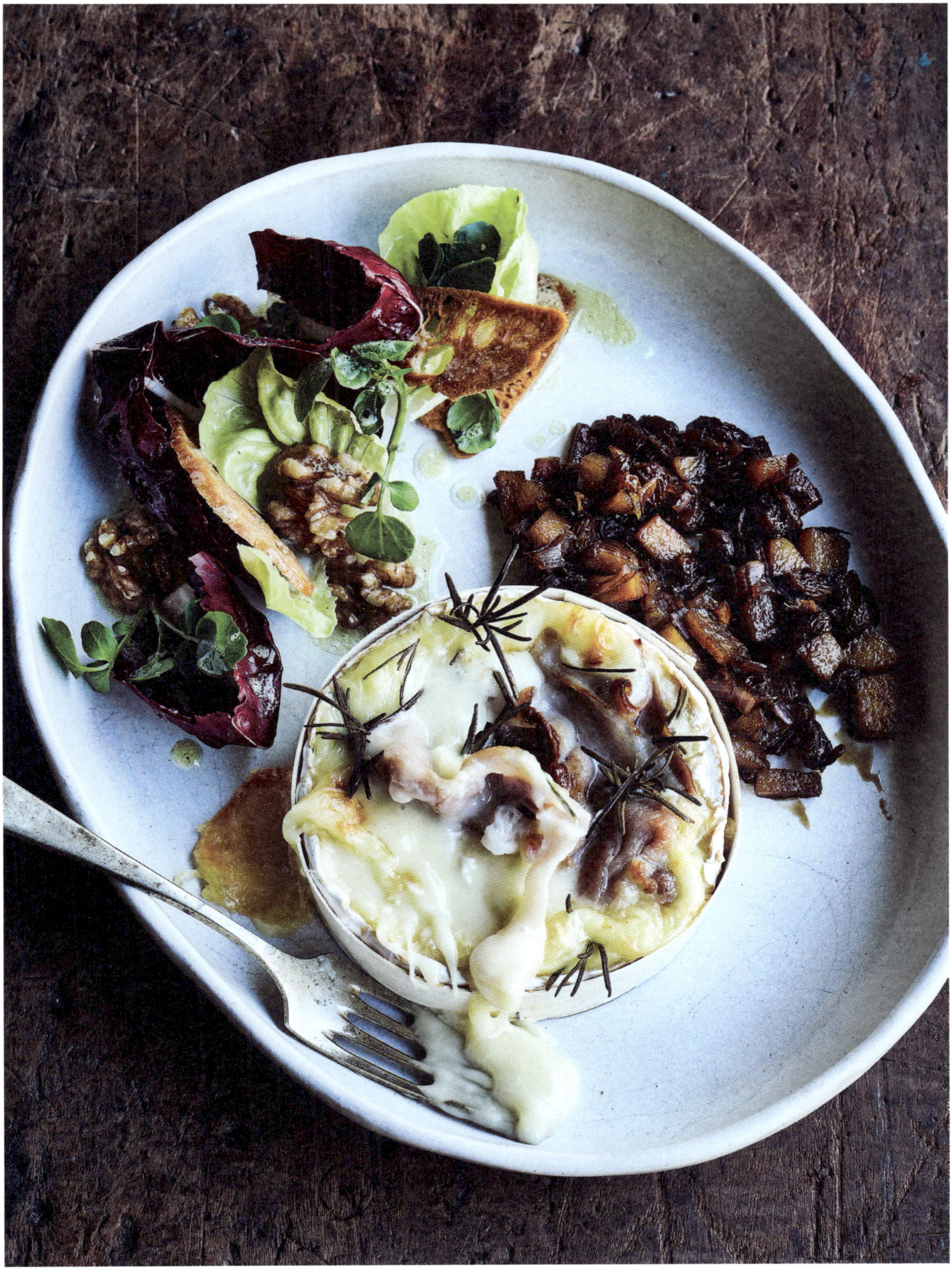

BEST-EVER CHEESEBOARD
\
SERVES 8

2 x 250g blocks of halloumi, sliced in half
1 teaspoon olive oil

FOR THE CHUTNEY
100g caster sugar
100g dark soft brown sugar
1 onion, sliced
100ml white wine vinegar
100g sultanas
250g fresh gooseberries

FOR THE VINE-LEAF BAKED CHEESE
6 fresh vine leaves
200g Sharpham Savour, cut into chunks
25ml Sauternes
100ml double cream
6 slices of speck

FOR THE ROSEMARY-BAKED CHEESE
2 Tunworth
freshly ground black pepper
a few sprigs of rosemary

FOR THE FRIED CHEESE
200g Sharpham Elmhirst
50g plain flour, seasoned
2 eggs, beaten
75g panko breadcrumbs

SUGGESTIONS TO SERVE
fresh vine leaves
Montagnolo Affine
honey and clover Gouda
Doddington Hotspur
Admiral Collingwood
figs, halved
pickled onions
crackers

A cheeseboard is the ultimate way to finish a meal in style or to showcase your favourite cheeses for a lighter bite. If you can't find those listed to serve, you can subsitute them with similar cheeses, but try to keep the mixture of soft, hard and blue the same.

Preheat the oven to 200°C (180°C fan)/400°F/gas 6.

To make the chutney, heat a non-stick pan over a medium heat and, when hot, add both sugars. Do not stir but carefully swirl in the pan until the sugars are brown and caramelised. This should take about 3–4 minutes. Once the sugars have caramelised, add the remaining ingredients and bring to the boil. Reduce the heat and simmer for 15 minutes. Remove from the heat and leave to cool.

First, to make the vine-leaf baked cheese, line a 20 x 15cm x 7cm deep ovenproof dish with the vine leaves. Pack in the cheese and pour over the wine and cream. Top with the ham and bake on the top shelf of the oven for 15 minutes.

Next, for the rosemary-baked cheese, slice the top off the cheeses and pop them into a 10cm round ovenproof dish, 3cm deep. Crack over black pepper and stud with the rosemary. Bake on the middle shelf of the oven for 10 minutes.

Place the halloumi on a griddle pan, drizzle in the oil and cook on both sides for 1–2 minutes.

Finally, for the fried cheese, heat a small pan of vegetable oil to 170°C (340°F). Dip the cheese in the flour, then the beaten egg and the panko breadcrumbs. Fry for about 1 minute until golden and crispy.

To serve, cover a very large board in fresh vine leaves, then position the Montagnolo, Gouda, Hotspur and Admiral Collingwood on the board. Add the two baked cheeses, the fried cheese and halloumi all over the board. Garnish with halved figs, pickled onions, small pots of the chutney and some crackers.

Pictured overleaf

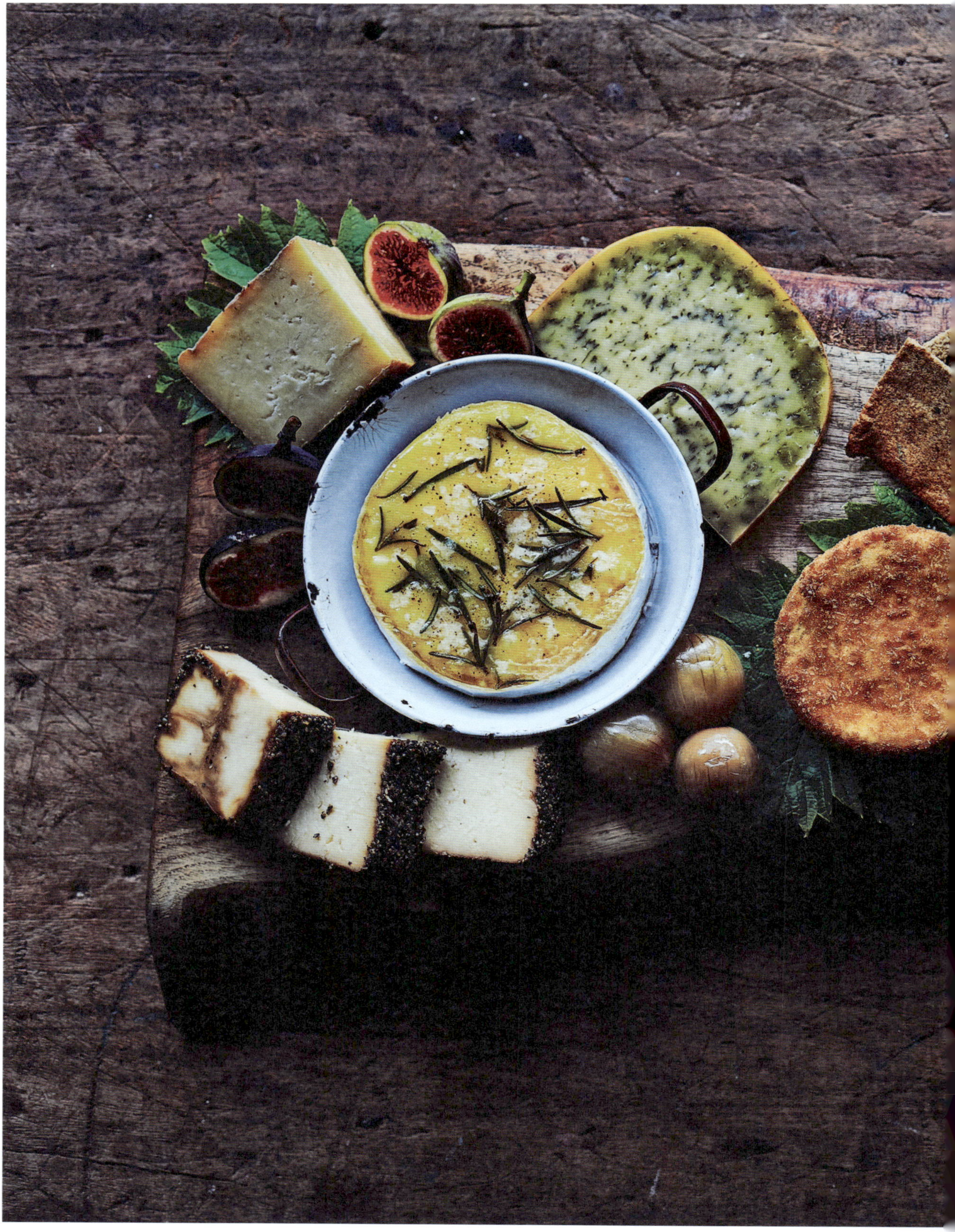

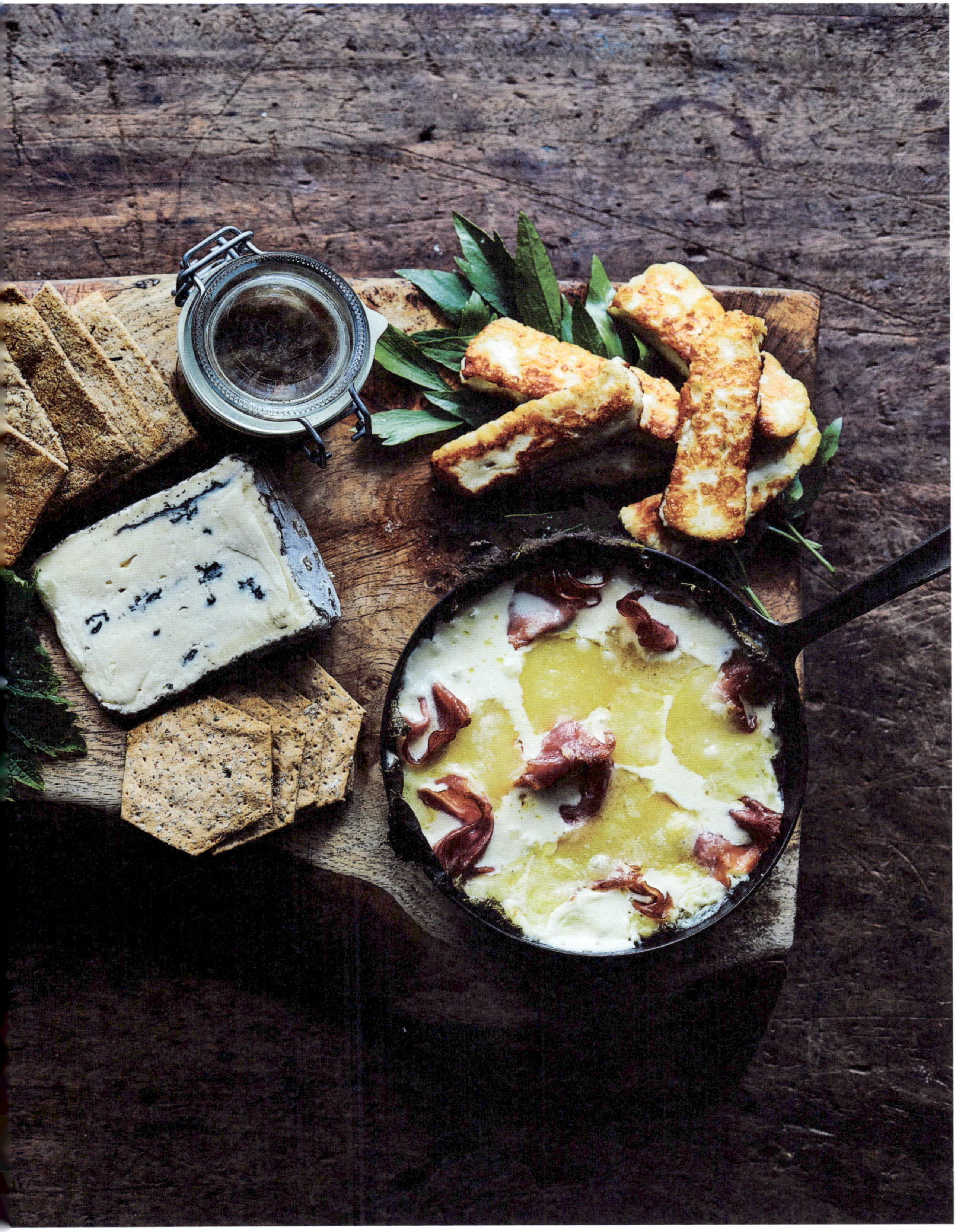

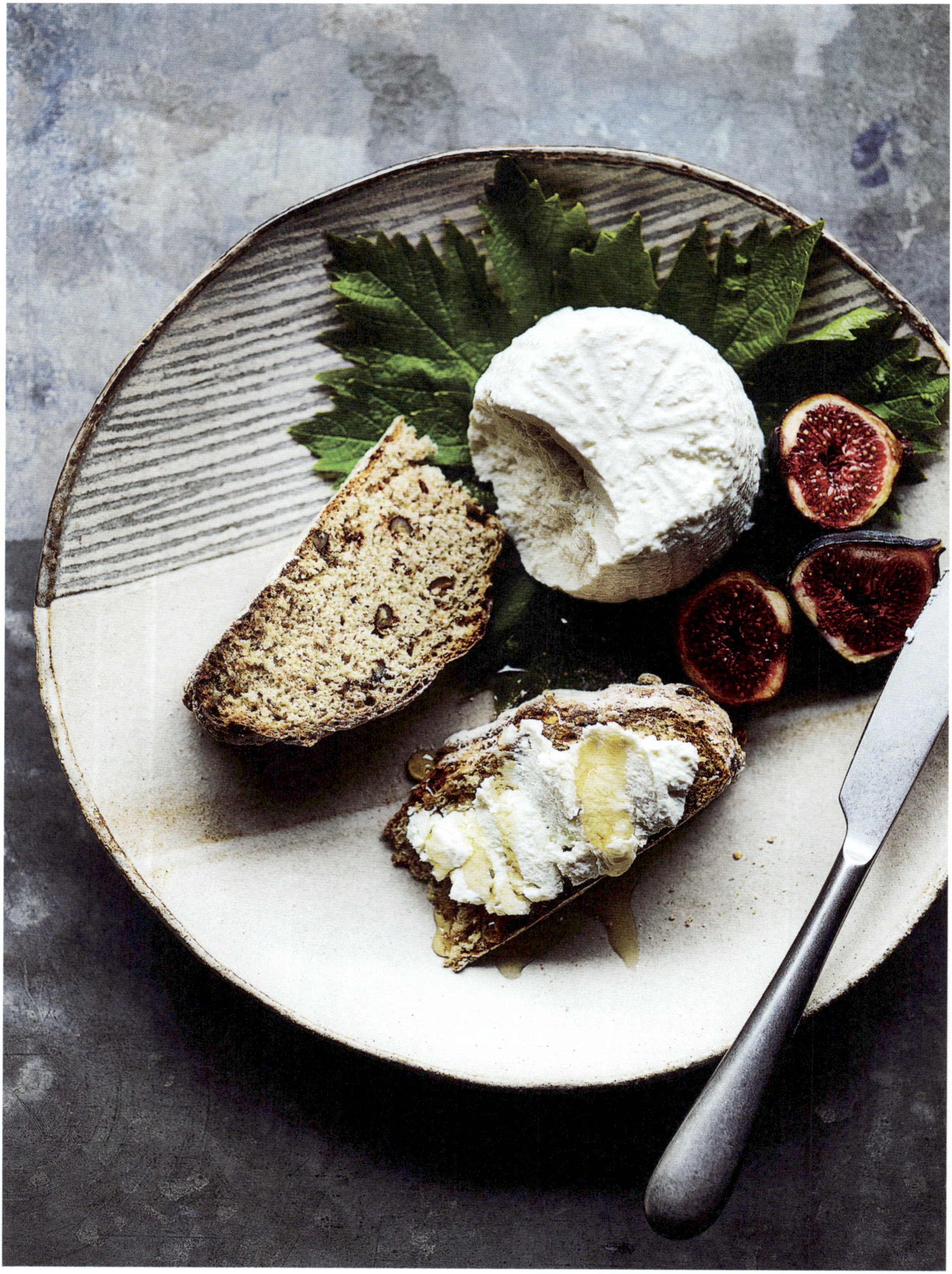

RICOTTA WITH FIGS AND PECAN SODA BREAD
\
SERVES 4

vine leaves (optional)
300g fresh ricotta
4 figs, halved
2 tablespoons runny honey

FOR THE PECAN SODA BREAD
170g wholemeal self-raising flour
170g plain flour, plus extra for dusting
½ teaspoon salt
1 teaspoon bicarbonate of soda
300ml buttermilk
100g pecans, chopped

Fresh, creamy ricotta works wonderfully spread on bread and here the nuttiness of the pecan soda bread provides the perfect flavour and texture combination. Drizzled with honey and accompanied with juicy figs, it's a simple but nonetheless luxurious light bite.

Preheat the oven to 200°C (180°C fan)/400°F/gas 6.

Put all the soda bread ingredients in a large bowl and mix by hand to form a dough. On a floured work surface, divide the dough in two, then shape into circles and push down. They should be 15cm round and 8cm deep. Dust a baking tray with flour and transfer the loaves to the tray. Dust with a little flour and cut a cross onto the top of each one. Bake for 15–20 minutes until the bottoms are crisp.

Arrange the vine leaves (if using) onto plates, top with ricotta and pop the figs on the side. Sit the wedges of soda bread alongside too, then smother in ricotta and drizzle over the honey.

CHEESE AND THYME STRAWS
\
SERVES 6–8

250g plain flour, plus extra for dusting
250g cold butter, diced
½ teaspoon salt
125ml cold water
1 egg, beaten
50g Parmigiano Reggiano or Parmesan, grated
50g Cheddar, grated
a few sprigs of thyme, leaves picked

Cheddar and Parmesan are a great cheesy pairing and work well with the thyme in these flaky straws. You could use all Cheddar or all Parmesan for a simpler flavour. Or change it up with Comté, Gruyère or Manchego.

To make the pastry, place the flour in a mound on a work surface. Make a deep well, add the butter and salt and, using your fingertips, work the ingredients together, drawing more flour into the well. Work the mixture until all the ingredients are combined but you can still see lumps of butter.

Gradually add the cold water and mix to form a rough dough. Shape the dough into a ball, wrap in clingfilm and chill in the fridge for 20 minutes.

When the dough is chilled, roll out onto a lightly floured work surface into a 40 x 20cm rectangle. With the short end facing you, fold into three as if you were folding a letter. Give a quarter turn, repeat the folding and then chill for 30 minutes. Repeat this process twice more and chill for a final 30 minutes.

Preheat the oven to 200°C (180°C fan)/400°F/gas 6.

On a lightly floured surface, roll out the dough into a large rectangle, about 30 x 20cm. To make the straws, brush the dough all over with the beaten egg and sprinkle over the Parmesan, Cheddar and thyme. Cut into 2cm-wide strips, then twist each one and pop onto a non-stick baking sheet. Bake for 8–10 minutes.

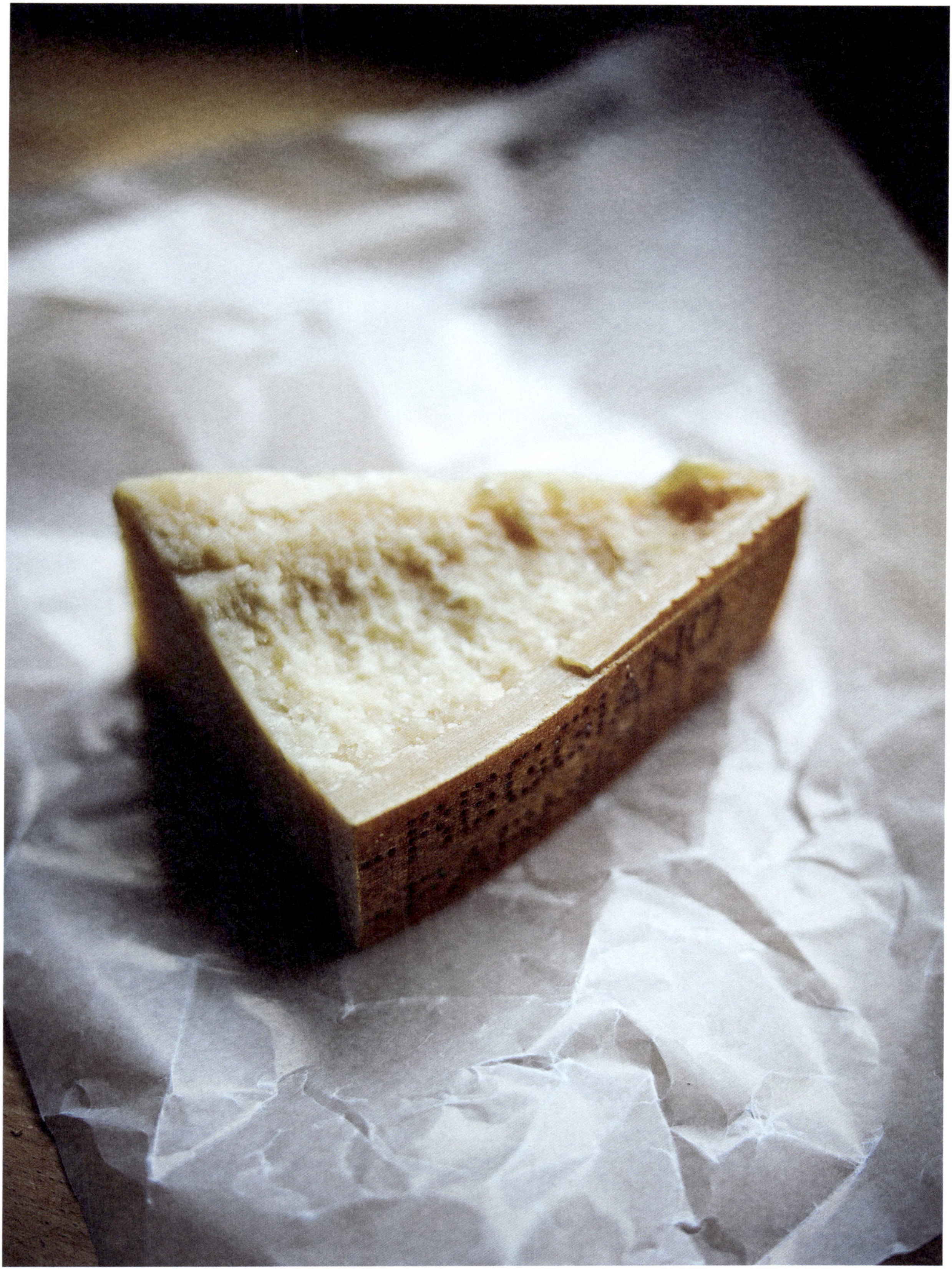

LARGE CHEESE, PANCETTA AND HAM TOASTIE
\
SERVES 8

30 slices of pancetta
vegetable oil, for cooking
1 oblong sourdough loaf
12 slices of good-quality ham

FOR THE SAUCE
25g butter
15g plain flour
100ml full-fat milk
150ml double cream
400g Cheddar, grated
freshly ground black pepper
1 small bunch of flat-leaf parsley

A childhood favourite, this cheese toastie is elevated with both ham and pancetta, as well as parsley, to cut through the richness of the cheesy sauce.

Preheat the oven to 200°C (180°C fan)/400°F/gas 6.

In a frying pan over a medium heat, fry the pancetta in a drizzle of vegetable oil until crisp. Set aside while you make the sauce.

Heat a pan over a medium heat, add the butter and, when foaming, whisk in the flour and cook out for a minute or two. Then whisk in the milk, cream and two-thirds of the grated Cheddar. When it is bubbling, take off the heat and season with pepper.

Cut the bread into 1cm slices, from the top to the bottom, just going 90 per cent through, so you don't quite reach the bottom. Place a large rectangular piece of baking parchment on a large rectangular piece of foil and sit the bread on top. Spoon the sauce in between each slice and fill with the ham, pancetta and parsley. Spoon over the remaining sauce and sprinkle the rest of the grated cheese over the top. Wrap the bread up tightly in the foil and bake in the oven for 15–20 minutes.

Remove from the oven and unwrap the loaf, cut the slices right through and serve immediately.

CHEESE AND PICKLE PIES
\
SERVES 12

1 x 450g jar of Branston pickle
150g firm mozzarella, grated
150g Cheddar, grated

FOR THE PASTRY
400g plain flour, plus extra for dusting
200g butter, plus extra for greasing
1 teaspoon salt
2 eggs, 1 whole, 1 beaten

TO SERVE
chutney (see pages 16 and 18 for homemade)
pickled onions
celery
tomatoes
pears

Cheese and pickle is a classic combination more usually found in a sandwich than encased in shortcrust pastry. These pies pair not one but two cheeses with tangy Branston for a different take on the duo.

Preheat the oven to 160°C (140°C fan)/325°F/gas 3. Grease a 12-hole muffin tin.

For the shortcrust pastry, place the flour in a bowl, add the butter and salt and rub between your fingers until the mixture looks like coarse breadcrumbs. Add the whole egg and mix with your fingers. Knead on a lightly floured surface until smooth, wrap in clingfilm and chill in the fridge for 30 minutes.

Roll out the pastry on a lightly floured surface and cut out 12 circles to fill the holes of the muffin tin. Re-roll the offcuts and cut out 12 lids to cover each of the pies.

Fill each pie with pickle and some of the cheeses, then brush the edges with beaten egg and top each one with a pastry lid. Cut a slit in each lid to allow steam to escape during cooking.

Bake for 30 minutes until golden. Serve with chutney, pickled onions, celery, tomatoes and pears.

Pictured overleaf

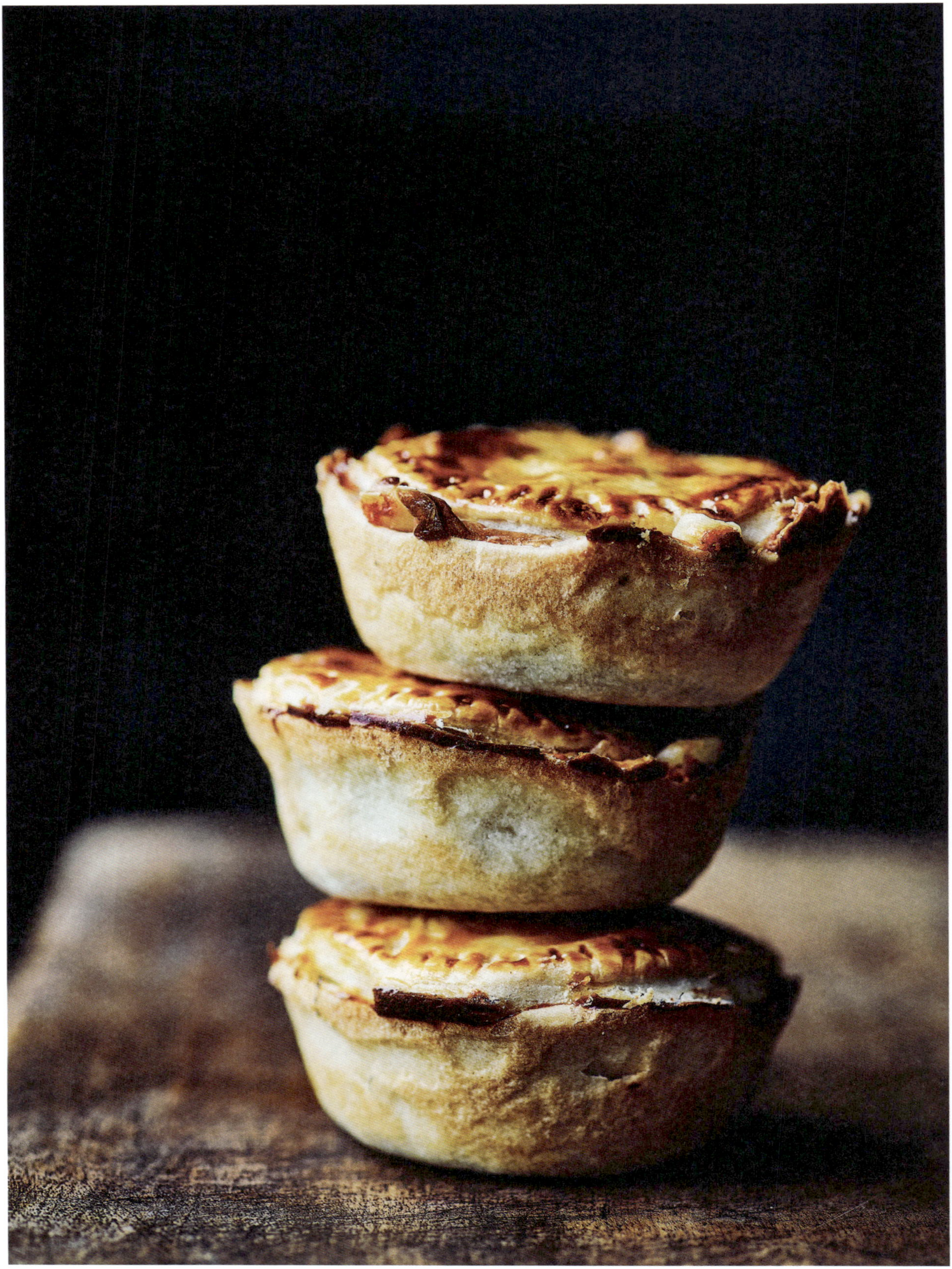

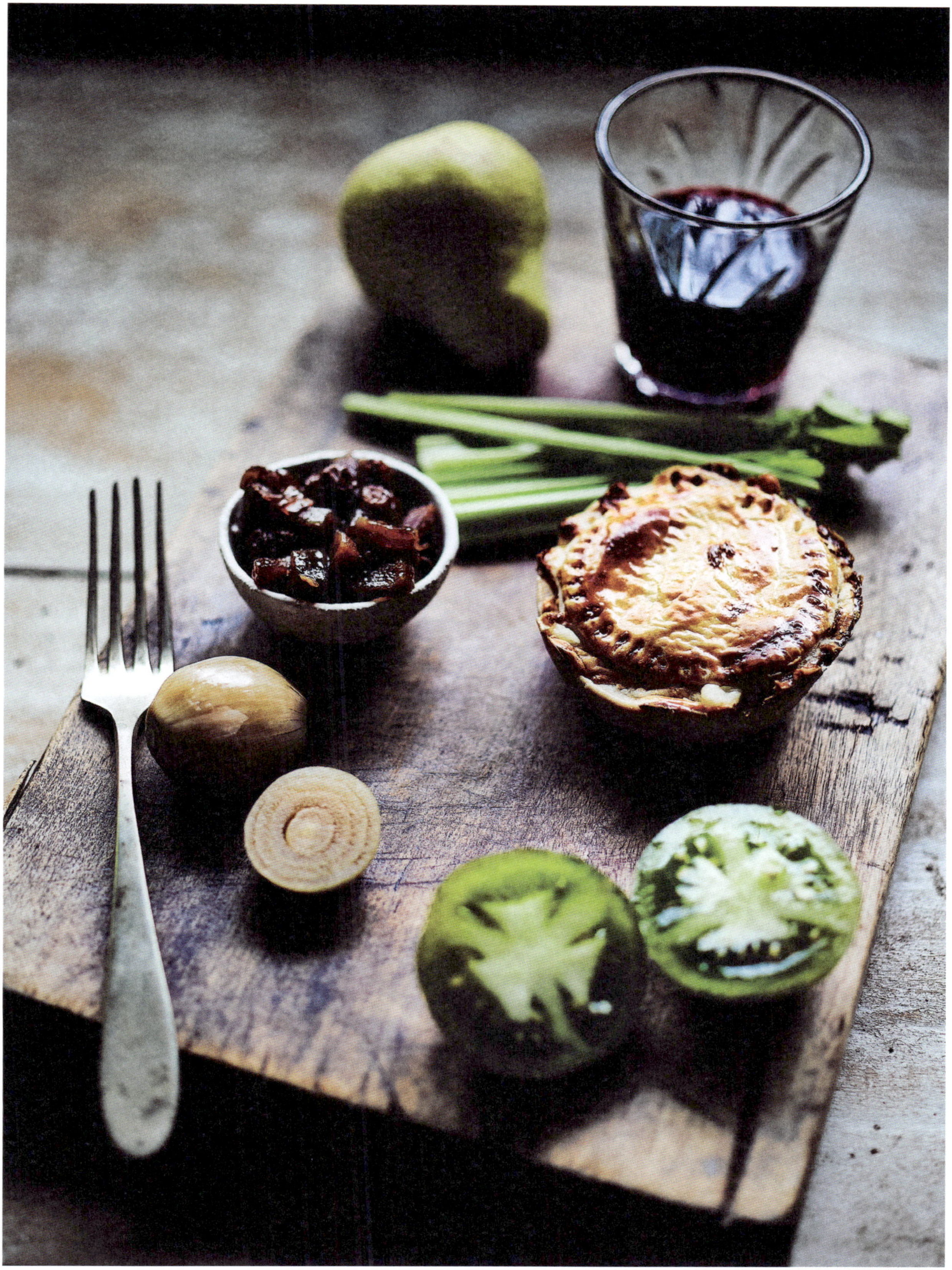

BUFFALO CHICKEN WINGS WITH CRUMBLED BLUE CHEESE

\
SERVES 4

1kg chicken wings
4 tablespoons koji paste
2 litres vegetable oil

FOR THE SAUCE
125ml sriracha sauce
100ml runny honey
125g butter
1 teaspoon onion powder
1 teaspoon garlic powder
juice of 1 lime

TO SERVE
100g Stilton, crumbled
a few chives, chopped
3 spring onions, sliced
1 green chilli, sliced

Blue cheese is often crumbled over dishes to finish and provide an extra layer of flavour and these spicy buffalo chicken wings are a prime example. If you haven't got Stilton, then Gorgonzola or Roquefort would work equally well here.

Coat the chicken wings in the koji and leave to marinate in the fridge for 1 hour.

In a deep-fat fryer or deep saucepan, heat the oil to 160°C (325°F). Pat the chicken dry with kitchen paper and deep-fry in batches for 6–8 minutes until crisp and golden.

Place all the ingredients for the sauce in a pan over a medium heat and bring to the boil. Use to coat the chicken wings as soon as they are cooked.

To serve, transfer the wings to a platter and sprinkle with the Stilton, chives, spring onions and chilli. This recipe will make a lot of sauce, so leftovers can be kept in an airtight jar in the fridge for up to a month.

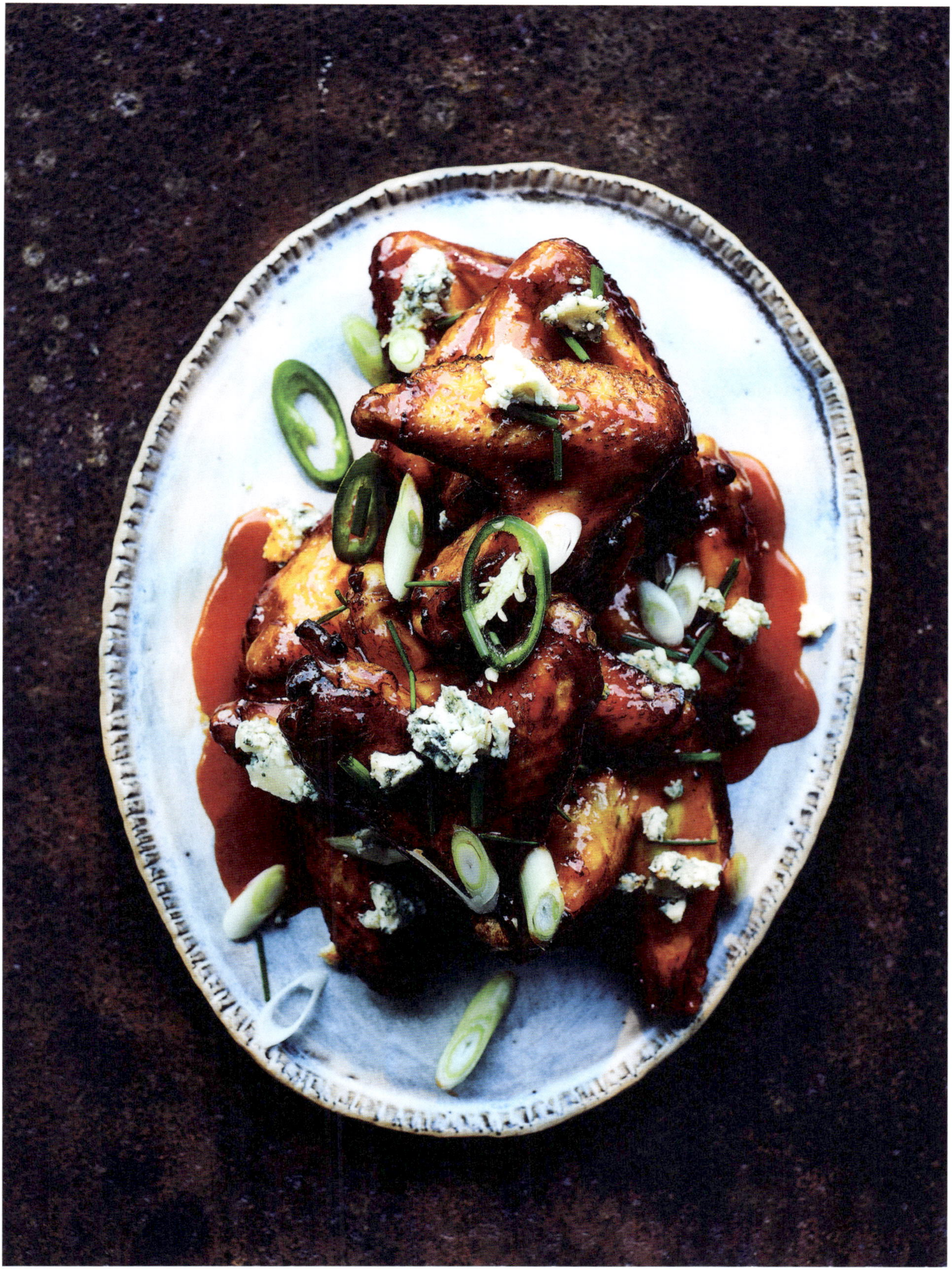

STRAWBERRIES AND MOZZARELLA WITH MINT PESTO
\
SERVES 4

500g hulled strawberries, half left whole and half sliced
50ml sweet wine

FOR THE MOZZARELLA CREAM
300g mozzarella
50ml full-fat milk
1 tablespoon white wine vinegar
1 tablespoon extra virgin olive oil
pinch of salt
200ml double cream, whipped

FOR THE PESTO
½ small bunch of basil, leaves picked
½ bunch of mint, leaves picked
40g caster sugar
40g pine nuts
20g Parmesan, finely grated
75ml extra virgin olive oil
pinch of salt

This simple but exquisite dish showcases mozzarella at its best. A mixture of mozzarella and cream, the cheese is used as a canvas for perfectly ripe strawberries and nutty mint pesto.

In a bowl, marinate the whole strawberries in the wine for 15 minutes. Then mix in the sliced strawberries.

In a blender, blend the mozzarella, milk, vinegar, oil and salt until smooth. Fold into the whipped cream.

Blitz all the ingredients together for the mint pesto.

To serve, spoon the cream onto plates, top with the strawberries and their juices, then the mint pesto.

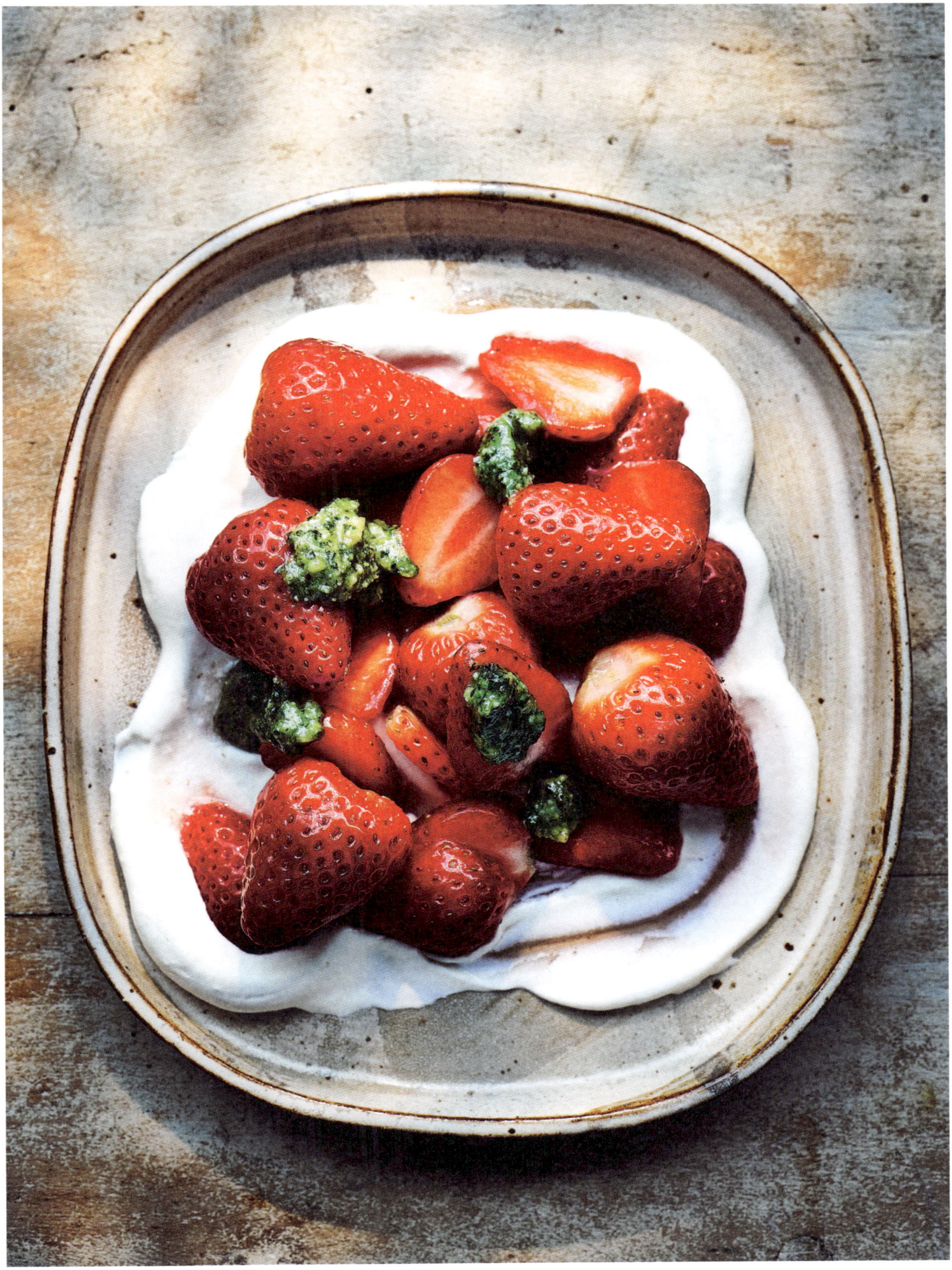

CHEESE, HAM AND TOMATO SANDWICH
\
SERVES 2

3 tomatoes
a few sprigs of thyme
100g butter
12 slices of pancetta
2 eggs
50ml full-fat milk
3 slices of sourdough bread
6 slices of Gruyère, rind removed
3 slices of Brie
50ml maple syrup
sea salt and freshly ground
　black pepper

A universally popular sandwich filling, this combines not one but two types of cheese with pancetta and tomato. The Gruyère and Brie complement and contrast each other without competing and both melt well when toasted.

Preheat the oven to 170°C (150°C fan)/340°F/gas 3½.

Slice the tomatoes in half horizontally and pop on a baking tray, cut-side up. Season, sprinkle with the thyme, dot with a little of the butter and bake for 1 hour.

To make the sandwich, fry the pancetta in a pan over a high heat until crisp.

Beat the eggs and milk together in a bowl. Layer up a slice of bread with both cheeses, top with a second slice of bread, then add the baked tomatoes and crispy pancetta. Finally, top with the remaining slice of bread and push down. Dip the sandwich in the egg mixture and pan-fry in the remaining butter over a medium heat until golden and crisp on both sides.

Drizzle over the maple syrup and serve.

GOUDA AND CHEDDAR CHEESE SCONES
\
MAKES 12

450g strong white bread flour, plus extra for dusting
2 teaspoons baking powder
pinch of salt
100g cold butter, diced
300ml full-fat milk
175g Cheddar, grated
125g Gouda, grated
a few sprigs of thyme, leaves picked
1 egg, beaten with a splash of milk
butter, to serve

A cheese scone is a simple way to enjoy cheese and while this recipe uses both Cheddar and Gouda, you could just use all of one type if you prefer. Feel free to experiment with other hard cheeses too – try Gruyère or Emmental.

Preheat the oven to 220°C (200°C fan)/425°F/gas 7.

Mix the flour, baking powder and salt together in a large bowl, then add the butter and, using your fingertips, rub it in until the mixture resembles breadcrumbs. Add the milk, 100g of the Cheddar, 50g of the Gouda and the thyme and mix until you have a smooth dough.

Roll out the dough on a lightly floured surface until 2cm thick. Cut out scones using a 7cm cutter. Re-roll the offcuts and repeat – you will get 12 scones. Transfer to a baking tray and brush the tops of the scones with the beaten egg mixture. Scatter over the remaining cheeses.

Bake for 10–12 minutes, then remove from the oven and allow to cool slightly. Alternatively, you can pop the scones in the fridge until you are ready to bake, or freeze, then defrost and bake as above.

Split and butter to serve.

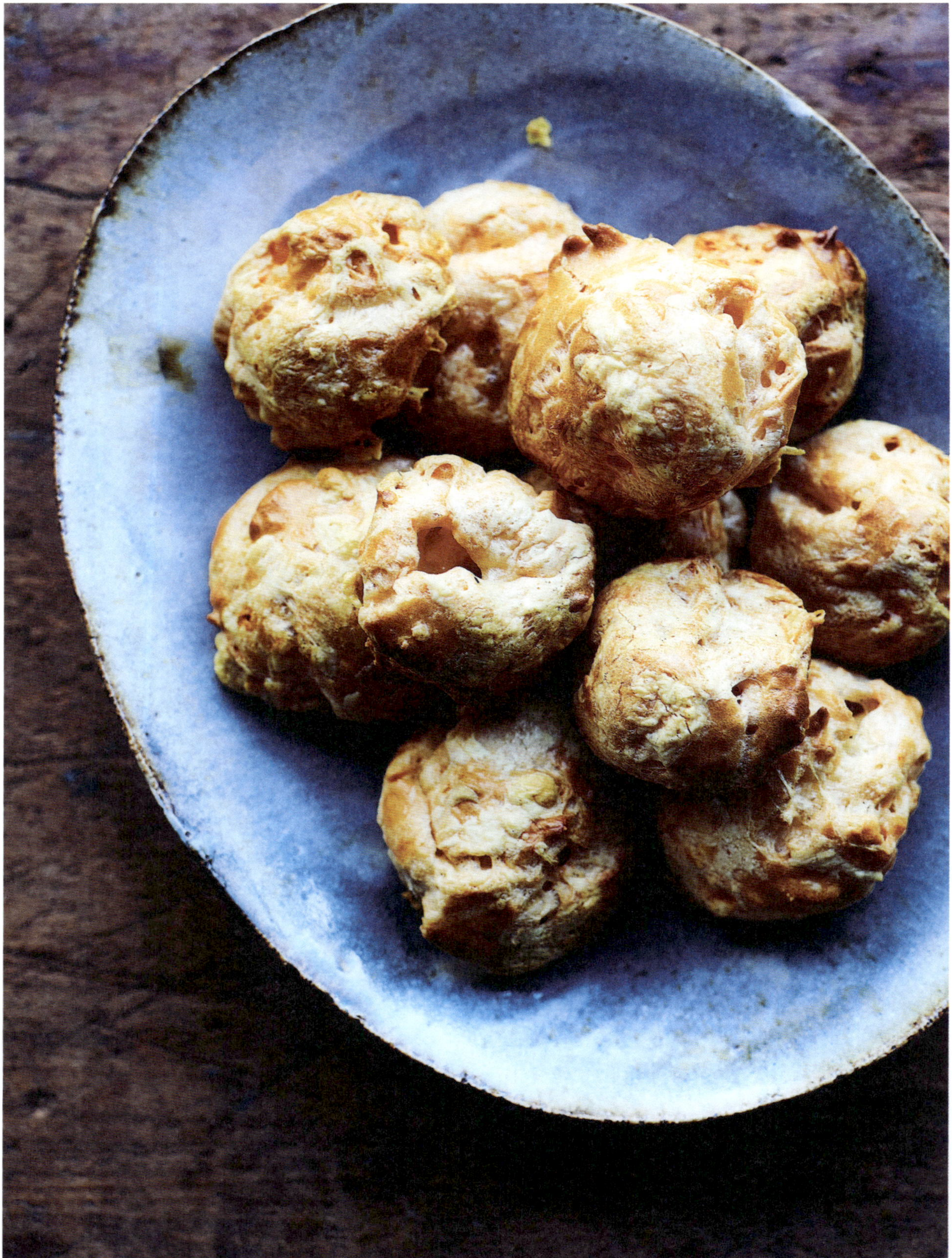

CHEESE GOUGÈRES
\
SERVES 8

200ml water
85g butter
115g plain flour
pinch of salt
3 eggs
150g Gruyère, grated
pinch of cayenne pepper

A gougère is a French baked savoury choux pastry where the dough has been mixed with cheese. Gruyère is commonly used, as I've done here, but Comté and Emmental are other popular options.

Heat the water and butter in a saucepan until the butter has melted.

Beat in the flour and salt until the mixture is smooth, then continue to cook for 2–3 minutes. Remove the pan from the heat and beat in the eggs, one at a time, until smooth and glossy. Set aside to cool.

Preheat the oven to 200°C (180°C fan)/400°F/gas 6. Line a baking tray with baking parchment.

Next, beat 100g of the cheese and the cayenne pepper into the cooled mixture and transfer to a piping bag. Pipe small circles onto the prepared baking tray. Sprinkle over the remaining 50g cheese, then bake for 15 minutes until golden and crispy. Serve warm.

HAZELNUT-FRIED BRIE WITH RHUBARB CHUTNEY
\
SERVES 4

vegetable oil, for frying
50g hazelnuts, blitzed to a crumb
75g panko breadcrumbs
50g plain flour, seasoned
2 eggs, beaten
2 x 200g Brie

FOR THE CHUTNEY
100g demerara sugar
100ml white wine vinegar
1 onion, diced
3 rhubarb sticks, diced
100g sultanas

TO SERVE
crackers
celery tops and sticks
grapes

Brie is wonderful melted and what better way to enjoy it than to encase it in hazelnut breadcrumbs and fry it to create the perfect crispy coating to contrast the oozing cheese? The rhubarb chutney provides an ideal accompaniment.

For the chutney, heat a non-stick pan over a medium heat and, when hot, add the sugar. Do not stir but carefully swirl in the pan until the sugar is brown and caramelised. This should take about 3–4 minutes. Once the sugar has caramelised, add the remaining ingredients and cook for 5 minutes. Remove from the heat and leave to cool.

For the brie, heat a small pan of vegetable oil to 170°C (340°F). Mix the hazelnuts through the panko breadcrumbs in a bowl. Then put the flour and beaten egg in another two separate bowls. Dip the Brie in the flour, then the beaten egg and finally in the breadcrumb mixture. Fry the Brie in the hot vegetable oil for about 1 minute on all sides until golden and crispy.

Serve the Brie with the chutney, some crackers, celery and grapes.

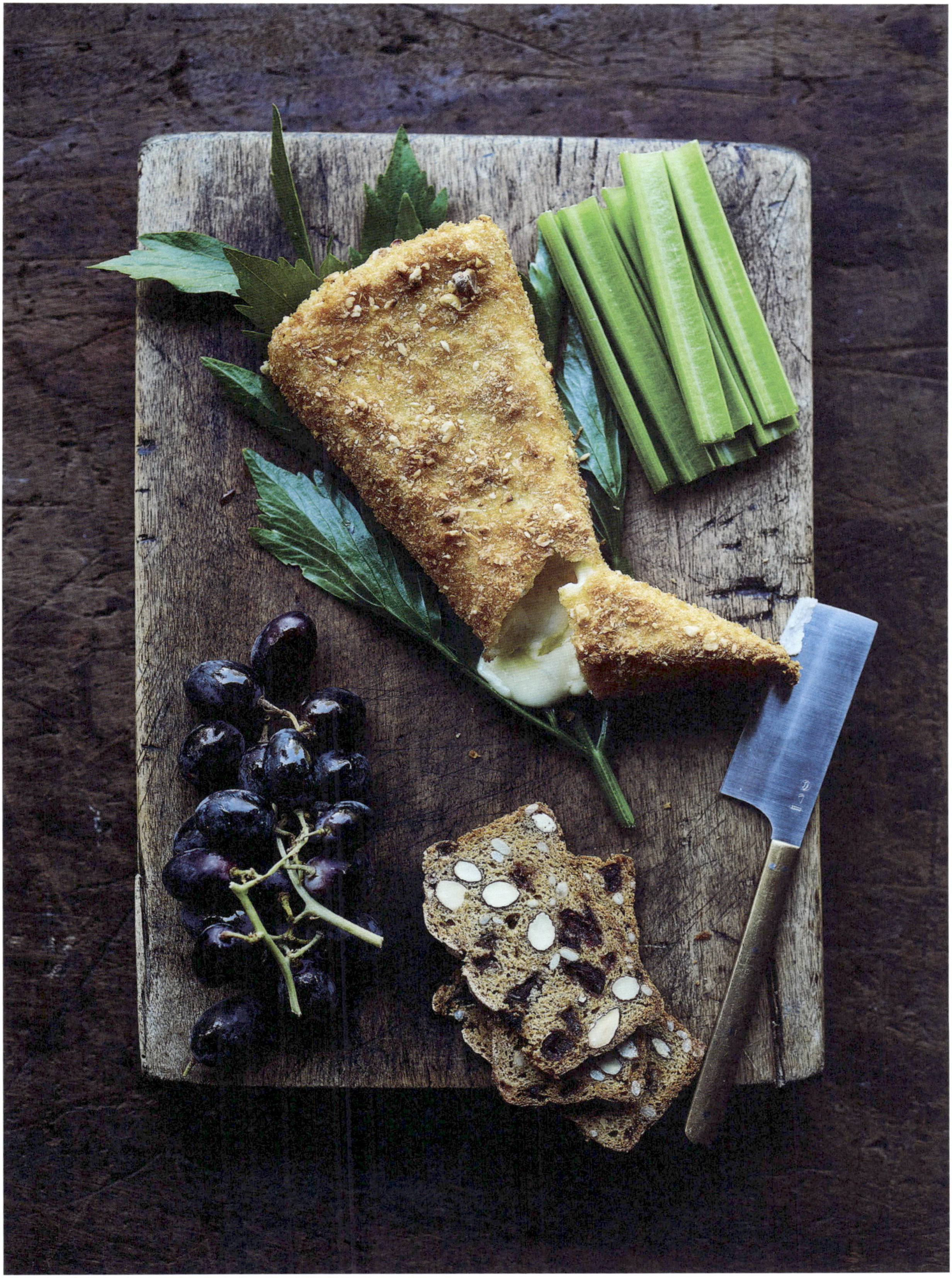

COMTÉ SOUFFLÉ
\
SERVES 8

100g butter, plus extra for greasing
150g plain flour
600ml full-fat milk
300g Comté, grated
120g egg yolks (about 5 egg yolks)
20g Dijon mustard
1 teaspoon salt
260g egg whites (about 10 egg whites), at room temperature
½ teaspoon cream of tartar
semolina, for dusting

This simple soufflé features Comté as the star of the show but you could easily change it up with a different hard cheese – Gruyère, Manchego or Cheddar would all take it in a slightly different flavour direction.

Preheat the oven to 170°C (150°C fan)/340°F/gas 3½.

Melt the butter in a large pan over a medium heat until foaming, then add the flour and cook out for 2–3 minutes. Whisk in the milk and bring to the boil. Remove from the heat and fold in the grated cheese as the mixture is cooling. Then fold in the egg yolks, Dijon mustard and salt until smooth.

In a bowl, softly whip the egg whites and cream of tartar until they reach a ribbon consistency, then fold the whipped egg white into the cheese mixture in three batches, incorporating each batch evenly before adding the next. Transfer the mixture to a piping bag.

Butter eight cold dariole moulds or ramekins and dust with fine semolina. Tap each mould on the work surface to get rid of any excess semolina. Pipe the mixture evenly between the moulds, tap on a cloth to level the mixture and use a palette knife to give an even finish.

Transfer the moulds to a roasting tin and fill halfway up the sides of the moulds with water. Bake for 25 minutes, or until risen and golden on top. Serve immediately.

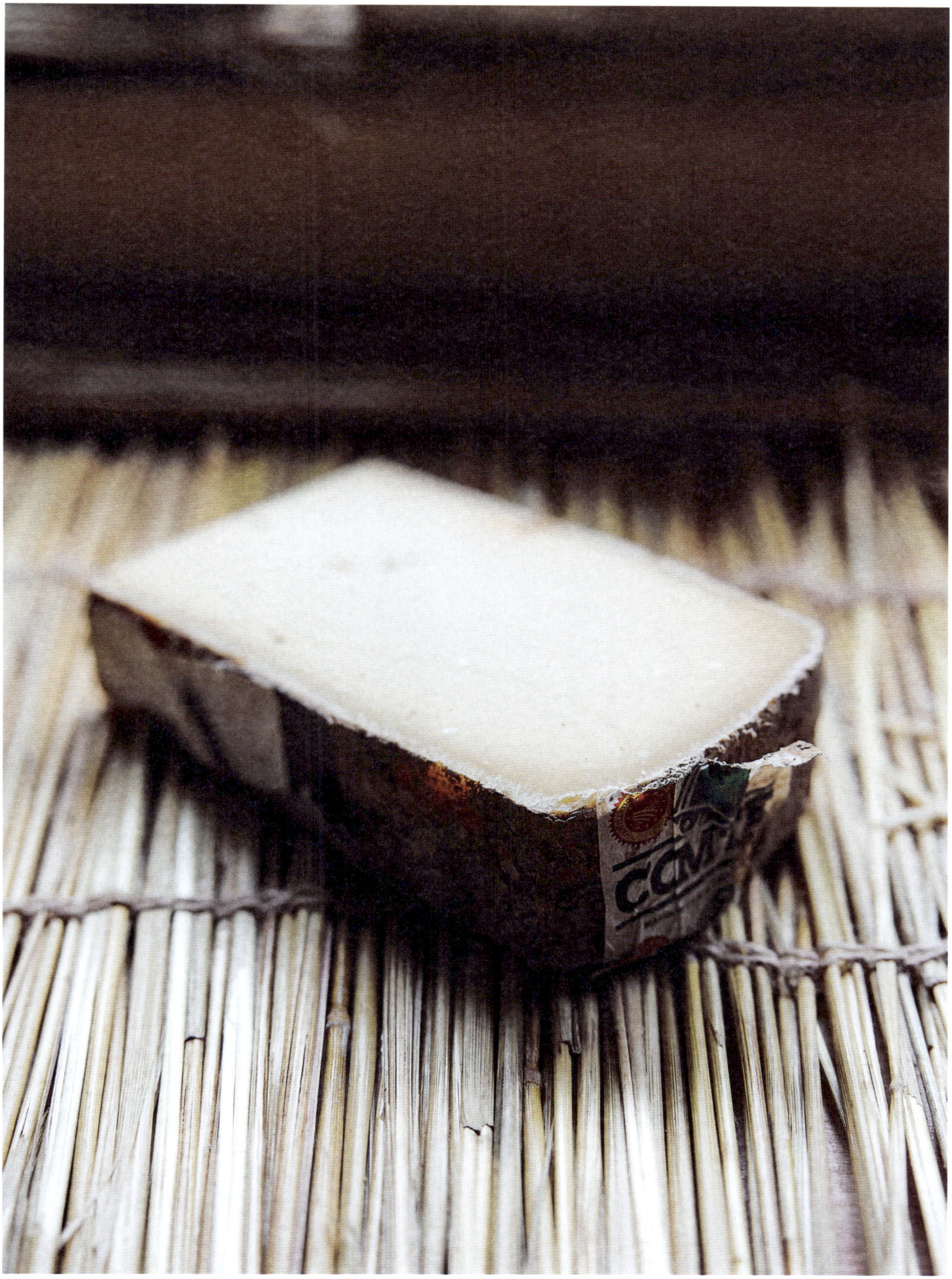

BRIE AND BACON CROISSANT BUTTER PUDDING

SERVES 6

50g butter
6 large croissants, sliced 1cm thick
300g bacon, cooked and sliced small
300g Brie, sliced
400ml double cream
400ml full-fat milk
4 eggs

Brie and bacon is a classic combination and the perfect filling for this savoury bread and butter pudding made with croissants. For a variation, you can swap the Brie for the same quantity of grated Cheddar.

Preheat the oven to 140°C (120°C fan)/275°F/gas 1.

Melt the butter in a pan over a medium heat until foaming. Tip the croissants into an 20 x 15cm ovenproof dish, pour over the melted butter and sprinkle over the bacon and Brie.

Warm the cream and milk in a pan over a medium heat. Whisk the eggs in a large bowl, then pour over the cream mixture and whisk together. Pour three-quarters of the cream mixture over the croissants and leave to soak for 10 minutes. Then pour over the remaining mixture.

Carefully pop into the oven and bake for 45 minutes. Remove from the oven and leave to cool a little. Slice and serve.

4-CHEESE SARNIE
\
SERVES 4

100g unsalted butter, softened
2 teaspoons Marmite
8 slices of sourdough or rye bread
100g mature Cheddar, grated
100g firm mozzarella, grated
100g Red Leicester, grated
½ tablespoon chilli flakes
2 twists of cracked black pepper
8 slices of mortadella
15 slices of salami
6 large gherkin pickles, sliced
Three-mustard mayonnaise (see below)
60g Parmesan, finely grated
olive oil, for frying

FOR THE THREE-MUSTARD MAYONNAISE
100g mayonnaise
2 teaspoons English mustard
2 teaspoons American mustard
2 teaspoons Dijon mustard

The ultimate cheese sandwich, featuring four cheeses: Cheddar, mozzarella, Red Leicester and Parmesan – and a three-mustard mayonnaise!

First make the three-mustard mayonnaise. Combine all the ingredients in a bowl, then set aside.

Place the butter and Marmite in a bowl and mix really well. Butter one side of every piece of sourdough or rye bread with the Marmite butter, making sure to go right to the edges. Add the Cheddar, mozzarella and Red Leicester cheeses to a bowl, then add the chilli flakes and black pepper and mix well.

Next, get everything ready in front of you on a work surface – your mortadella, your salami, your pickles and your three-mustard mayonnaise. Start to build your sandwiches by placing an even amount of the cheese mixture on all eight slices of buttered bread. On four slices of the bread, lay the slices of pickled gherkins evenly over the cheese. Then place the salami evenly on top of the pickles, followed by the mortadella. Complete the sandwiches by carefully picking up each of the other four-cheese topped slices and quickly flip them onto the mortadella-topped slices. Push down on the top of your sandwiches to lightly compress all the ingredients together.

Continued overleaf

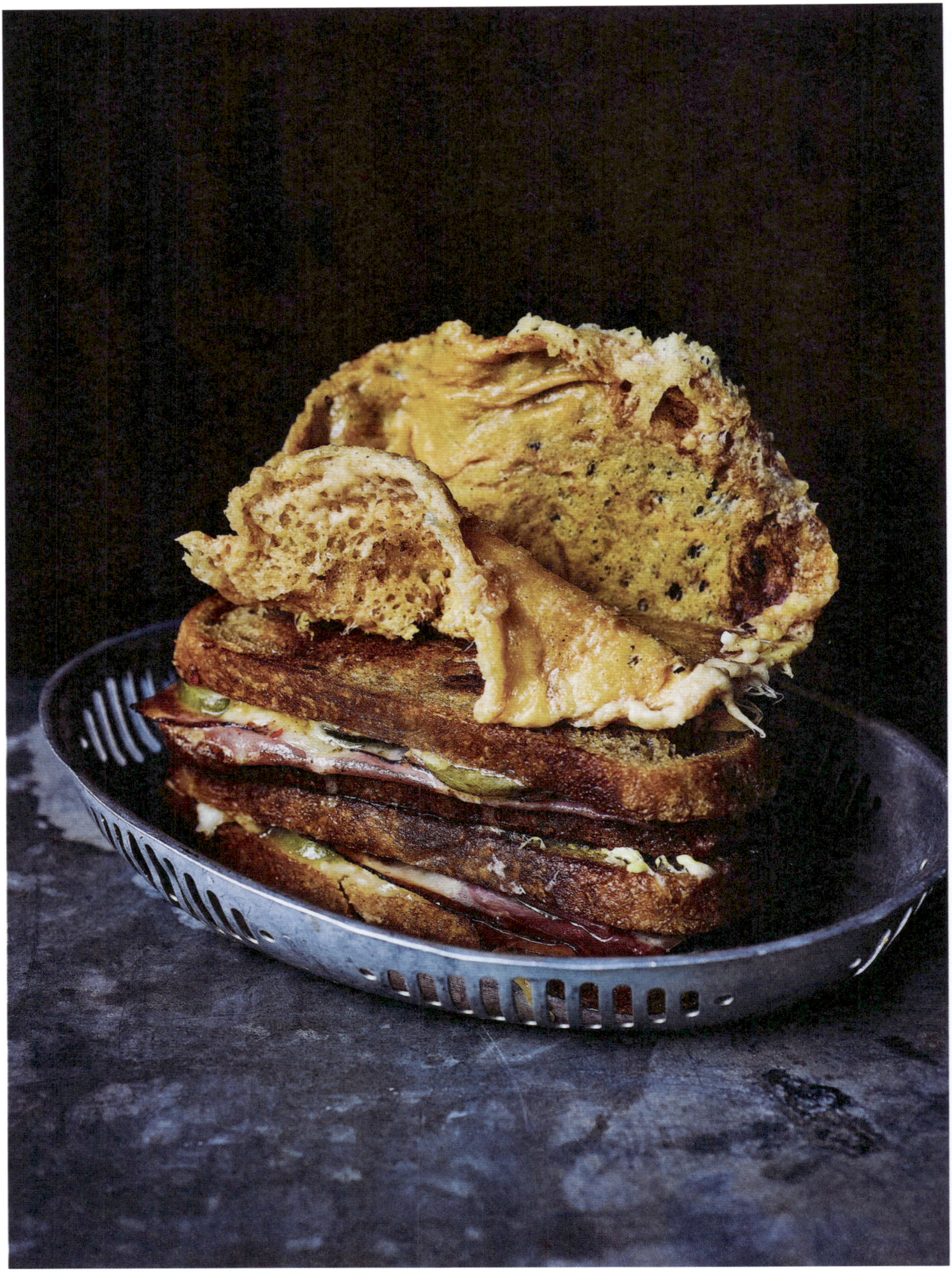

Place a large non-stick frying pan over a medium heat and add a little olive oil. Place the sandwiches in the pan, probably two at a time. Keep the heat medium and just allow the first side of the sandwiches to toast and go crisp. Turn the sandwiches and repeat the process.

While the sandwiches are toasting on the second side, spread the mustard mayonnaise all over the already-toasted side. Once the second side is toasted, turn the sandwiches again and toast the mayonnaise side of the sandwich. Again, repeat the process and spread the mustard mayonnaise on the second toasted side of the sandwiches.

Turn the sandwiches one last time to toast the last mayonnaise side. All the while, your sandwiches have been cooking in the middle and your cheeses should now be starting to melt. Once the sandwiches are oozing with the melted cheese and the bread is totally crisp, remove the sandwiches, wipe the pan with some kitchen paper, and then sprinkle in around 15g of the finely grated Parmesan per sandwich. Gently melt, then place your sandwiches on top and don't move them. Once the Parmesan is golden, using a palette knife, lift the sandwiches out, hold each one on your palette knife, and just allow the Parmesan to go crisp – this will take seconds. Repeat with the remaining sandwiches and Parmesan.

To serve, turn the sandwiches over and slice in half.

CHEESY COB CROUTE-STYLE

SERVES 4–6

50ml white wine
1 cob loaf, top sliced off carefully and most of the crumb removed
500g Cheddar, grated
500g Gruyère, grated
100ml crème fraîche
sea salt and freshly ground black pepper
50g salad leaves, to serve

FOR THE DRESSING
25ml vegetable oil
1 tablespoon white wine vinegar
1 teaspoon Dijon mustard

Cheese and bread are a winning combination and in this twist, instead of making a sandwich or toastie, a whole hollowed-out cob is filled with a creamy, cheesy filling. Serve with a simply dressed salad to cut through the richness.

Preheat the oven to 220°C (200°C fan)/425°F/gas 7.

Pour the wine all over the bread and leave for 5 minutes until the wine is absorbed.

Layer half the cheeses into the bread and top with crème fraîche. Sprinkle over the rest of the cheeses and put the bread onto a baking tray. Pop into the oven for 15–20 minutes.

To make the dressing, whisk all the ingredients together, then add a splash of water. Pour over the salad leaves and serve alongside the baked bread.

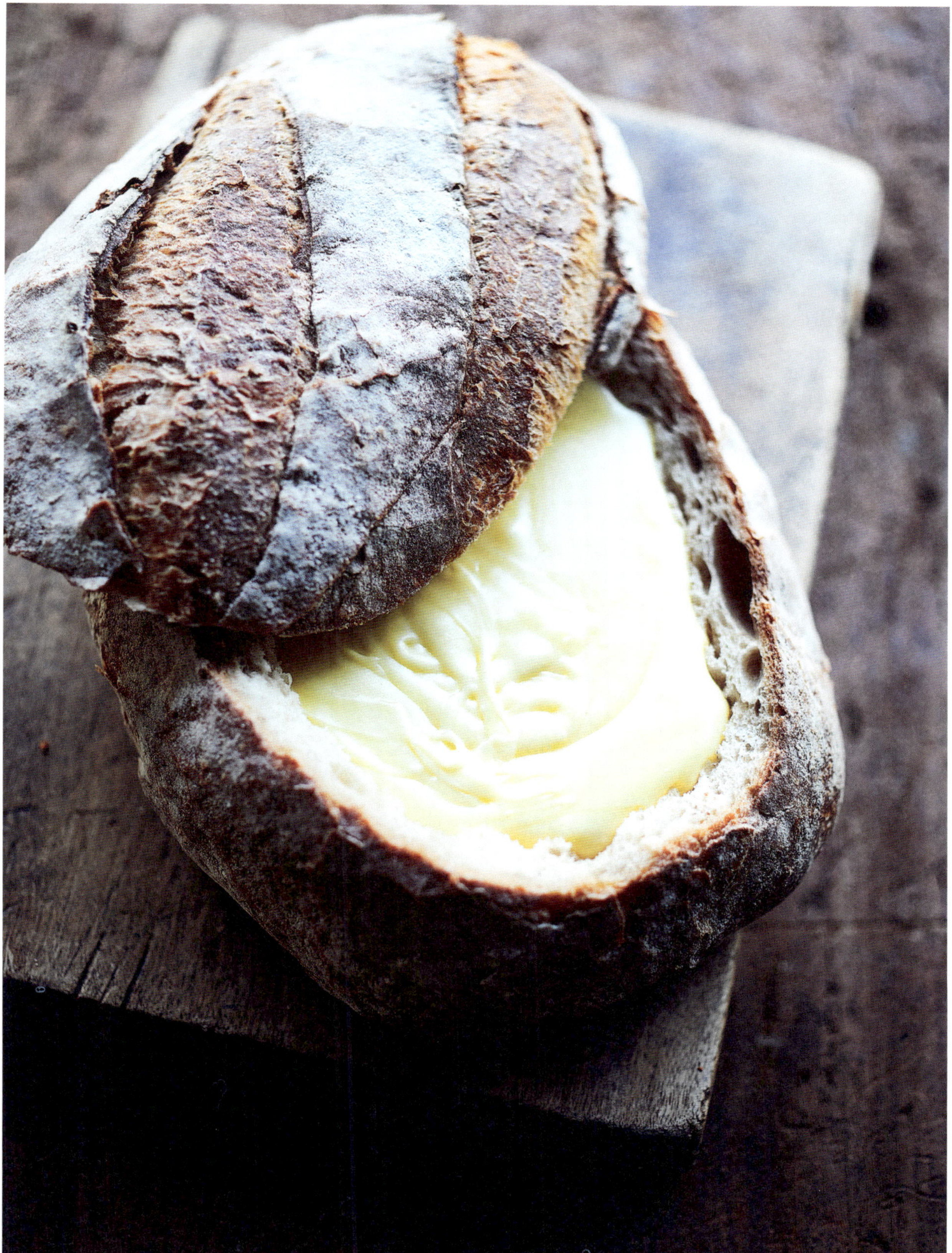

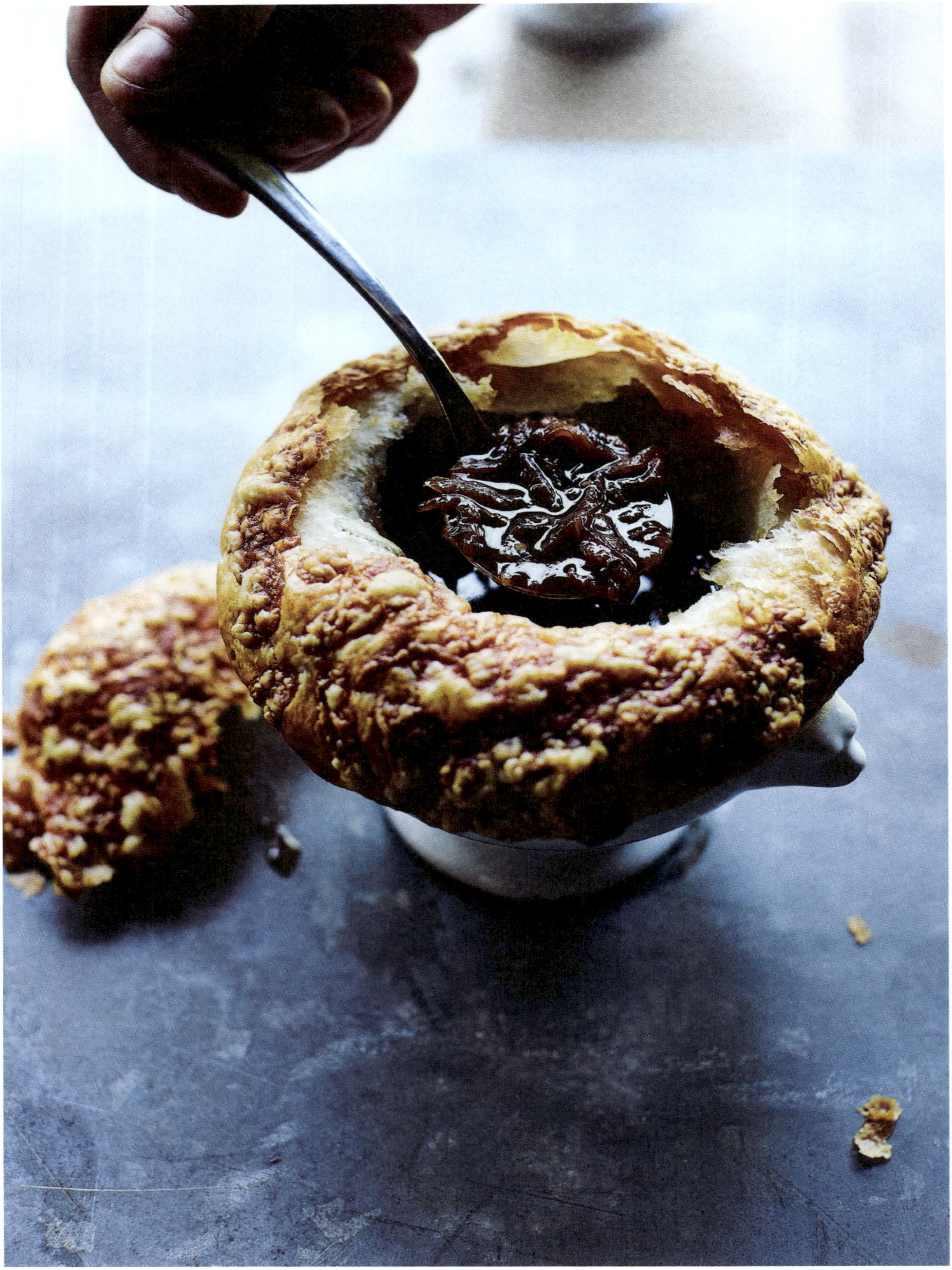

FRENCH ONION SOUP WITH CHEESE LIDS
\
SERVES 4

5 ruscoff onions, peeled and sliced
25g butter
2 garlic cloves, crushed
a few sprigs of thyme
50ml sherry
50ml white wine
25ml brandy
500ml beef stock
1 tablespoon brown sugar
sea salt and freshly ground
    black pepper

FOR THE TOPPING
plain flour, for dusting
300g all-butter puff pastry
200g Comté, grated

The cheesy tops are an essential element of a classic French onion soup and these Comté versions are a fitting final touch to this dish. Feel free to switch the Comté for another hard cheese like Gruyère or Cheddar.

Put the onions into a hot saucepan with the butter, garlic and thyme. Cook over a medium heat until coloured, then add the sherry, wine, brandy, stock and sugar and season. Cook for 10–15 minutes. Spoon the soup into deep ovenproof soup bowls and leave to cool.

Preheat the oven to 200°C (180°C fan)/400°F/gas 6.

On a lightly floured surface, roll out the pastry and cut into four circles slightly bigger than the soup bowl tops. Brush the edges of the soup bowls with water, then press the pastry circles on top and seal. Sprinkle with the cheese and bake for 20 minutes.

SMALL PLATES AND SNACKS

DOUBLE-BAKED CHEESE SOUFFLÉ
\
SERVES 4

40g butter, plus extra for greasing
40g plain flour, plus extra for dusting
250ml full-fat milk
200g Cheddar, grated
1 tablespoon Dijon mustard
1 teaspoon chopped rosemary
1 egg
3 egg whites
400ml double cream
1 small bunch of watercress
1 red or white chicory (endive), chopped
2 Little Gem lettuces, chopped
sea salt and freshly ground black pepper

FOR THE DRESSING
1 egg yolk
25ml white wine vinegar
100ml vegetable oil

Soft, pillowy soufflés smothered in a golden, bubbling cheesy sauce? Yes, please!

Preheat the oven to 200°C (180°C fan)/400°F/gas 6. Grease four soufflé moulds with butter and dust all over with flour.

Melt the butter in a pan over a medium heat, then whisk in the flour and cook out for a couple of minutes. Slowly add the milk and cook for 2 minutes. Then whisk in half the Cheddar, the mustard, rosemary and egg, season and transfer to a bowl to cool.

In a bowl, whisk the egg whites until stiff, then fold into the cheese mixture. Spoon into the prepared moulds, level off the tops and run your finger around the top of the moulds. Put into a baking tray lined with kitchen paper and pour water into the tray to about two-thirds of the way up the sides of the moulds. Bake for 12–14 minutes.

Remove from the oven and leave to cool slightly. Transfer the soufflés to an ovenproof dish, pour over the cream and sprinkle with the remaining Cheddar. Bake for 10–12 minutes.

To make the dressing, in a bowl, whisk the egg yolk, vinegar and oil together, season and then add a splash of water.

Put the watercress, chicory and Little Gem into a bowl and dress with 2 tablespoons of the dressing. (The remaining dressing can be stored in the fridge for up to a week.)

Spoon the soufflés onto plates and serve with the salad on the side.

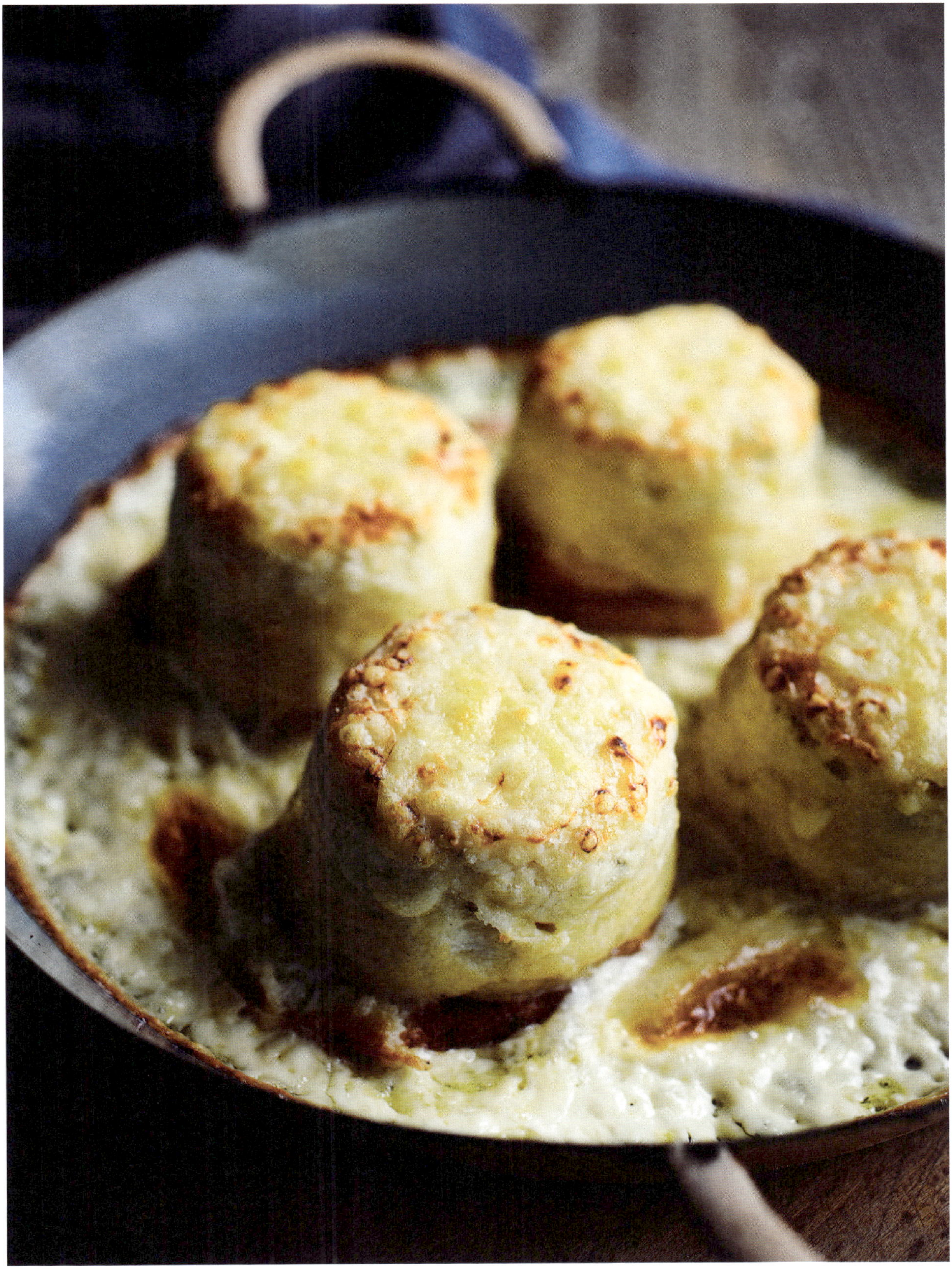

CRAB RAREBIT TOASTS
\
SERVES 4

4 slices of sourdough bread
300g white crab meat
zest and juice of 1 lime
2 tablespoons crème fraîche
100g tomato chutney
4 tomatoes, sliced
sea salt and freshly ground
　　black pepper
watercress, to serve

FOR THE RAREBIT
350g Cheddar, grated
50ml beer
1 teaspoon Worcestershire sauce
2 tablespoons English mustard
a few drops of Tabasco green
　　pepper sauce
2 tablespoons plain flour
2 egg yolks

Rarebit is a Welsh dish usually consisting of a hot cheese sauce served on toasted bread. I've taken things up a notch here by adding crab meat and zesty lime to the mix as well as tomatoes and tomato chutney to contrast the richness.

Preheat the grill to high.

First, make the rarebit. Gently melt the cheese in a medium pan over a medium heat. Then add the remaining ingredients and continue to cook and whisk for 3–4 minutes until all the cheese has melted and mixed in.

Toast the bread on both sides.

In a bowl, mix the crab, lime juice and crème fraîche together and season. Top the toast with the tomato chutney and sliced tomatoes. Then add the crab mixture and sprinkle over the lime zest. Spoon over the rarebit and grill for 5 minutes until hot and bubbling.

Serve the crab rarebit toasts with watercress on the side.

DEEP-FRIED COURGETTE FLOWERS WITH SAUCE VIERGE

\
SERVES 2

1.5 litres vegetable oil
6 courgette flowers
150g ricotta

FOR THE BATTER
150g gluten-free self-raising flour
100ml cider
pinch of salt

FOR THE SAUCE VIERGE
100ml olive oil
1 teaspoon coriander seeds, crushed
1 small bunch of flat-leaf parsley, chopped
1 small bunch of tarragon, chopped
juice of ½ lemon
a few sprigs of samphire
2 tomatoes, skinned, deseeded and diced
sea salt and freshly ground black pepper

Creamy, soft Italian ricotta is the ideal filling for these beautiful courgette flowers, fried in a light and crispy batter. Sauce vierge is a simple French sauce made from olive oil, lemon juice, chopped tomato and herbs, which finishes the dish off perfectly.

First make the sauce vierge. Put all the ingredients, except the tomatoes, into a pan and warm gently for a minute. Add the tomatoes, season and stir, then take off the heat and set aside.

Heat the vegetable oil in a deep-sided saucepan to 170°C (340°F).

For the batter, whisk the ingredients together in a bowl.

Fill the courgette flowers with the ricotta. Dip the stuffed flowers in the batter, then deep-fry for 2 minutes. Drain on kitchen paper.

To serve, sit the deep-fried courgette flowers in the middle of a plate and top with the sauce vierge.

Pictured overleaf

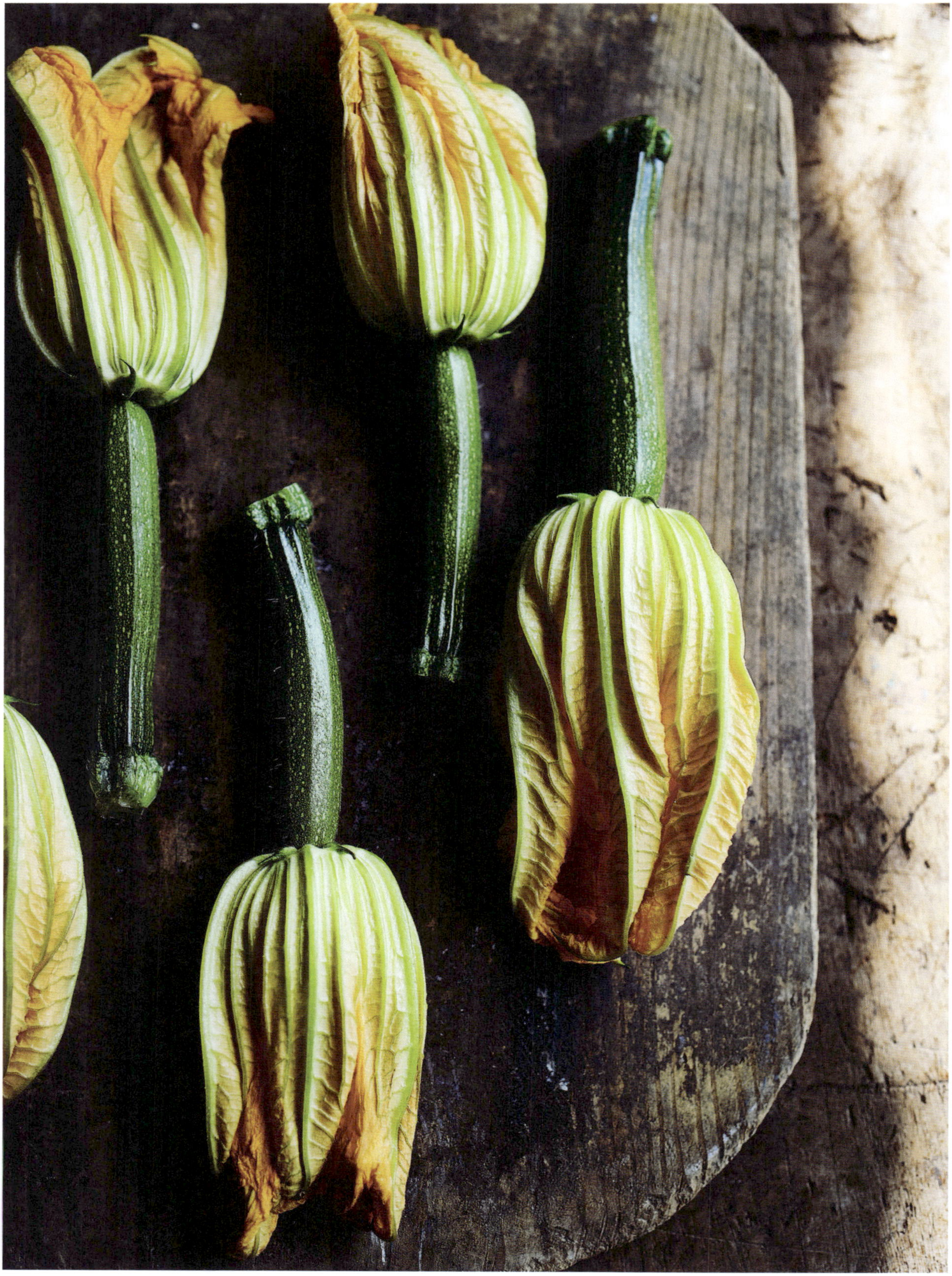

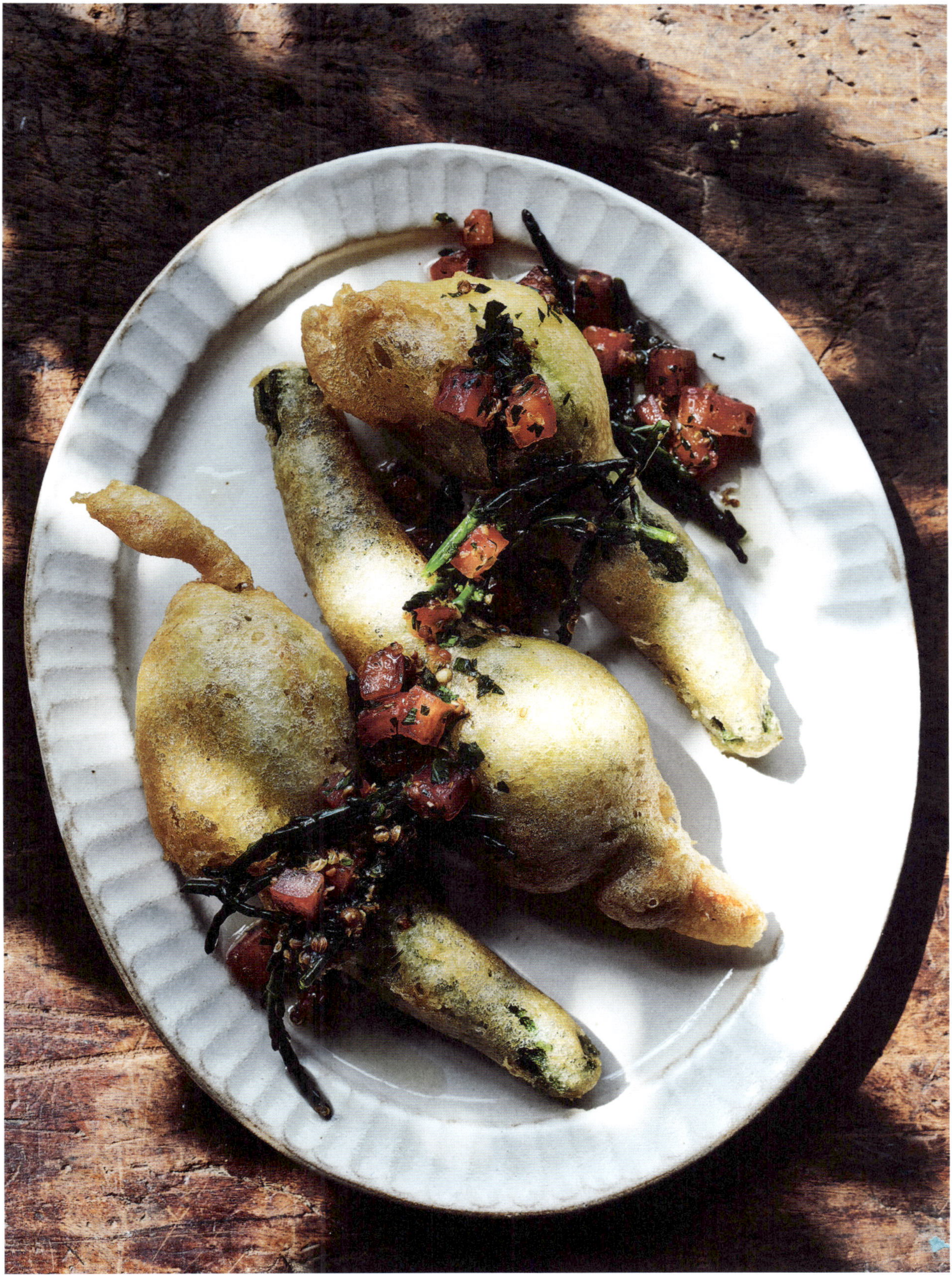

CROQUETAS WITH IBÉRICO HAM AND MANCHEGO
\
SERVES 4

100g butter
150g plain flour
1 teaspoon sweet paprika
550ml full-fat milk
100g Manchego, cubed
6 slices of Ibérico ham, sliced
2 tablespoons chopped flat-leaf parsley
75g plain flour
2 eggs, beaten
100g panko breadcrumbs
1.5 litres vegetable oil, for deep-frying
sea salt and freshly ground
    black pepper

TO SERVE
Manchego
lemon mayonnaise

These croquetas feature two of Spain's most well-known (and loved) culinary exports: Ibérico ham and Manchego cheese. Serve with even more Manchego grated over the top and a zesty lemon mayo to complement and contrast the cheesiness.

Put the butter into a pan over a medium heat and, when foaming, add the flour and sweet paprika and cook for a couple of minutes. Whisk in the milk and cook gently over a very low heat for 3 minutes, stirring constantly.

Remove the mixture from the heat and leave it to cool for a few minutes. Then beat in the Manchego, ham, parsley, ½ teaspoon of salt and some black pepper to taste. Cover with clingfilm and chill the mixture in the fridge for 2 hours.

Shape the mixture into sausage shapes. Put the flour, beaten egg and breadcrumbs in three separate bowls. Coat the croquetas first in the flour, then dip in the beaten egg and finally coat in the breadcrumbs.

Heat the oil to 180°C (350°F) in a deep-sided saucepan. Drop the croquetas into the hot oil and cook for 1–2 minutes until crisp and golden, working in batches. Drain on kitchen paper, then grate over some Manchego and serve immediately with lemon mayo.

HOMEMADE CRUMPETS WITH CHEESE AND MARMITE
\
SERVES 8

175g strong white bread flour
175g plain flour
2 x 7g sachets fast action yeast
1 teaspoon caster sugar
½ teaspoon bicarbonate of soda
1 teaspoon salt
350ml full-fat milk, warmed
100ml warm water

FOR THE TOPPING
100g butter, softened, plus extra for frying and greasing
200g Cheddar, grated
1 tablespoon Marmite

A cheesy comfort-food classic, featuring a golden Cheddar and Marmite sauce atop homemade crumpets. The perfect teatime treat or light bite.

Whisk together all the crumpet ingredients, cover and leave to prove in a warm place for 2–3 hours.

Warm a large, flat griddle pan over a low heat and brush with butter. Butter as many crumpet rings as you can comfortably fit in your pan – you will need to cook the crumpets in batches. Pour the crumpet batter into the prepared rings and cook over a medium heat for 3 minutes. Remove the rings, and flip over and cook for a further 2 minutes. Keep warm while you cook the remaining crumpets.

Preheat the grill to high.

Beat the butter, Cheddar and Marmite together, then spread the mixture over the crumpets. Grill the crumpets until the topping is golden and bubbling.

DUCK CONFIT SALAD
\
SERVES 6

4 duck legs
15g table salt
1 small bunch of thyme
2 garlic cloves
500g duck fat
2 tablespoons runny honey

FOR THE PECANS
100g caster sugar
100ml water
200g pecans
500ml vegetable oil
1 teaspoon cayenne pepper
sea salt

FOR THE DRESSING
200ml crème fraîche
200g soft blue cheese, such as Dolcelatte
1 tablespoon Worcestershire sauce
200g mayonnaise
a few drops of Tabasco

FOR THE SALAD
2 Cos lettuces
100g grapes of your choice
6 large croutons

In this stunning salad the blue cheese dressing pulls all the elements together – rich duck confit, crispy lettuce, crunchy croutons and sweet caramelised pecans. It's important to use a soft blue cheese here to give the right texture to the dressing.

Rub the duck legs with the salt and chill in the fridge for 24 hours. Remove from the fridge, wash off the salt and then pop into a deep saucepan with the thyme and garlic. Cover in the duck fat and simmer for 2 hours. Remove from the heat and chill in the fridge until the fat is hard.

Preheat the oven to 220°C (200°C fan)/425°F/gas 7.

Remove the duck legs from the pan, remove any excess fat and pop onto a roasting tray. Drizzle over the honey, then roast for 10 minutes. Remove from the oven and transfer to a plate. Remove the bones and shred the duck meat.

For the pecans, heat the sugar and water together in a saucepan over a high heat and, when the sugar has dissolved, stir through the pecans. Drain. Heat the vegetable oil to 170°C (340°F) in a deep-sided frying pan. Deep-fry the pecans for 30 seconds, then drain on kitchen paper and season with the cayenne pepper and some salt.

Blitz all the dressing ingredients together in a blender or food processor.

To serve, shred the lettuce and pile up on plates with the pecans, grapes and croutons. Top with the shredded duck and drizzle over the dressing.

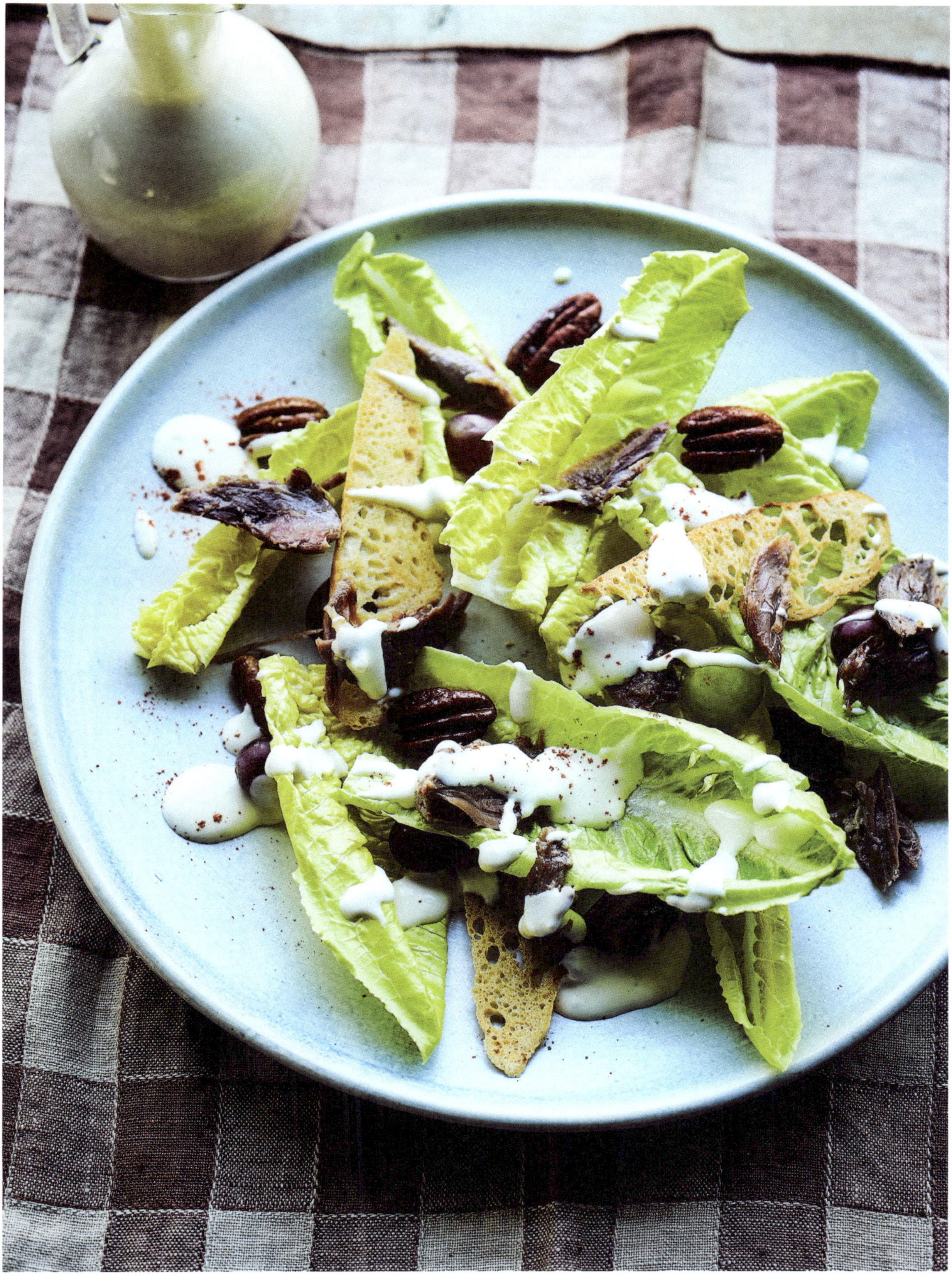

WARM CHEESE FONDUE WITH NIBBLES
\
SERVES 6

100ml dry white wine
3 teaspoons cornflour
500g Cheddar, grated
500g Gouda, grated
100ml crème fraîche
sea salt and freshly ground
   black pepper

TO SERVE
400g baby potatoes
12 slices of pancetta, halved lengthways
400g chorizo chunks
300g radishes
400g bread, cut into chunks and fried
   in garlic butter
200g jar cornichons, drained
2 red or white chicory (endives),
   leaves separated

A fondue is one of the best ways to showcase and enjoy cheese. Originating in Switzerland, it's the ultimate sharing dish and you can dip almost anything you want into the melting pot of cheesy deliciousness.

Preheat the oven to 200°C (180°C fan)/400°F/gas 6.

Cook the potatoes in boiling salted water for 12–15 minutes until just soft. Drain and leave to cool. Wrap each potato in a slice of pancetta, pop into a roasting tray and roast for 15 minutes.

Put the chorizo into a small roasting tray and roast for 15 minutes alongside the potatoes.

Whisk all the fondue ingredients together in a non-stick pan and warm through gently, whisking continuously, until melted and combined. Pour into a fondue dish and keep warm.

Serve the cheese fondue alongside the radishes, chorizo, pancetta-wrapped potatoes, bread chunks, cornichons and chicory.

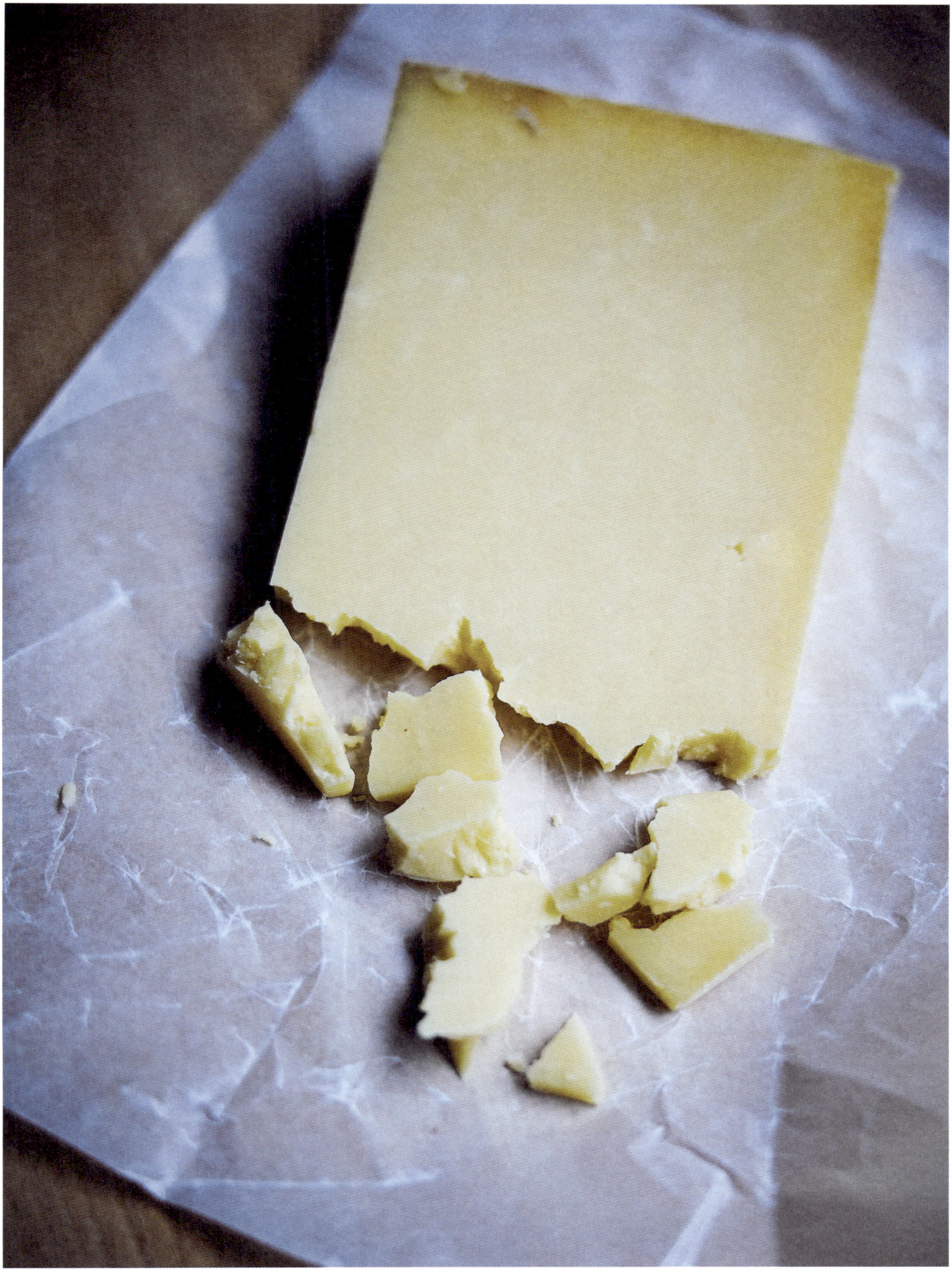

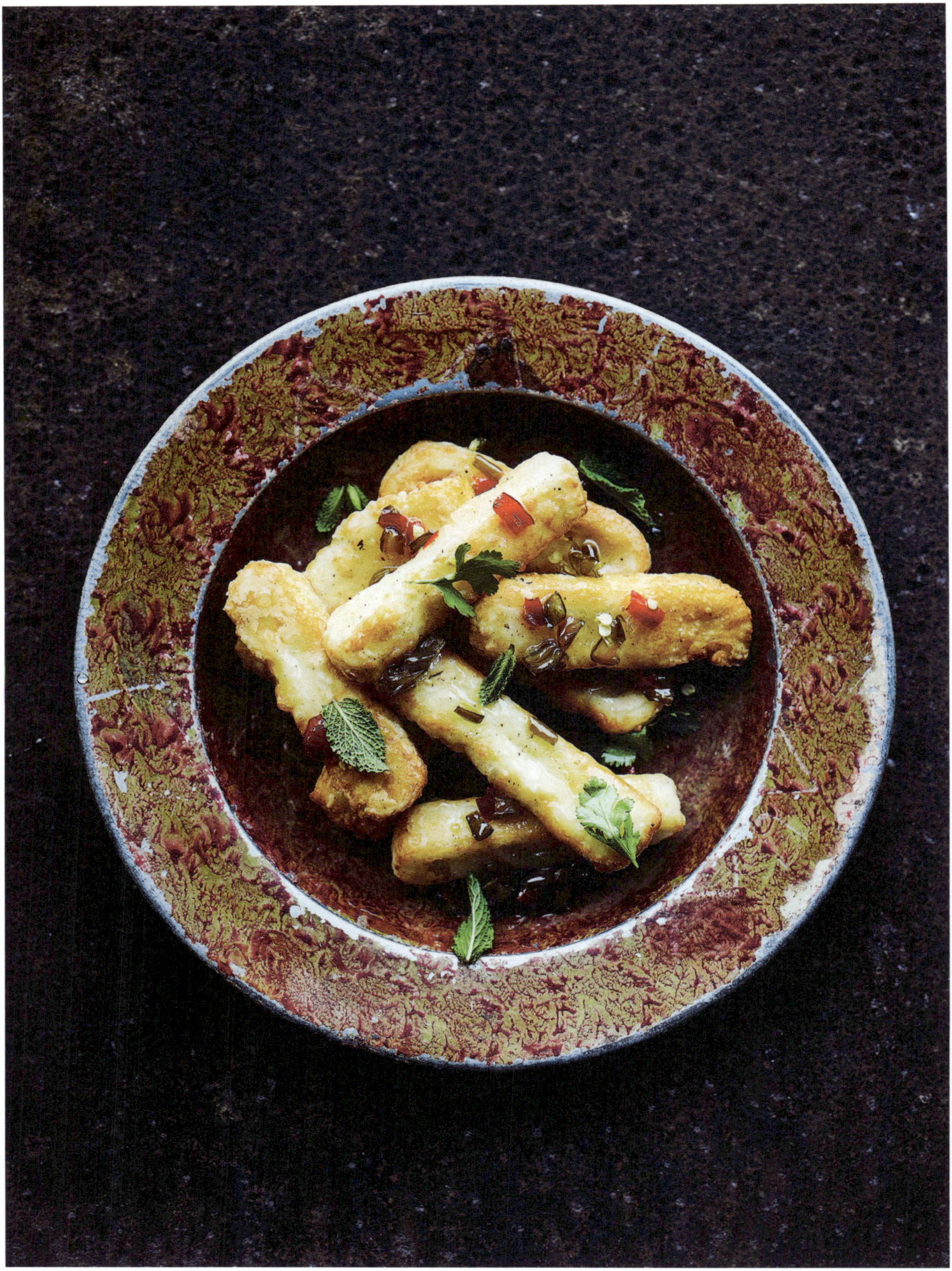

HALLOUMI FRIES WITH CHILLI SAUCE
\
SERVES 4

2 litres vegetable oil
2 tablespoons za'atar
75g plain flour
2 x 250g blocks of halloumi, cut into fingers
sea salt and freshly ground black pepper

FOR THE SAUCE
100g caster sugar
50ml white wine vinegar
1 green chilli, chopped
1 red chilli, chopped
1 small bunch of mint, chopped, plus extra to serve
1 small bunch of coriander, chopped, plus extra to serve

The firm, 'squeaky' texture of halloumi means it works best when griddled or fried. In this recipe I've coated it in flavoursome za'atar and served it with a herby chilli sauce that is perfect with the mild taste of the cheese.

In a deep-fat fryer or deep-sided saucepan, heat the oil to 180°C (350°F).

Mix the za'atar and flour together and season. Dip all the halloumi fingers in the flour mixture. Fry in batches until golden, then drain on kitchen paper. Season with sea salt.

For the sauce, heat the sugar and vinegar in a small pan over a medium heat until the sugar has dissolved. Remove from the heat, then add the remaining ingredients and stir through.

Pile the halloumi fries onto plates, spoon over the chilli sauce and scatter with herbs.

FRENCH TOAST SANDWICH
\
SERVES 2

12 slices of pancetta
2 eggs
100ml full-fat milk
6 slices of brioche
6 slices of Gruyère, rind removed
150g butter
50ml maple syrup, to serve

The classic combination of cheese and ham is utilised again here in a savoury version of French toast. In this instance I've paired Gruyère with pancetta, but you could easily switch it for Comté or Manchego.

In a large frying pan over a medium heat, fry the pancetta until crisp. Set aside, leaving the fat in the pan.

In a small bowl, beat together the eggs and milk.

On a board, top a slice of brioche with three slices of cheese, then a slice of brioche, then six slices of pancetta and then another slice of bread. Squash together, then dip into the egg mixture. Repeat to make the other sandwich.

Heat the pancetta fat with the butter in the frying pan until gently foaming, then fry the sandwiches on both sides until golden, crisp and the cheese has melted.

To serve, cut in half, pop onto plates and drizzle with the maple syrup.

CHEESE AND ONION BREAD WITH PICKLES
\
SERVES 8

a knob of butter, plus extra for greasing
2 large onions, sliced
2 Camemberts, sliced
pickles, to serve

FOR THE DOUGH
300ml full-fat milk
500g strong bread flour, plus extra for dusting
1 egg
15g caster sugar
5g salt
2 teaspoons fast action yeast

Not just a crisp flavour, cheese and onion is an ever-popular pairing. I've used Camembert to contrast with the caramelised onions in this bread, but similar cheeses would work well here, such as Brie or English Tunworth.

Melt the butter in a pan over a low heat and cook the onions until caramelised, about 30 minutes.

For the bread, put all the ingredients into the bowl of a stand mixer fitted with a dough hook and knead for 5 minutes. Cover, then leave to prove at room temperature until doubled in size.

On a floured work surface, divide the dough into 18 pieces and roll each one into a ball. Arrange the balls next to each other on a greased baking tray to form a circle and leave to prove at room temperature until doubled in size.

Preheat the oven to 200°C (180°C fan)/400°F/gas 6.

Dot the dough with the caramelised onions and slices of Camembert, then bake for 15–20 minutes until golden and bubbling.

Turn out the bread onto a board and allow to cool slightly before tearing. Serve with pickles.

GOAT'S CHEESE AND BEETROOT WITH HAZELNUT BREADCRUMBS
\
SERVES 2

100g soft goat's cheese
75g mascarpone
3 mixed coloured beetroots
25ml olive oil, plus extra for drizzling
3 sprigs of thyme, leaves picked
sea salt and freshly ground
    black pepper
edible garden flowers and herbs, such
    as pansies or fennel fronds,
    to garnish (optional)

FOR THE HAZELNUT
BREADCRUMBS
1 slice of stale sourdough bread,
    roughly torn
25g hazelnuts, lightly crushed
25g butter

FOR THE DRESSING
100ml fresh beetroot juice
25ml olive oil
10ml red wine vinegar (preferably
    Cabernet Sauvignon vinegar)
pinch of sugar
pinch of salt

Soft goat's cheese is wonderful in salads, here providing the perfect flavour and colour contrast to vibrant multicoloured beetroot, fresh herbs and edible flowers. The hazelnut breadcrumbs add a satisfying and complementary crunch. You can always roast the beetroot instead of using the BBQ.

Heat a BBQ until hot and the coals are white.

In a bowl, mix the goat's cheese and mascarpone together until smooth. Transfer to a piping bag and snip the end off.

On a large piece of foil, roll the beetroot in some olive oil and season heavily with salt and pepper. Keep the beetroot apart so the colours do not bleed into each other. Add the thyme and evenly distribute around the beetroot. Seal the foil parcel and bake directly on the coals of the BBQ for about 1 hour or until cooked. Allow to cool, then remove the skins and slice into wedges.

Whizz the sourdough in a food processor to form breadcrumbs. Mix together with the crushed hazelnuts. Melt the butter in a pan over a medium heat, then gently fry the breadcrumb mixture until golden and crispy, turning frequently to toast and soak up all the butter.

In a pan over a high heat, reduce the beetroot juice by half. Then pour into a bowl and whisk together with the oil, vinegar, sugar and salt.

To serve, divide the beetroot between plates, top with the hazelnut breadcrumbs and drizzle over the beetroot reduction. Pipe on the goat's cheese mixture, then decorate with garden herbs and flowers and drizzle with oil.

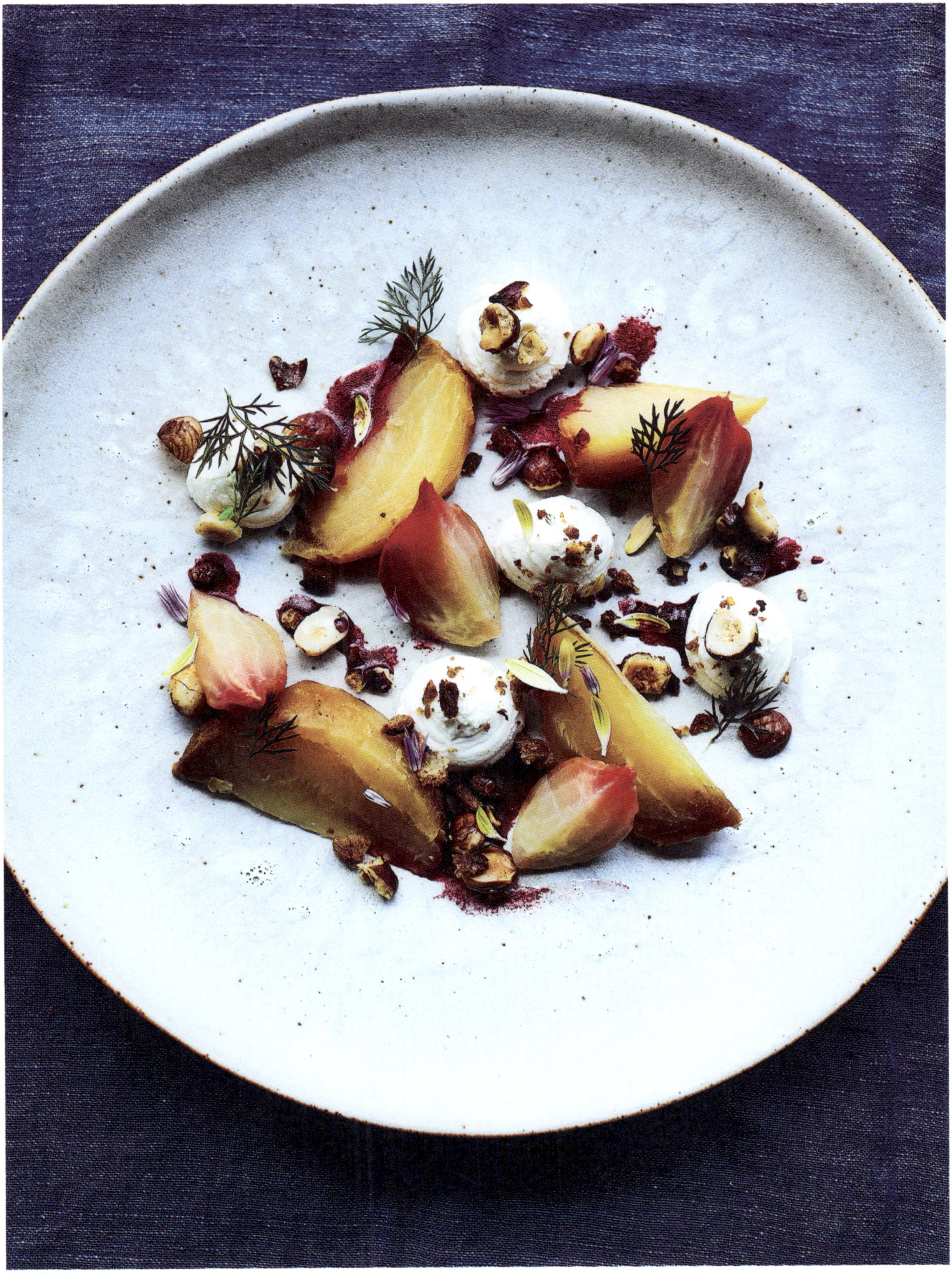

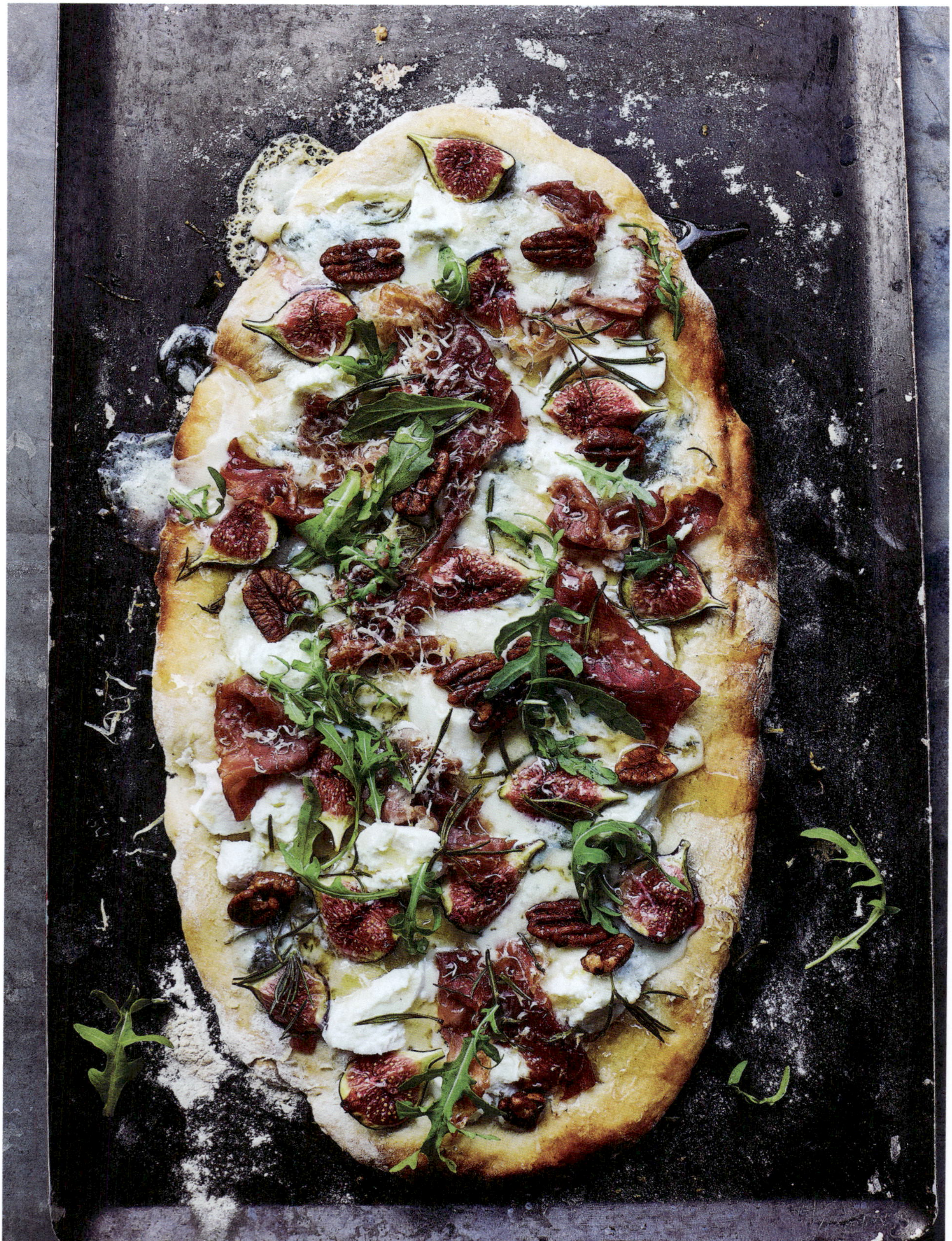

FLATBREAD WITH RICOTTA, FIGS, PARMA HAM AND PECANS

\
SERVES 4

300g self-raising flour, plus extra for dusting
100g thick Greek yoghurt
pinch of salt
200g ricotta
200g blue cheese, such as Gorgonzola
200g soft pecorino (also known as pecorino dolce)
4 figs, quartered
8 slices of Parma ham
a few sprigs of rosemary
olive oil, for drizzling

FOR THE CANDIED PECANS
200g pecans
100g caster sugar
150ml water
vegetable oil, for deep-frying

TO SERVE
50g rocket
50g runny honey

This flatbread features three Italian cheeses – the mild ricotta and a bit of bite from the pecorino and Gorgonzola. All three contrast wonderfully with the sweet figs and candied pecans, while the salty Parma ham cuts through it all.

Preheat the oven to 220°C (200°C fan)/425°F/gas 7 or heat a pizza oven to 500°C (930°F).

To make the candied pecans, put the sugar and water into a pan and bring to the boil. Add the pecans, cook for 1 minute, then drain. Heat a small pan of vegetable oil to 170°C (340°F). Add the pecans and deep-fry for 2 minutes, then drain on kitchen paper.

Mix the flour, yoghurt, salt and enough water to bring the dough together. Stretch out the dough on a baking sheet dusted in flour – it should be 30 x 20cm and 1cm thick. Top with the cheeses all over, then scatter over the figs, ham and rosemary. Drizzle with olive oil, then bake in the oven for 10–12 minutes or the pizza oven for 4–5 minutes.

To serve, top with the rocket, honey and candied pecans.

HOMEMADE NACHOS WITH CHEESE SAUCE
\
SERVES 4

4 large white tortillas
25ml olive oil
1 tablespoon sea salt

FOR THE SAUCE
200g Cheddar, grated
100g Red Leicester, grated
2 tablespoons cornflour
500ml double cream
75ml maple syrup
1 teaspoon sriracha sauce

TO SERVE
crispy bacon, chopped
guacamole
soured cream
tomato salsa
chopped coriander
jarred sliced jalapeños

What better dish to share with friends and family than a platter of crispy homemade nachos, drizzled with a golden cheesy sauce? Bacon, guacamole, soured cream, coriander and jalapeños add layers of flavour.

Preheat the oven to 200°C (180°C fan)/400°F/gas 6.

Cut each tortilla into eight triangles, then spread out in a single layer on a baking tray. Drizzle with the oil, season with the salt and bake for 5–6 minutes until crisp. Remove from the oven and leave to cool.

Place all the sauce ingredients into a medium pan and warm gently over a medium heat, whisking continuously until all the cheese has melted.

To serve, pile the nachos into a bowl, then top with the cheese sauce, bacon, guacamole, soured cream, salsa, coriander and jalapeños.

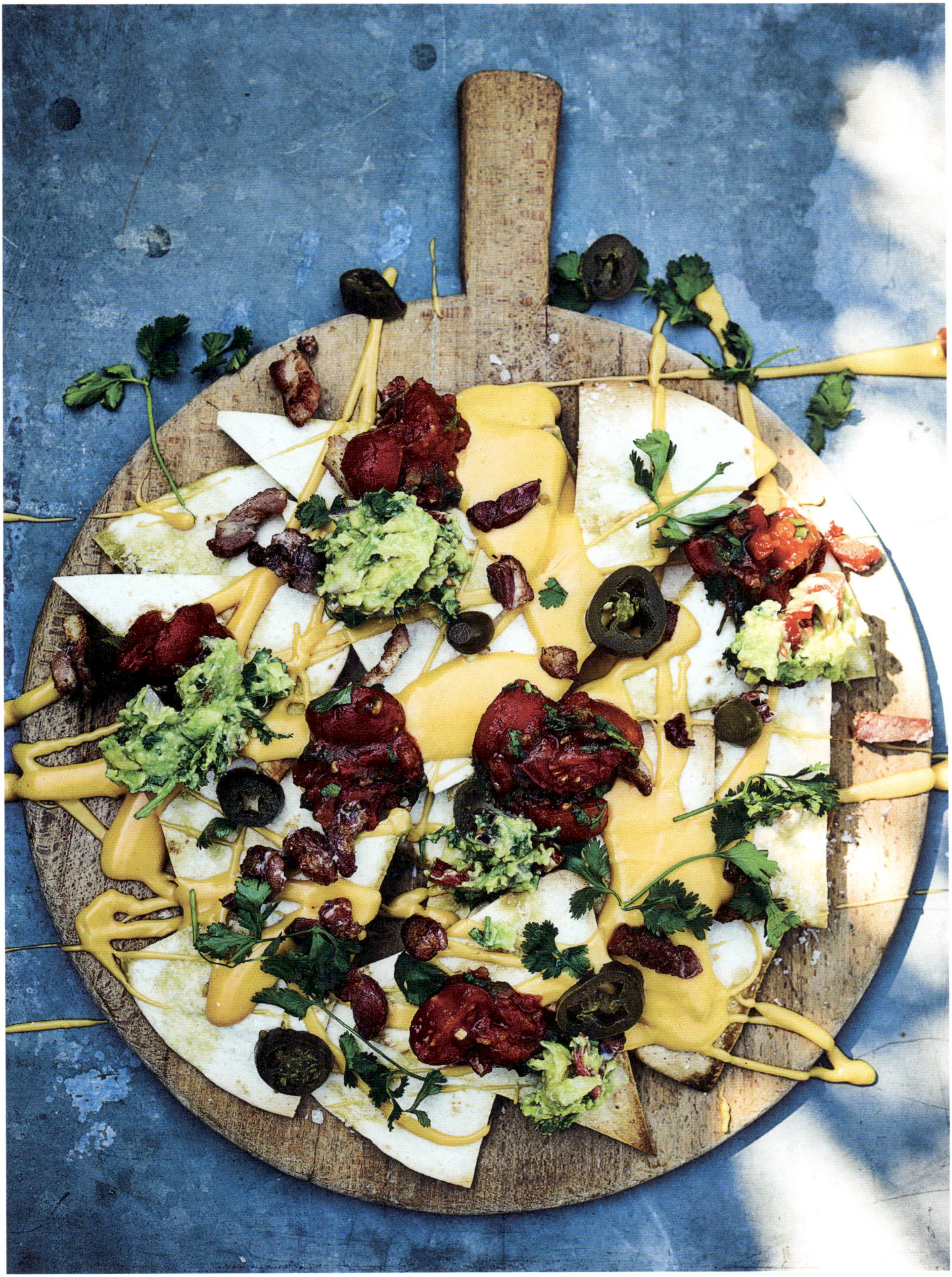

MUFFALETTA WITH SLAW
\
SERVES 6

1 round loaf of crusty bread
100g basil pesto
200g sliced ham
100g provolone, sliced
100g sliced salami
4 balls of mozzarella, sliced
100g pitted olives of your choice
sea salt and freshly ground
 black pepper

FOR THE PICKLE
100g caster sugar
100ml white wine vinegar
2 carrots
¼ green cauliflower, shredded
½ red onion, diced

FOR THE SLAW
25ml soy sauce
25ml runny honey
1 tablespoon white sesame seeds
1 tablespoon black sesame seeds
½ teaspoon chilli flakes
½ red cabbage, thinly sliced
1 corn on the cob, kernels removed
½ red onion, diced

This might just be the ultimate cheese and ham sandwich. Made in a hollowed-out loaf of crusty bread, it combines two types of mild Italian cheese with both ham and salami, as well as salty olives and herby pesto.

Take the bread and cut a 20cm wide and 3cm deep circle from the top. Keep this lid to one side and hollow out the soft crumb from the middle of the loaf.

To make the pickle, put the sugar and vinegar into a pan and bring to the boil. Remove from the heat. Using a potato peeler, peel ribbons off the carrots and put into a big bowl. Add the cauliflower and onion, pour over the pickle liquid and leave to cool.

In a bowl, whisk the soy sauce, honey, sesame seeds and chilli flakes together and mix through the cabbage, corn and red onion.

Layer up the pesto, ham, provolone, salami, mozzarella and olives in the hollowed-out loaf, seasoning between layers. Repeat until the bread is filled up, press down and pop the bread lid on top.

Slice and serve with the slaw and pickle.

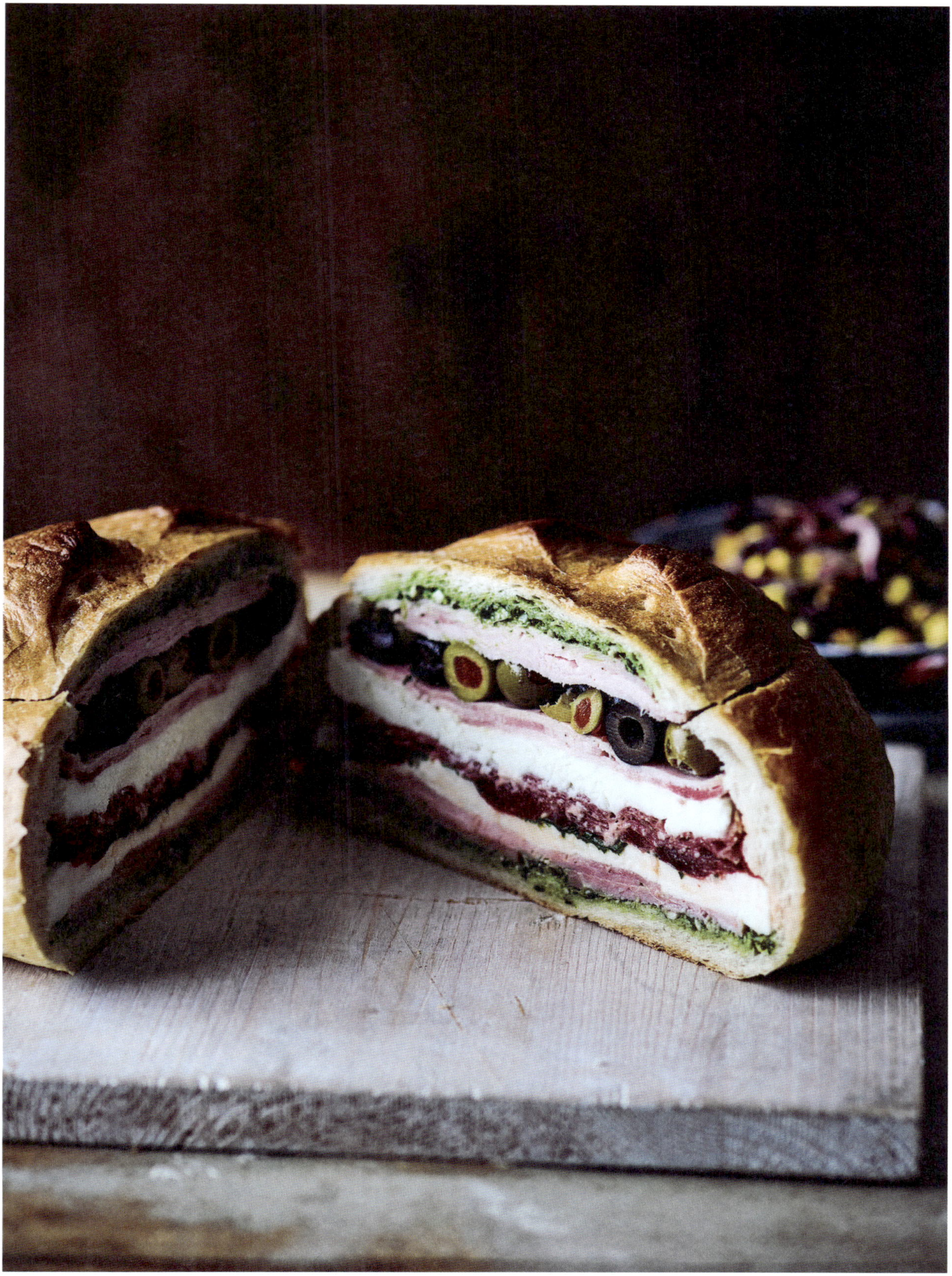

MACKEREL PÂTÉ WITH MELBA TOAST

SERVES 4

150g full-fat cream cheese
300g smoked mackerel, skin and pin bones removed
zest and juice of 1 unwaxed lemon
a few chives, chopped
6 slices of white bread
sea salt and freshly ground black pepper
lemon wedges, to serve

Soft cream cheese mixed with smoked mackerel and lemon makes the perfect pâté for melba toast.

To make the pâté, put the cream cheese, smoked mackerel, lemon zest and juice and chives into a bowl and mix together. Season and spoon into bowls.

Preheat the grill to high.

Toast the bread on both sides, then cut off the crusts. With each piece laying flat, slice each in piece half horizontally. Rub the untoasted sides to remove any excess crumbs. Cut into triangles, then grill, untoasted side up, until golden and the edges have curled up.

To serve, pile the melba toast alongside the pâté and dot with lemon wedges for squeezing.

HALLOUMI WITH CHILLI JAM

SERVES 4

1 teaspoon vegetable oil
2 x 250g blocks of halloumi
4 large or 8 small pickled onions, cut in half lengthways
1 large bunch of watercress
1 tablespoon nigella seeds, to garnish

FOR THE CHILLI JAM
1 teaspoon vegetable oil
1 red onion, thinly sliced
2 red peppers, deseeded and thinly sliced
2 garlic cloves, thinly sliced
1 lemongrass stalk, outer husk removed and thinly sliced
190g sweet chilli sauce
100g dark soft brown sugar
100ml red wine vinegar

FOR THE DRESSING
75ml vegetable oil
1 teaspoon Dijon mustard
1 tablespoon white wine vinegar
1 tablespoon water
sea salt and freshly ground black pepper

In this recipe, I've fried the halloumi alongside some pickled onions to serve with a sweet and spicy chill jam. Halloumi is mild in taste, so works well as a canvas for flavoursome sauces and dips.

To make the chilli jam, add the oil to a pan over a medium heat, then add the onion, peppers, lemongrass and garlic and cook for 5 minutes until soft. Then add the chilli sauce, sugar and vinegar and bring to the boil. Reduce the heat and simmer for 5 minutes. Remove from the heat and set aside to cool.

Whisk together the ingredients for the dressing in a bowl.

Heat a non-stick frying pan until hot, then add the oil. Slice the halloumi into 1cm-thick slices and pop in the pan with the pickled onions, flat-side down. Cook for 1–2 minutes, then flip over, they should be coloured and charred slightly.

To serve, pull the pickled onions into petals, put the watercress in a bowl and drizzle over the dressing. Place the halloumi onto plates with a spoonful of chilli jam, the watercress on the side and dot the onion petals around. Finally, sprinkle over the nigella seeds to garnish.

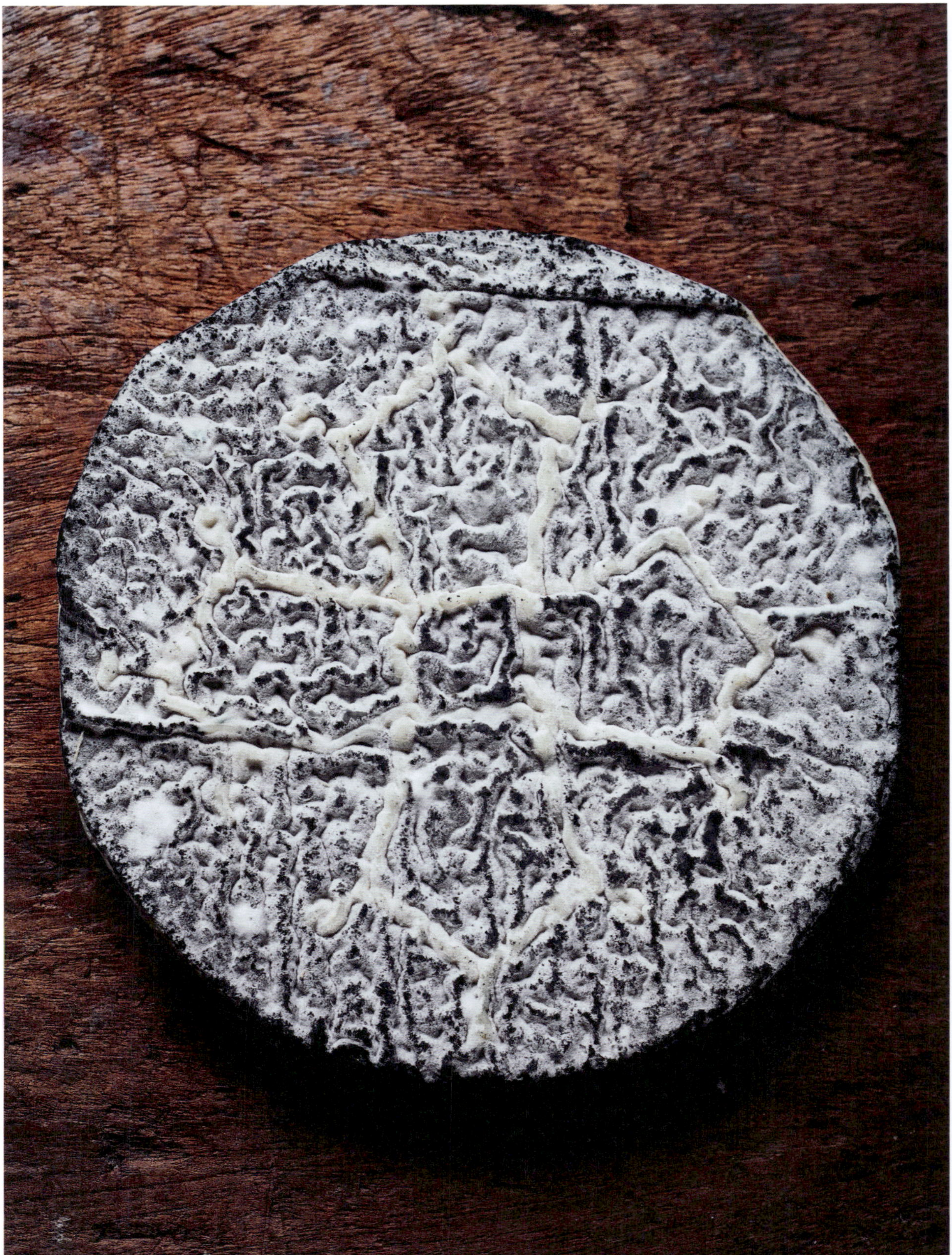

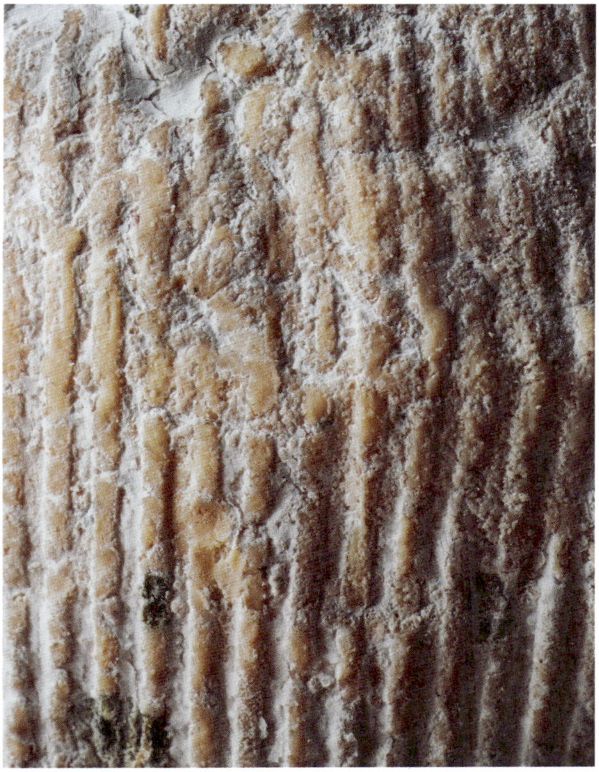

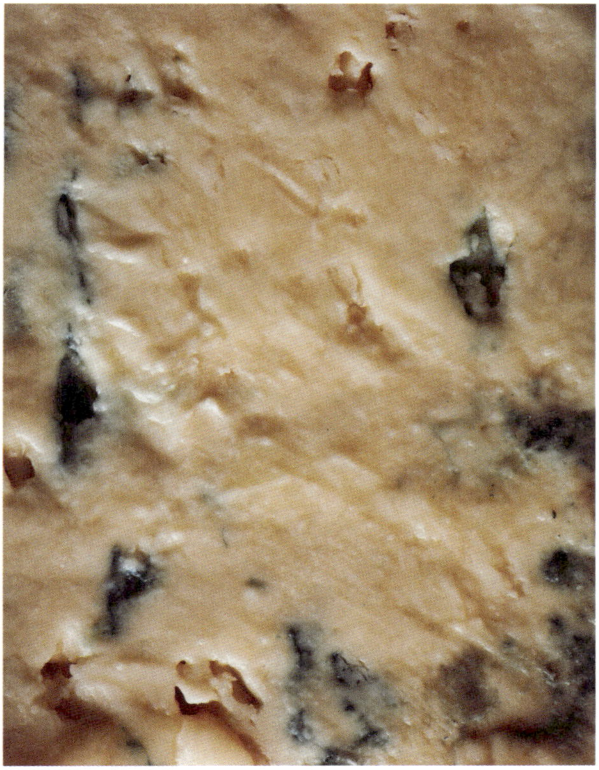

NECTARINE AND BURRATA SALAD WITH CANDIED ALMONDS
\
SERVES 6

25g butter
100g caster sugar
100g flaked almonds, toasted
6 large nectarines, halved and stoned
100g rocket
1 small bunch of basil, leaves picked
3 burrata
50ml thick balsamic vinegar
extra virgin olive oil, for drizzling
freshly ground black pepper

There are few better ways to serve burrata than on top of a simple combination of nectarines and rocket. With basil for extra freshness and toasted flaked almonds for a bit of crunch, this is the perfect summer salad.

Line a baking tray with baking parchment. Heat a small pan over a medium heat, add the butter and sugar and when it reaches a deep caramel colour, add the flaked almonds. Coat all over carefully, then pour onto the prepared tray and leave to cool.

Heat a large frying pan over a high heat and cook the nectarines, flat-side down, until charred.

Slice the charred nectarines, then pile onto a platter and top with the rocket, flaked almonds, basil and burrata. Drizzle over the balsamic, then drizzle some extra virgin olive oil over the burrata and season with black pepper. Serve.

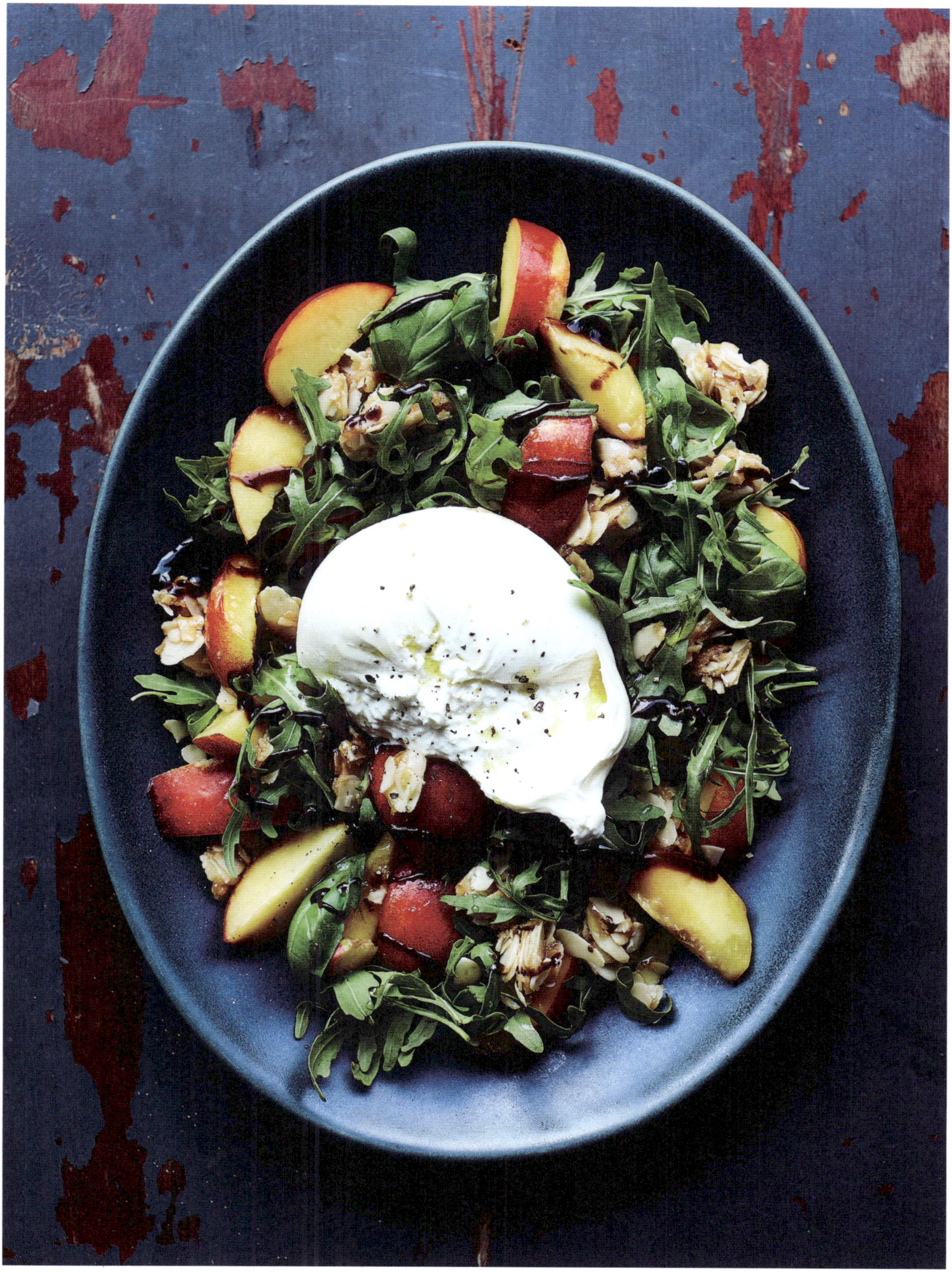

LEEK AND POTATO SOUP WITH CRISPY BACON AND BLUE CHEESE TOASTS

SERVES 4

2 leeks, sliced
300g potatoes, peeled and sliced
100ml double cream
500ml full-fat milk

FOR THE TOASTS
300g Stilton, sliced
50ml double cream
4 slices of sourdough bread, toasted
4 slices of bacon, cooked until crisp and crumbled

TO SERVE
1 leek, cut into very thin strips (julienned)
oil, for deep-frying
1 tablespoon double cream
1 tablespoon olive oil

The blue cheese toasts topped with crispy bacon are a wonderful contrast to the creamy simplicity of a leek and potato soup. If you don't have Stilton, Gorgonzola or Roquefort would work equally well here. The crispy leeks add another layer, but are not completely necessary.

Put the sliced leeks, potatoes, cream and milk in a pan over a high heat and bring to the boil. Reduce the heat and simmer for 6–8 minutes. Remove from the heat and blitz in the pan with a stick blender until completely smooth.

For the crispy leeks, heat the oil in a deep saucepan over a medium heat. When the temperature gets to 160°C/325°F, deep-fry the leek in batches – each batch will take about 2 minutes. Using a slotted spoon, carefully drain onto kitchen paper and season with salt.

Preheat the grill to high.

Mix the Stilton and cream together, then spread over the toasted sourdough. Grill until hot and bubbling. Halve the toasts and sprinkle with the crispy bacon.

Divide the soup between four bowls, then drizzle with the cream and oil and top with some crispy leeks. Serve with the crispy bacon and blue cheese toasts alongside.

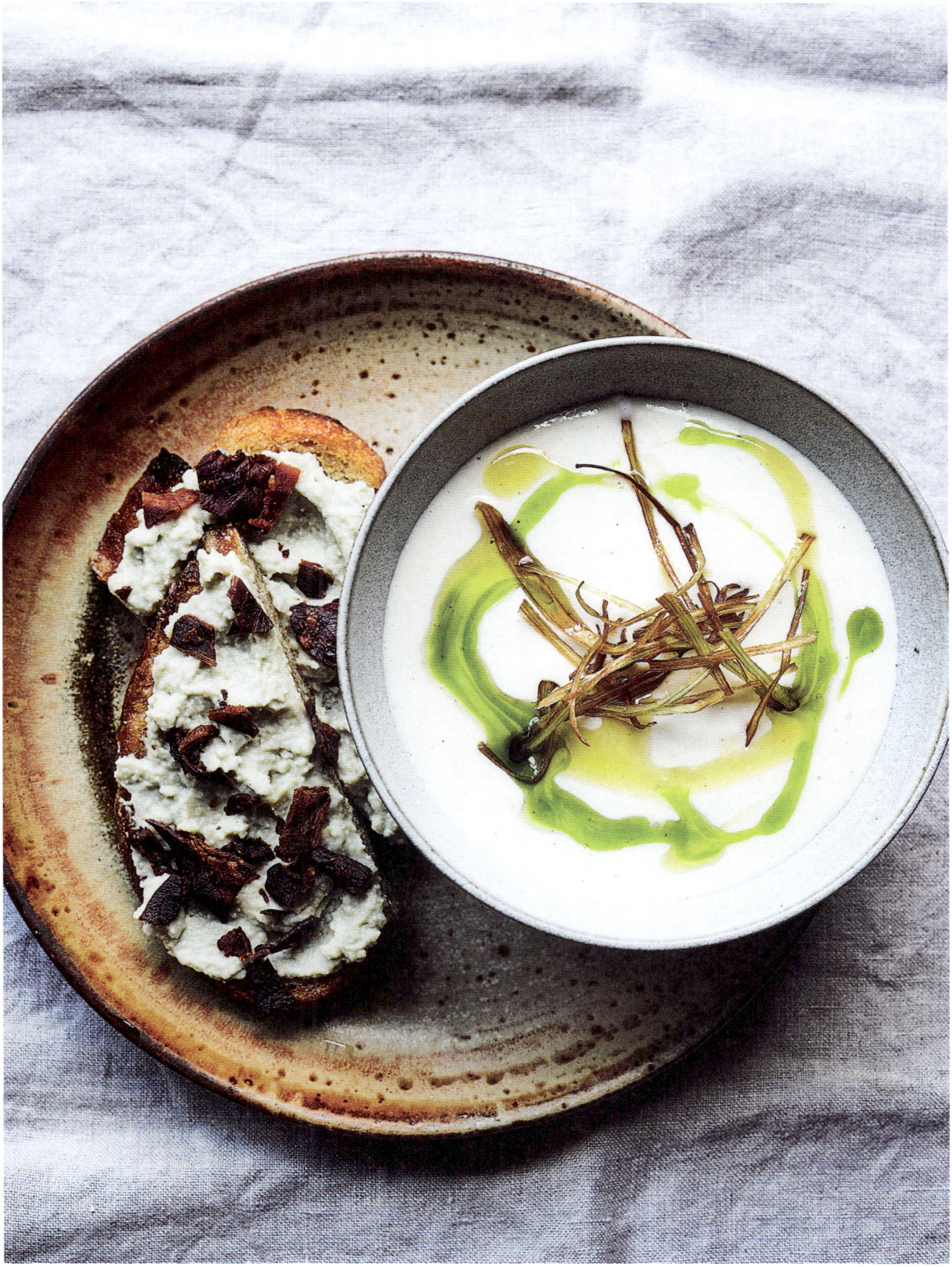

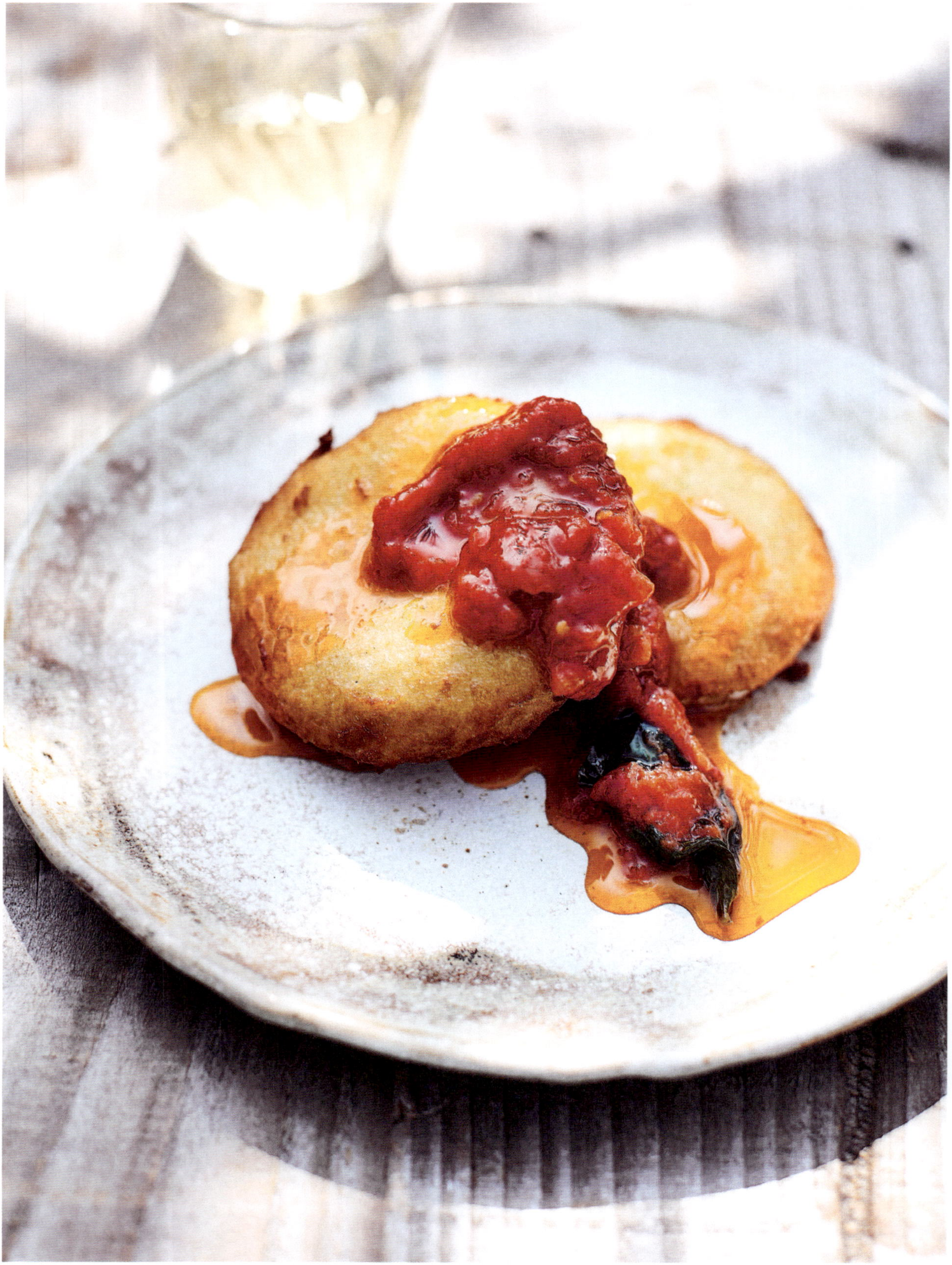

MOZZARELLA SANDWICHES WITH ARRABBIATA SAUCE
\
SERVES 6

2 litres vegetable oil
2 eggs
200ml full-fat milk
12 slices of white bread
2 balls of mozzarella, sliced
12 basil leaves

FOR THE SAUCE
400g can chopped tomatoes
2 tomatoes, chopped
1 teaspoon chilli flakes
50ml olive oil
1 small bunch of basil, leaves picked
sea salt and freshly ground
   black pepper

Here I've encased mozzarella in eggy bread and then deep-fried the sandwiches to add a pleasing crunchy texture to contrast with the creamy cheese. Topped off with an easy 5-minute tomato sauce, this is a simple but satisfying dish.

Whisk the eggs and milk together. Flatten the bread slices with a rolling pin and cut into 12 circles. Dip each piece of bread into the egg mixture, then top six pieces with cheese and basil and pop the remaining circles on top. Squeeze together to seal.

In a deep-fat fryer or deep-sided saucepan, heat the vegetable oil to 170°C (340°F).

Place all the sauce ingredients in a pan over a medium heat and bring to the boil. Reduce the heat and simmer for 5 minutes.

Deep-fry the sandwiches for a couple of minutes until golden brown, then drain on kitchen paper. Season with sea salt.

Sit the sandwiches on plates, then spoon over the sauce.

PARMESAN AND ROSEMARY BISCUITS WITH BAKED CAMEMBERT, FIGS AND HONEY

\

MAKES 12–16 BISCUITS/SERVES 6

3 Camemberts, in wooden boxes
75g pistachios
75g walnuts, chopped
9 figs, quartered
100g runny honey

FOR THE BISCUITS
150g butter, plus extra for greasing
75g Parmesan, grated
75g Cheddar, grated
1 teaspoon mustard powder
1 tablespoon rosemary leaves, chopped
1 egg yolk
150g plain flour, plus extra for dusting

These savoury biscuits combine Cheddar and Parmesan and can be enjoyed on their own or, for extra cheesiness, alongside oozing baked Camembert. Try switching the Camembert for Brie or Tunworth too.

Preheat the oven to 180°C (160°C fan)/350°F/gas 4. Grease a baking tray with butter.

Use a stand mixer to beat the butter, both cheeses, mustard and rosemary together. Beat in the egg yolk, then fold in the flour. Tip onto a floured surface and knead lightly. Roll into one or two long sausage shapes, about 6cm in diameter, then wrap in clingfilm and chill in the fridge for 30 minutes.

Unwrap the dough and slice into 1cm-thick circles. Pop onto the prepared baking tray and bake for 10–12 minutes until golden and crisp round the edges. Remove from the oven and leave to cool.

Meanwhile, take the Camemberts out of their wrapping, and discard the paper. Slice the top off the cheeses and pop them back into the wooden boxes (lids off). Cover in the nuts and figs and bake for 10 minutes. Drizzle with the honey and serve with the biscuits. Any leftover biscuits will keep in an airtight container for a couple of days.

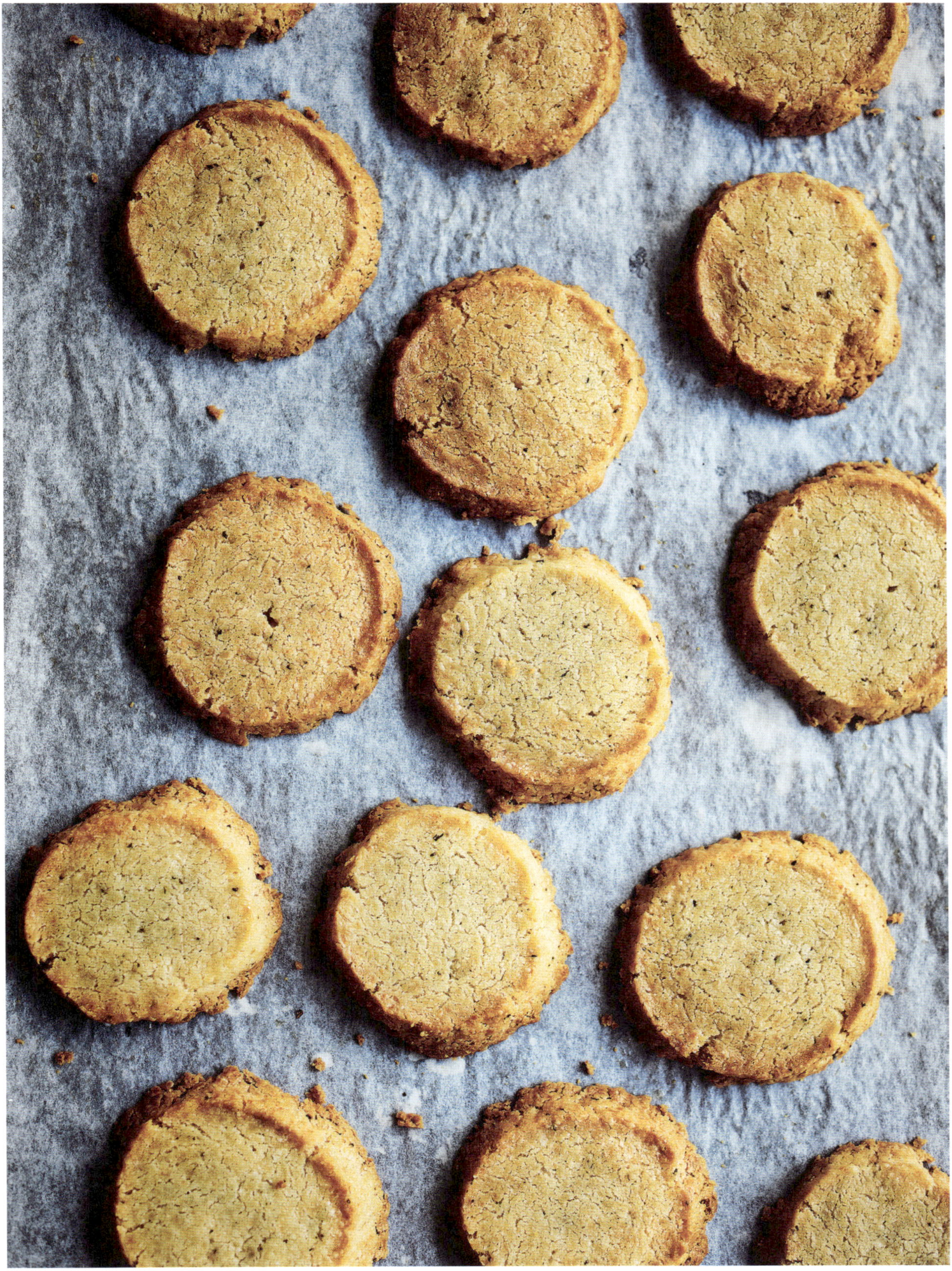

SMOKED HADDOCK WELSH RAREBIT
\
SERVES 2

2 x 200g undyed smoked haddock fillets
milk, to cover
2 slices of sourdough bread, toasted
4 tablespoons chutney of your choice
sea salt and freshly ground black pepper

FOR THE RAREBIT
350g Cheddar, grated
50ml full-fat milk
1 teaspoon Worcestershire sauce
2 tablespoons English mustard
a few drops of Tabasco
4 tablespoons plain flour
3 egg yolks

TO SERVE
a few chives, chopped
2 tablespoons olive oil
1 teaspoon white wine vinegar

Here I've added salty, smoky haddock to the classic Welsh rarebit. The chutney also adds another layer of flavour and it's all finished off with a simple drizzle of chive dressing.

First make the rarebit. Line a 20 x 15cm baking tray with baking parchment. Gently melt the cheese in a medium pan over a medium heat. Add the remaining rarebit ingredients and cook for 1–2 minutes. Pour onto the prepared tray and chill in the fridge for about 1 hour until set.

Preheat the grill to high.

Put the haddock into a pan, cover with milk and poach over a medium heat for 2–3 minutes. Transfer to a tray using a fish slice and season.

Meanwhile, mix together the chives, olive oil and vinegar and set aside.

Put the sourdough into the bottom of a 20 x 15cm ovenproof dish. Dot with the chutney, then sit the haddock on top. Put the rarebit on top of the fish. Grill for 2–3 minutes until the rarebit is heated through and starting to char on top.

To serve, portion the rarebit on plates, ensuring each serving has a fillet of haddock, and spoon over the chive dressing.

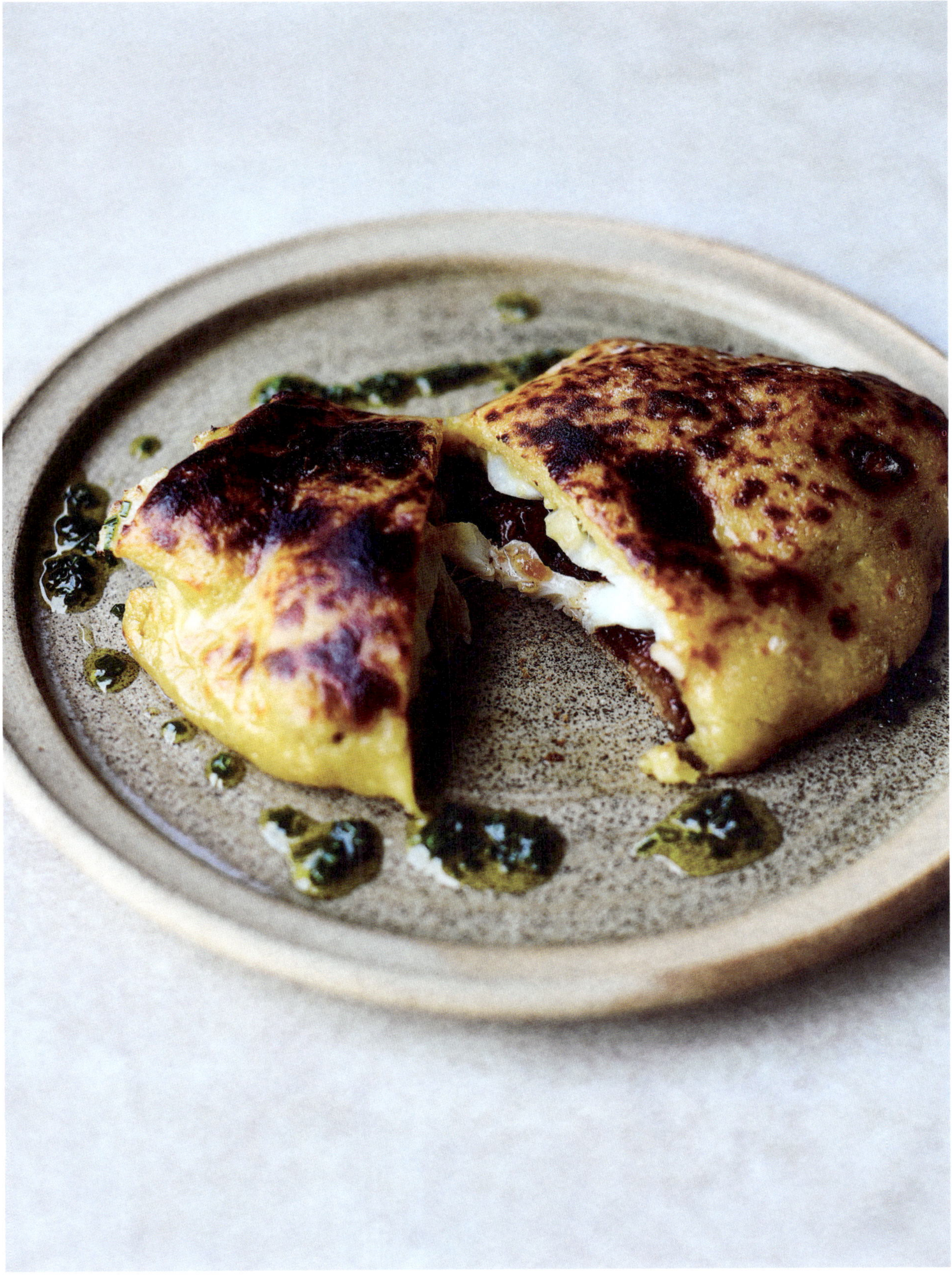

SALMON MOUSSE
\
SERVES 6-8

12 slices of smoked salmon
watercress, to serve

FOR THE MOUSSE
400g smoked salmon
400g full-fat cream cheese
200ml double cream
zest and juice of 1 unwaxed lemon
freshly ground black pepper

Cream cheese helps form the base of this simple salmon mousse which takes less than 10 minutes to throw together. All you need to do then is pop it in the fridge to chill and firm up. Make it in the morning and enjoy for lunch, or prep ahead and serve as a dinner party starter.

Line a 20cm savarin mould with clingfilm, allowing plenty of overlap. Then use the slices of salmon to line the sides and base of the mould.

To make the mousse, add all the ingredients to a food processor and whizz for 20–30 seconds. Use the mousse to fill the salmon-lined mould. Loosely cover with the clingfilm, then transfer to the fridge to chill for 2 hours.

To serve, unwrap the mousse and invert it onto a plate. Fill the centre with watercress.

STUFFED TOMATOES
\
SERVES 5

½ onion, diced
2 garlic cloves, diced
400g minced lamb
1 courgette, diced
1 small aubergine, diced
1 teaspoon ground cinnamon
100ml chicken stock
2 tablespoons chopped mint
5 beef tomatoes
100g cooked long-grain rice
5 mozzarella pearls
olive oil, for drizzling (optional)
sea salt and freshly ground
    black pepper

These stuffed tomatoes take full advantage of fresh mozzarella's wonderful ability to melt when baked as it perfectly tops off the lamb, vegetable and rice filling.

Preheat the oven to 200°C (180°C fan)/400°F/gas 6.

In a dry frying pan over a medium heat, fry the onion, garlic, lamb, courgette, aubergine and cinnamon until the lamb is crisp and browned. Add the stock and mint and cook for 8 minutes.

Cut the tops off the tomatoes and scoop out the centres. Chop and add the scooped-out tomato flesh to the lamb mixture, cook for 5 minutes and stir through the rice.

Fill the tomatoes with the lamb mixture, add a ball of mozzarella to each one and replace the tomato tops. Transfer to a baking tray and cook in the oven for 5 minutes until the cheeese has melted.

To serve, drizzle with olive oil, if desired.

Pictured overleaf

SMALL PLATES AND SNACKS

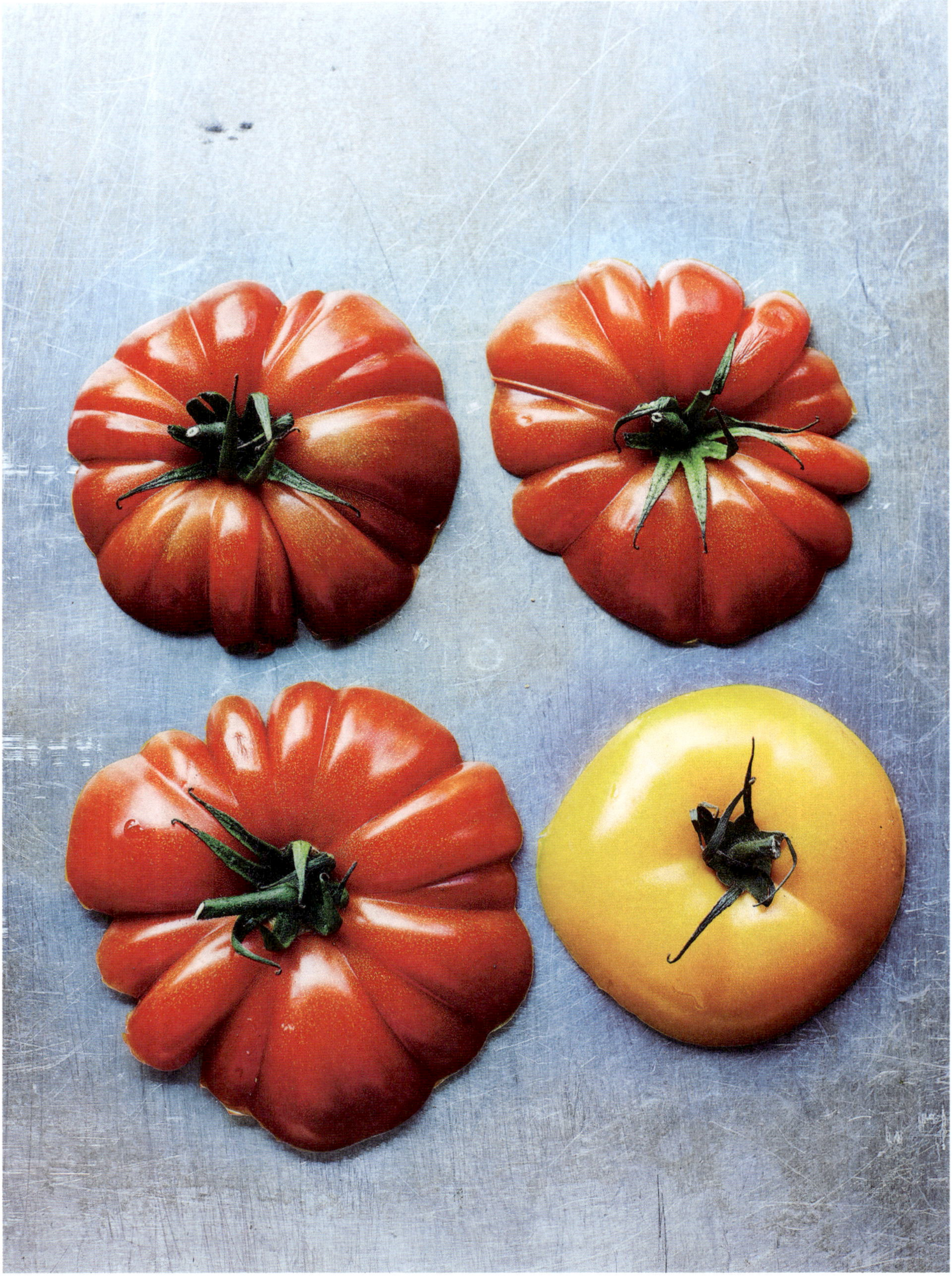

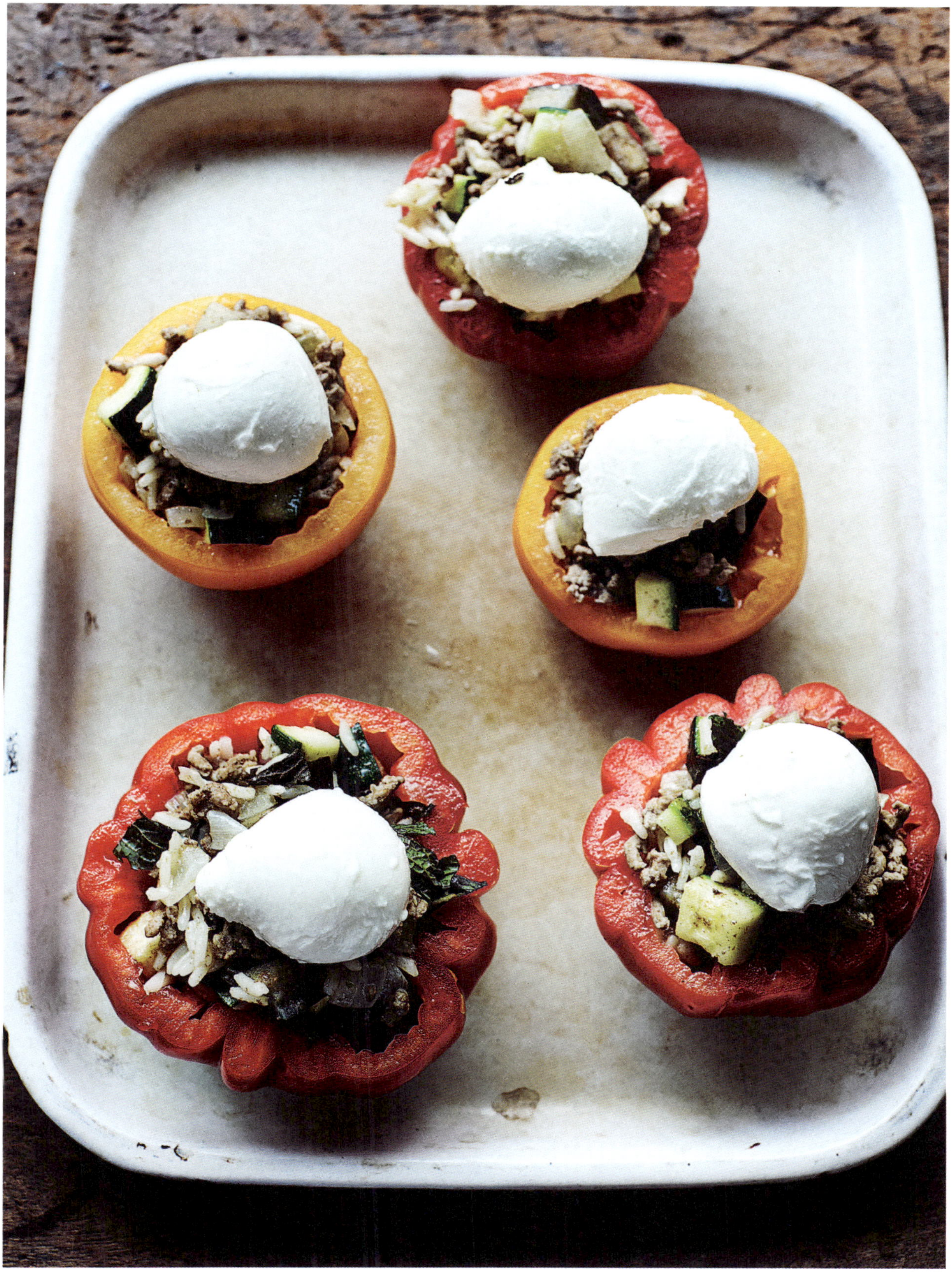

WARM BULGUR WHEAT SALAD WITH FETA
\
SERVES 4

50ml olive oil
200g cooked bulgur wheat
50g pistachios, chopped
50g pine nuts
50g almonds, chopped
50g dried apricots, chopped
50g mixed sultanas, raisins and currants
1 small bunch of mint, chopped
1 small bunch of coriander, chopped
100g pomegranate seeds
pinch of chilli flakes
pinch of za'atar
juice of 2 lemons
200g feta, crumbled

One of the best ways to use feta is crumbled over salads, like in this nutty, fruity bulgur wheat dish. Here it adds a tangy, salty note to the sweet fruit, fresh herbs, zesty lemon and crunchy array of nuts.

Warm a large frying pan over a medium heat and add the oil. Fry the bulgur wheat, pistachios, pine nuts and almonds until hot, then stir through the remaining ingredients, except the feta.

To serve, spoon the warm bulgur wheat mixture into bowls and top with the feta.

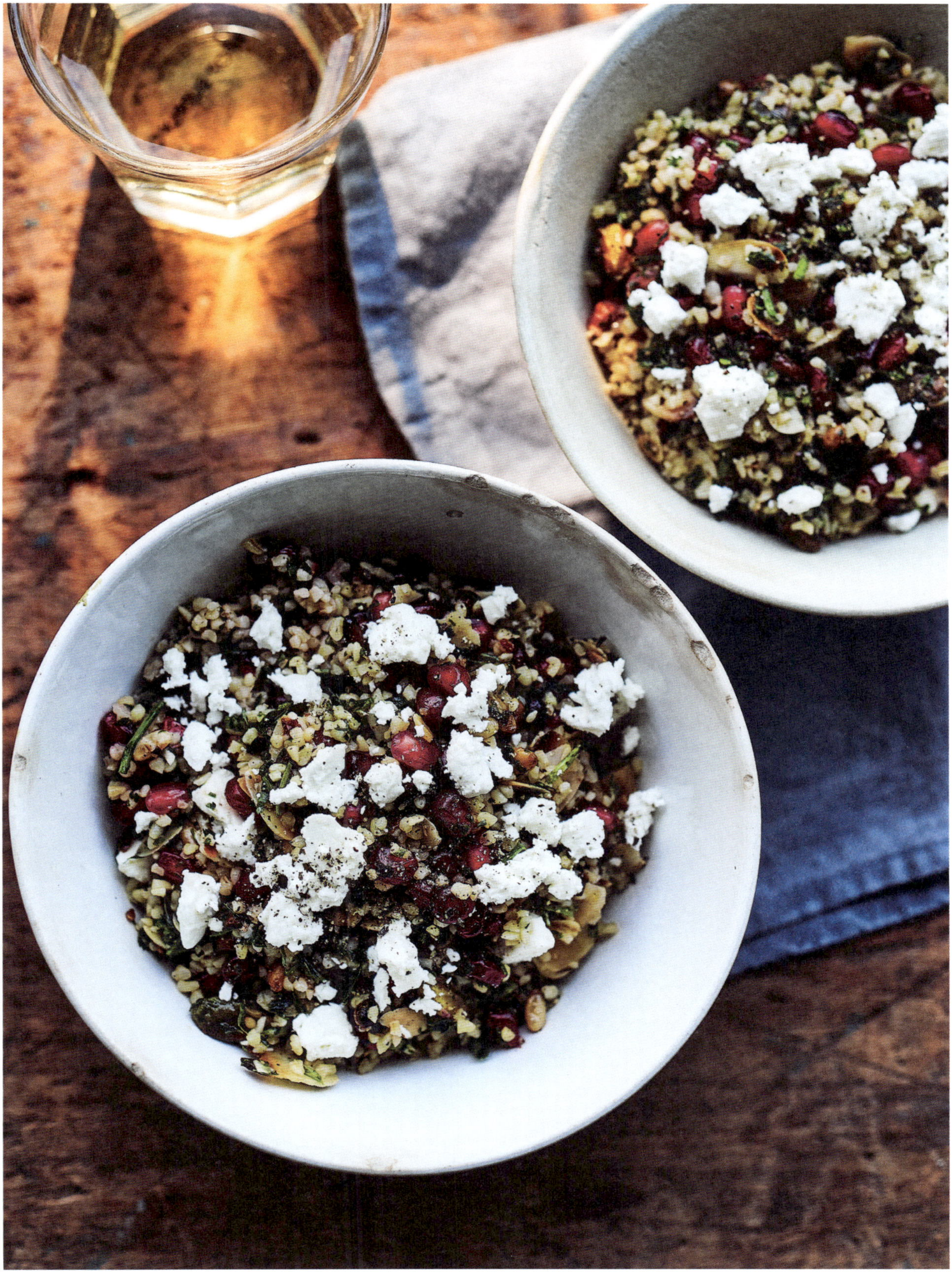

Pont-l'Évêque AOP
au lait cru
400g
UNE HISTOIRE DE FAMILLE
GRATIOT
Fabriqué en Normandie
Soft ripened cheese. Product of France

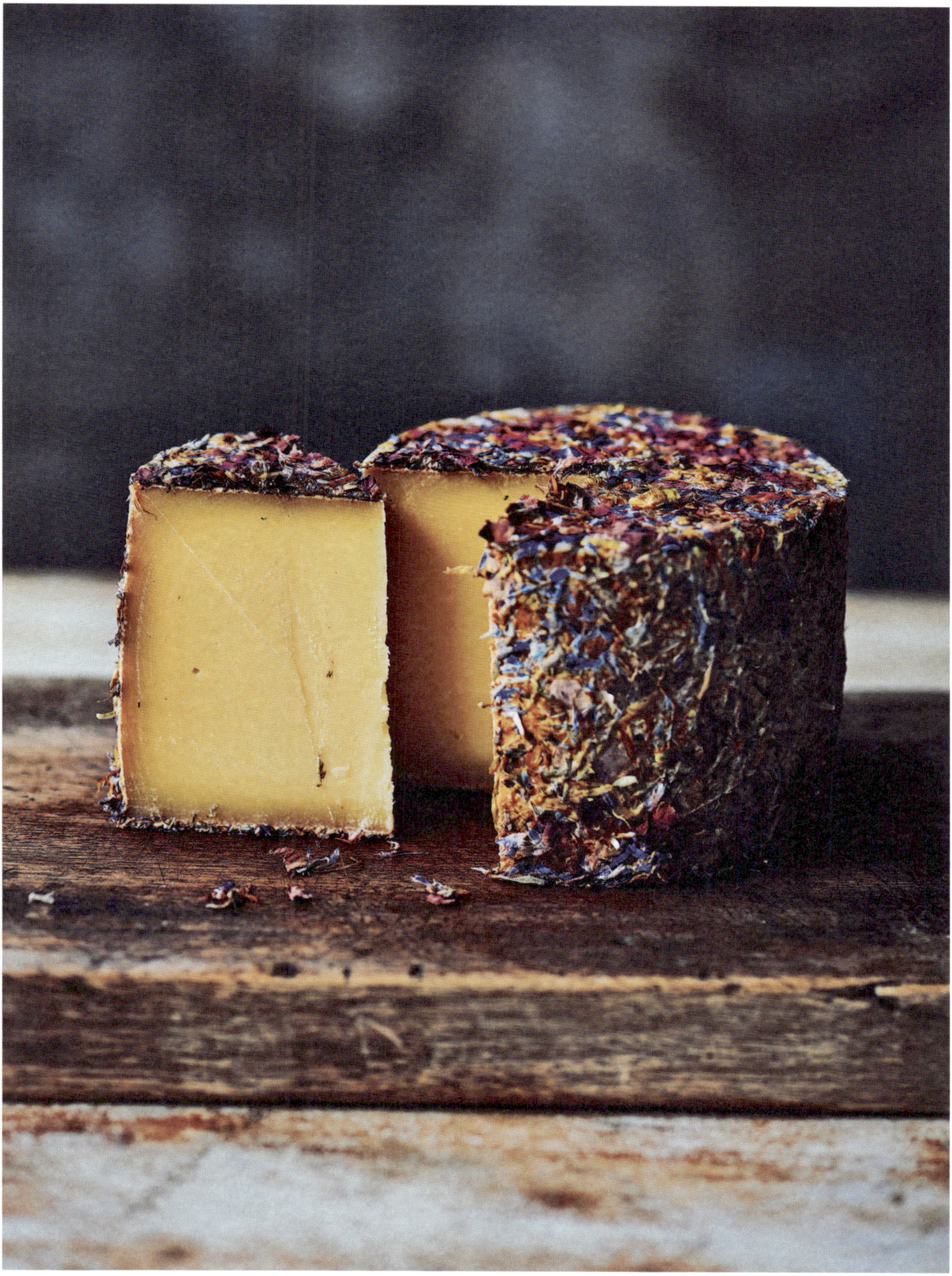

WARM LENTIL SALAD WITH WHIPPED GOAT'S CHEESE BUTTER

SERVES 4

25g butter
2 garlic cloves, chopped
1 shallot, diced
½ carrot, peeled and diced
½ celery stick, diced
50g bacon lardons
½ leek, diced
1 teaspoon ground cumin
1 teaspoon ground coriander
150g green lentils
a few sprigs of thyme
300ml chicken stock
50ml red wine
25g butter
1 tablespoon sherry vinegar
1 small bunch of coriander, chopped

TO SERVE
100g goat's butter, softened
200g soft goat's cheese
freshly ground black pepper

Here I've combined soft goat's cheese with goat's butter, perfect for topping a warm salad so the cheese can melt into the lentils.

Melt the butter in a large pan over a medium heat, then add the garlic, shallot, carrot, celery, bacon, leek and spices and cook for a minute. Add the remaining ingredients, bring to the boil, then simmer for 30 minutes.

Whisk together the goat's butter and cheese, and season with pepper.

To serve, spoon the lentils onto plates and dot with the goat's cheese butter.

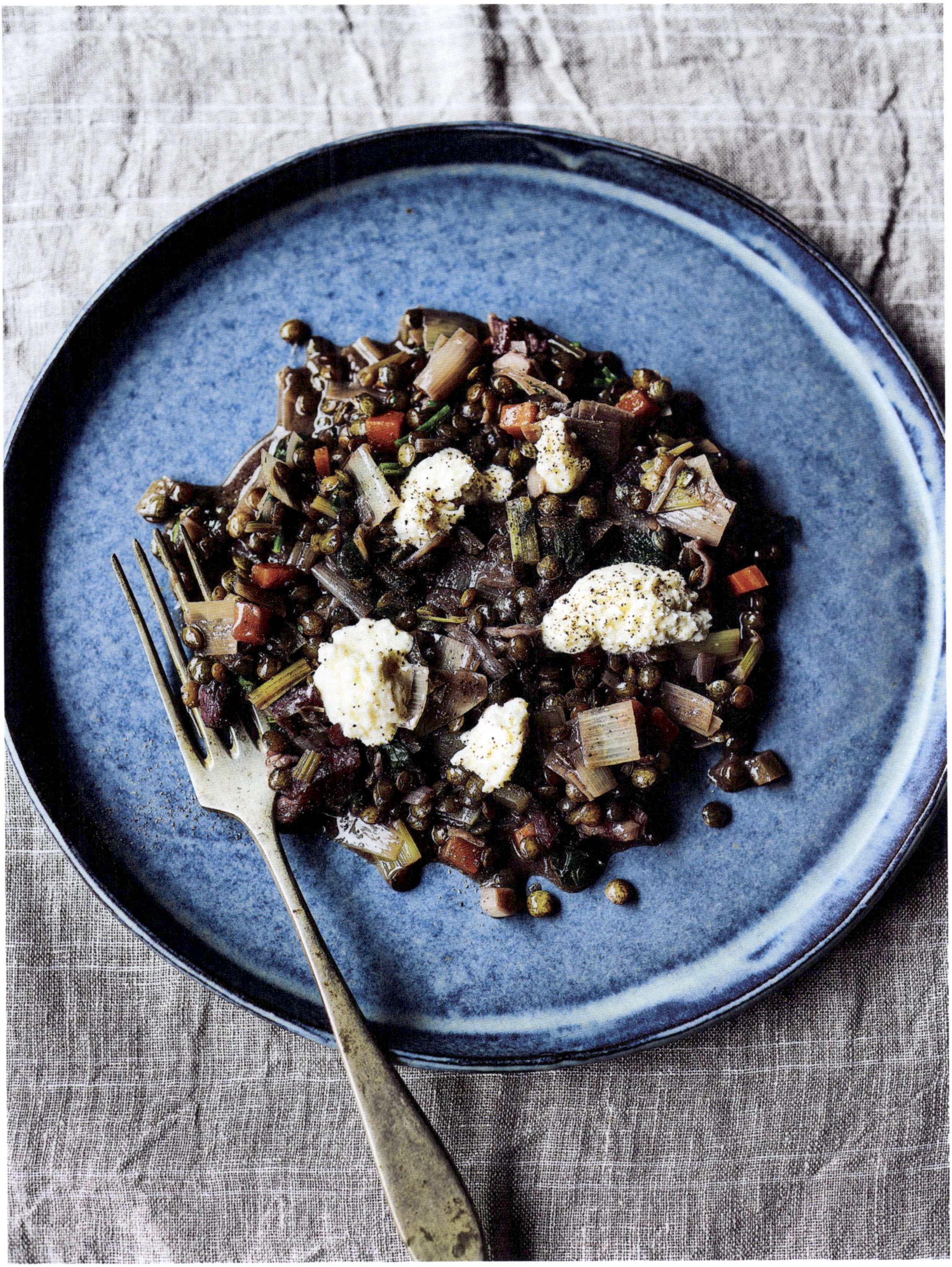

SPANISH SALAD
\
SERVES 4–6

300g broad beans
200g fresh peas
100g sugar snap peas, sliced
100g mangetout, sliced
1 bunch of spring onions, sliced
100g butter
2 tablespoons chopped sage
2 tablespoons sherry vinegar

FOR THE CROUTONS
8 thin slices of baguette
50g butter

TO SERVE
12 slices of Spanish ham
12 slices of Manchego

As with several other recipes in this chapter, this dish uses the classic cheese and ham combination, but with a twist. Taking the deconstructed elements of a sandwich, including bread in the form of croutons, this salad combines them with fresh summer vegetables for a satisfying lunch.

In a large pan over a medium heat, fry the bread in the butter until golden and crisp on both sides. Drain on kitchen paper.

Bring a large pan of water to the boil and cook the broad beans for 2 minutes. Then add the peas, sugar snaps and mangetout and cook for another minute. Stir through the spring onions and remove from the heat. Drain.

In a second large pan over a medium heat, warm the butter and sage and stir through the vegetables and vinegar. Spoon onto a platter, then top with the ham, cheese and croutons and serve.

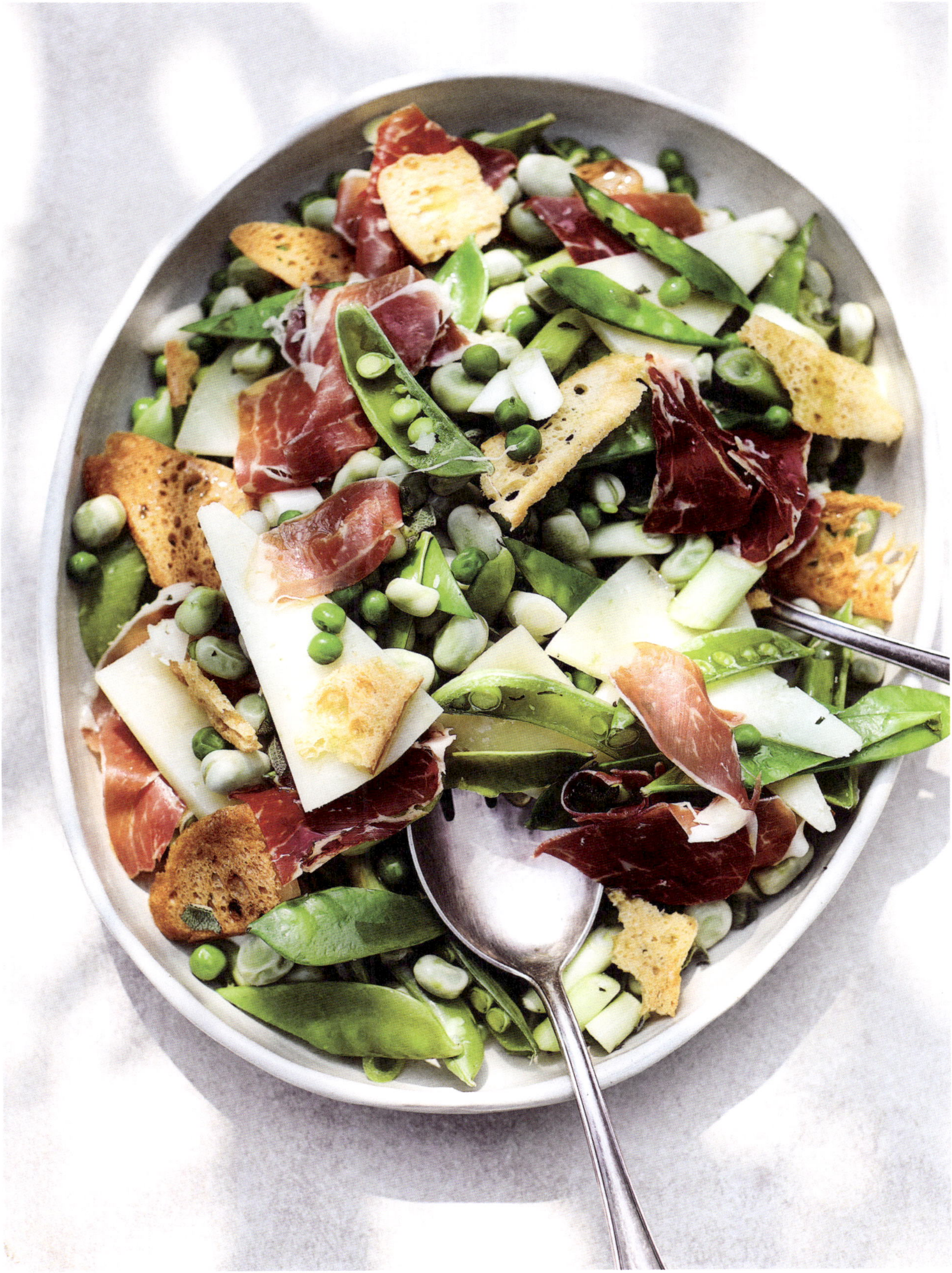

WELSH RAREBIT TOASTIE
\
SERVES 2

2 thick slices of bread of your choice
green salad dressed with a
   French vinaigrette

FOR THE RAREBIT
500g Cheddar, grated
100ml bitter (beer)
1 teaspoon Henderson's Relish
1 teaspoon English mustard
a few drops of Tabasco
4 tablespoons plain flour
1 egg yolk

This is more of a traditional take on the rarebit than other recipes in this chapter (see pages 52 and 86). With a simple cheese sauce and no added extras, the contrast is provided by a fresh, dressed green salad.

Preheat the oven to 200°C (180°C fan)/400°F/gas 6.

First make the rarebit. Gently melt the cheese in a medium pan over a medium heat. Add all the remaining rarebit ingredients and stir together.

Put the bread on a baking tray and toast on both sides until golden. Spoon the rarebit over both slices of toast, then bake in the oven for 5 minutes until bubbling and starting to char.

To serve, spoon the salad alongside the rarebit.

CHICORY, FETA AND POMEGRANATE SALAD
\
SERVES 6

400g red and white chicory (endive), sliced
100g pomegranate seeds
100g pine nuts, toasted
1 small bunch of mint, chopped
1 small bunch of coriander, chopped
200g feta, crumbled

FOR THE DRESSING
150ml vegetable oil
50ml white wine vinegar
1 tablespoon Dijon mustard
splash of water
2 tablespoons pomegranate molasses

In this salad I've used the salty, creamy feta as a foil for bitter endive, sweet pomegranate seeds, fresh herbs and crunchy pine nuts.

Place the chicory in a large serving bowl and top with the pomegranate seeds, nuts, herbs and feta.

Whisk all the dressing ingredients together and spoon over the salad. Serve.

MAINS

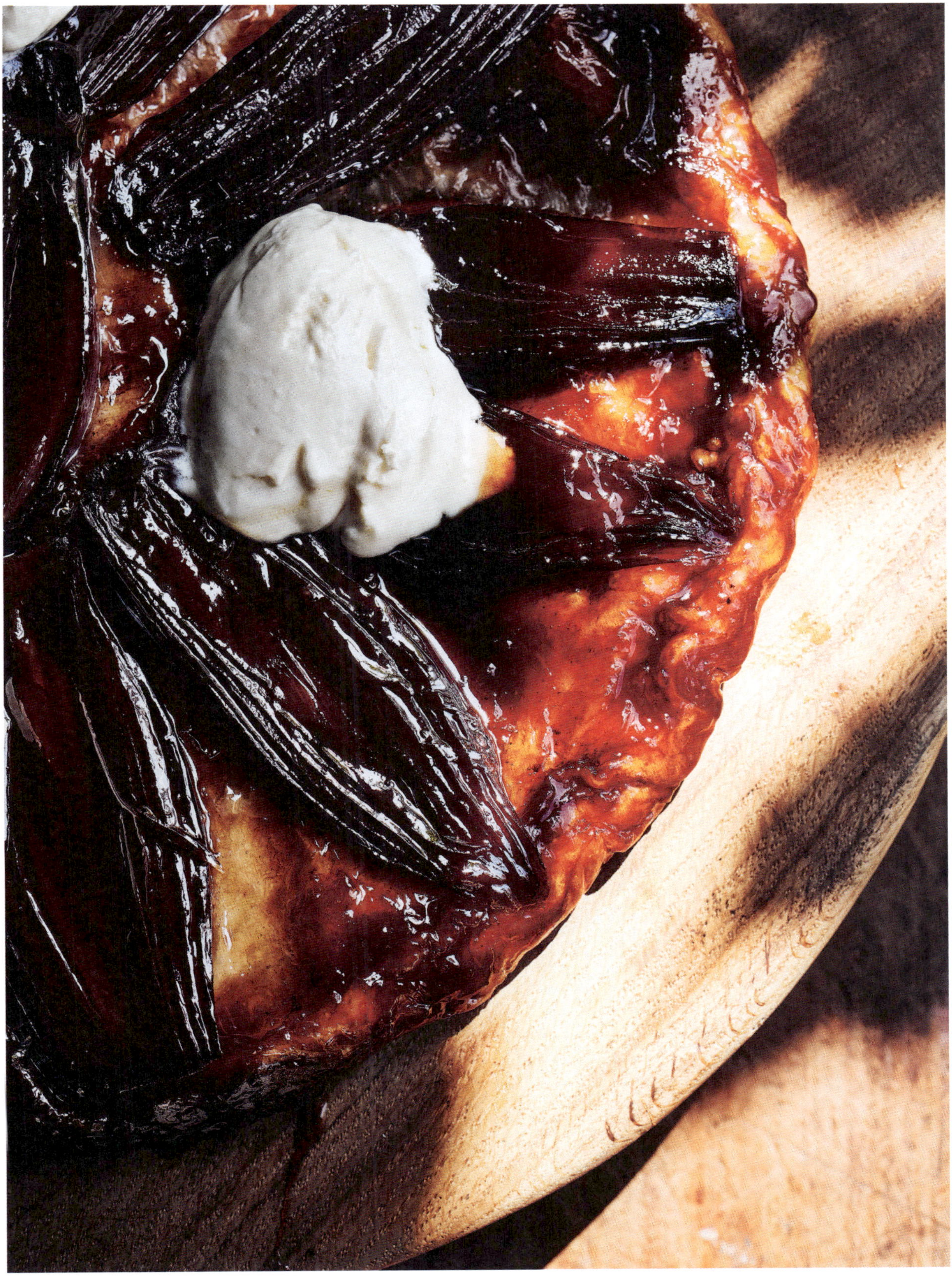

COTTAGE PIE
\
SERVES 8

1kg minced beef
1 onion, diced
1 garlic clove, chopped
450ml beef stock
1.5kg potatoes, peeled and diced
125g butter
300g Cheddar, grated
sea salt and freshly ground
   black pepper

TO SERVE
300g frozen peas
25g butter

The golden, cheesy mashed potato topping is the crowning glory of a traditional cottage pie and the dish just wouldn't be the same without it.

Place a large non-stick pan over a high heat and fry the beef, onion and garlic for 6–8 minutes until deep brown in colour. Then add the stock, season and simmer for 1 hour. Pour into a large ovenproof dish and leave to cool.

Preheat the oven to 200°C (180°C fan)/400°F/gas 6.

Meanwhile, boil the potatoes in salted boiling water until soft. Drain, then pass through a ricer into a bowl. Add the butter and season. Pipe or fork on top of the meat, then top with the grated cheese. Bake in the oven for 30–40 minutes.

Plunge the peas into boiling water for 2 minutes. Drain and dot with the butter. Serve alongside the cottage pie.

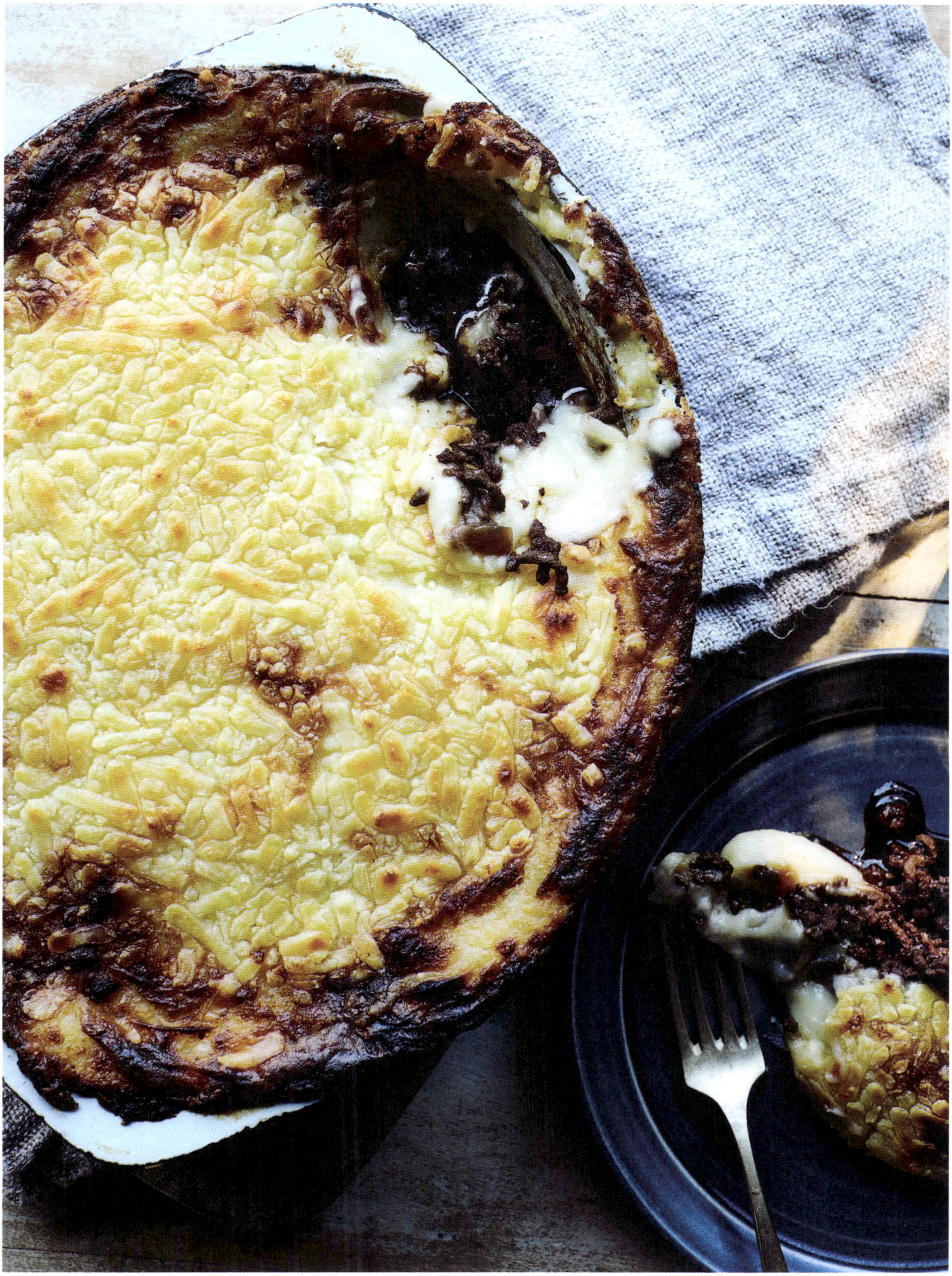

TART BRIOCHE WITH SMOKED HADDOCK AND TUNWORTH \
SERVES 6

1 egg
100ml full-fat milk
250g strong bread flour, plus extra for dusting
25g caster sugar
5g salt
25g fast action yeast
25g butter, plus extra for greasing

FOR THE FILLING
1 Tunworth cheese
a few sprigs of rosemary
300g smoked haddock, skinned and flaked
25g butter, melted

This tart brioche showcases one of our finest cheeses – Tunworth – as a whole round is placed in the middle to create a gloriously gooey sauce for the haddock.

To make the brioche, put the egg and milk into the bowl of a stand mixer fitted with a dough hook. Add the flour, sugar, salt and yeast and mix until the dough comes together. Then add the butter and pull and stretch the dough by hand until it is elastic and passes the windowpane test when you can stretch it into a thin, translucent membrane without breaking. Cover the dough with clingfilm or a clean tea towel and leave to rest at room temperature for 1 hour.

On a lightly floured work surface, roll the dough into a circular shape. Cover with clingfilm, transfer to a tray, then rest in the fridge for 3 hours, or ideally overnight.

Butter and line a 25cm tart ring, 4.5cm deep, with baking parchment. Grease a baking tray and sit the tart ring on top.

Roll the dough into an even circle, roughly 25cm diameter, on a lightly floured surface, then place into the prepared tart ring on the tray. Sit the cheese in the middle and leave to prove at room temperature until doubled in size.

Preheat the oven to 170°C (150°C fan)/340°F/gas 3½.

Dot the tart with the rosemary leaves and haddock. Bake for 15–20 minutes until golden and baked through. Brush with melted butter and serve warm.

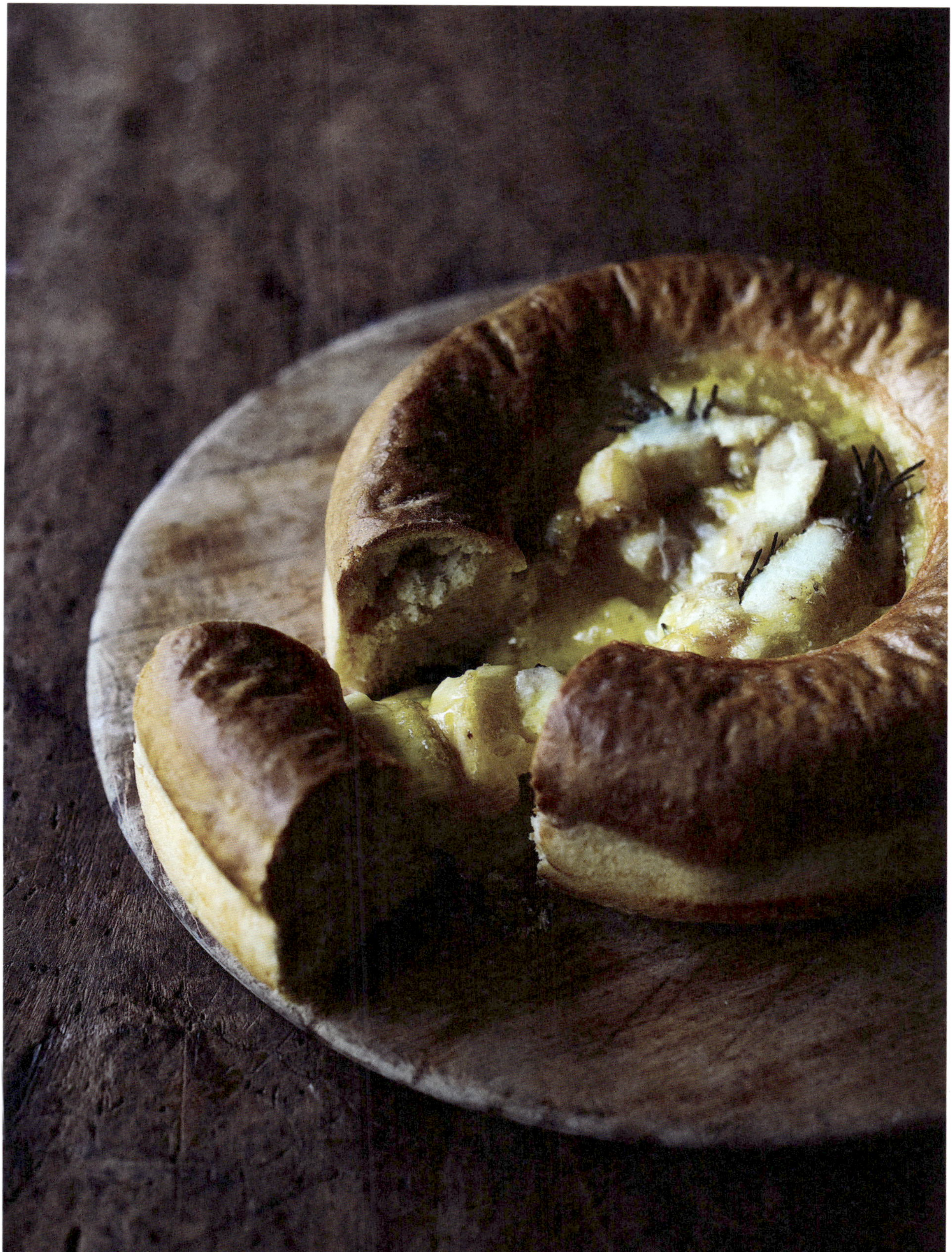

ASPARAGUS AND WENSLEYDALE TART
\
SERVES 8

4 eggs
4 egg yolks
300ml double cream
300ml full-fat milk
2 shallots, diced
25g butter
600g asparagus, woody ends snapped off
200g Wensleydale, crumbled
sea salt and freshly ground black pepper

FOR THE PASTRY
400g plain flour, plus extra for dusting
200g butter, plus extra for greasing
pinch of salt
3 sprigs of thyme, leaves picked (optional)
1 egg

Wensleydale is a creamy cheese, associated with Yorkshire in particular but now made throughout the UK. Despite being thought of as an iconic English cheese, it was actually first made by French Cistercian monks, who settled in Jervaulx in lower Wensleydale. This simple tart pairs it with asparagus – perfect for a spring or summer dinner.

First make the pastry. Put the flour into a bowl, add the butter, salt and thyme (if using), then rub between your fingers until the mixture looks like coarse breadcrumbs. Add the egg and mix with your fingers, adding a splash of water if needed to bring the dough together. Knead the dough on a floured work surface until smooth, then wrap in clingfilm and chill in the fridge for 30 minutes.

Preheat the oven to 170°C (150°C fan)/340°F/gas 3½. Grease a 27cm tart tin.

Roll out the pastry on a lightly floured surface and use to line the tin, allowing it to overhang slightly.

For the filling, in a bowl, whisk together the eggs, egg yolks, cream and milk, then season.

Set a pan over a medium heat and cook the shallots in the butter for 5 minutes. Leave to cool, then spread over the base of the tart.

Pour the custard into the tart tin, top with the asparagus and sprinkle the Wensleydale over the top. Bake in the oven for 30–40 minutes.

Once cooked, let the tart sit for 5 minutes and trim the edge of the pastry crust. Serve warm or cold.

BEST-EVER CHEESEBURGER
\
SERVES 4

600g minced beef
sea salt and freshly ground
    black pepper

FOR THE CHUTNEY
3 onions, sliced
a knob of butter
1 tablespoon vegetable oil, plus
    extra for drizzling
50g demerara sugar
1 large tomato, sliced
50ml white wine vinegar
25g sultanas

TO SERVE
500g Cuddy's Cave, sliced
4 brioche buns, halved
1 Little Gem lettuce
a few pickles

For my ultimate burger, I've topped it with Cuddy's Cave, which has a strong, slightly nutty flavour. I'd strongly advise you try to get your hands on some, but if you can't then Cheddar or another hard cheese which melts well would make a good substitute.

To make the chutney, in a pan over a medium heat, cook the onions in the butter and oil for 30 minutes until caramelised.

Heat a non-stick pan over a medium heat and, when hot, add the sugar. Do not stir but carefully swirl in the pan until the sugar is brown and caramelised. This should take about 3–4 minutes. Once the sugar has caramelised, pop in the caramelised onions and tomato, drizzle in the vinegar and sprinkle in the sultanas. Remove from the heat and leave to cool.

Mix the beef with some salt and pepper and mould into four patties. Drizzle with oil, then place the burgers into a large frying pan and cook gently for 5 minutes. Flip the burgers over, top with a square of cheese and continue to cook for a further 5 minutes.

Toast the brioche buns, sliced-side down.

To serve, layer up the burgers, starting with a brioche bun base, then lettuce, chutney, pickles and a beefburger. Top with the brioche bun lid before securing with a stick.

Pictured overleaf

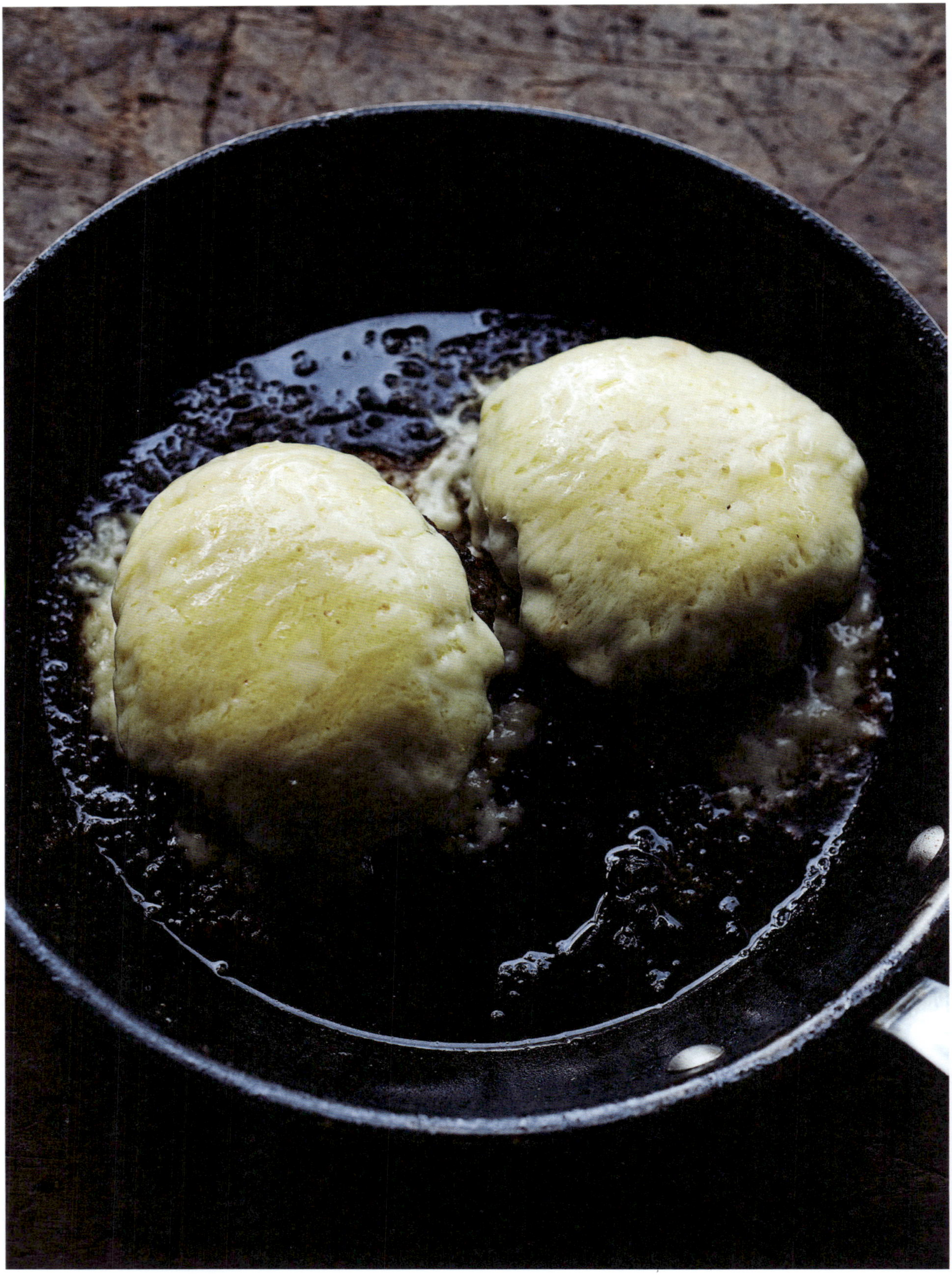

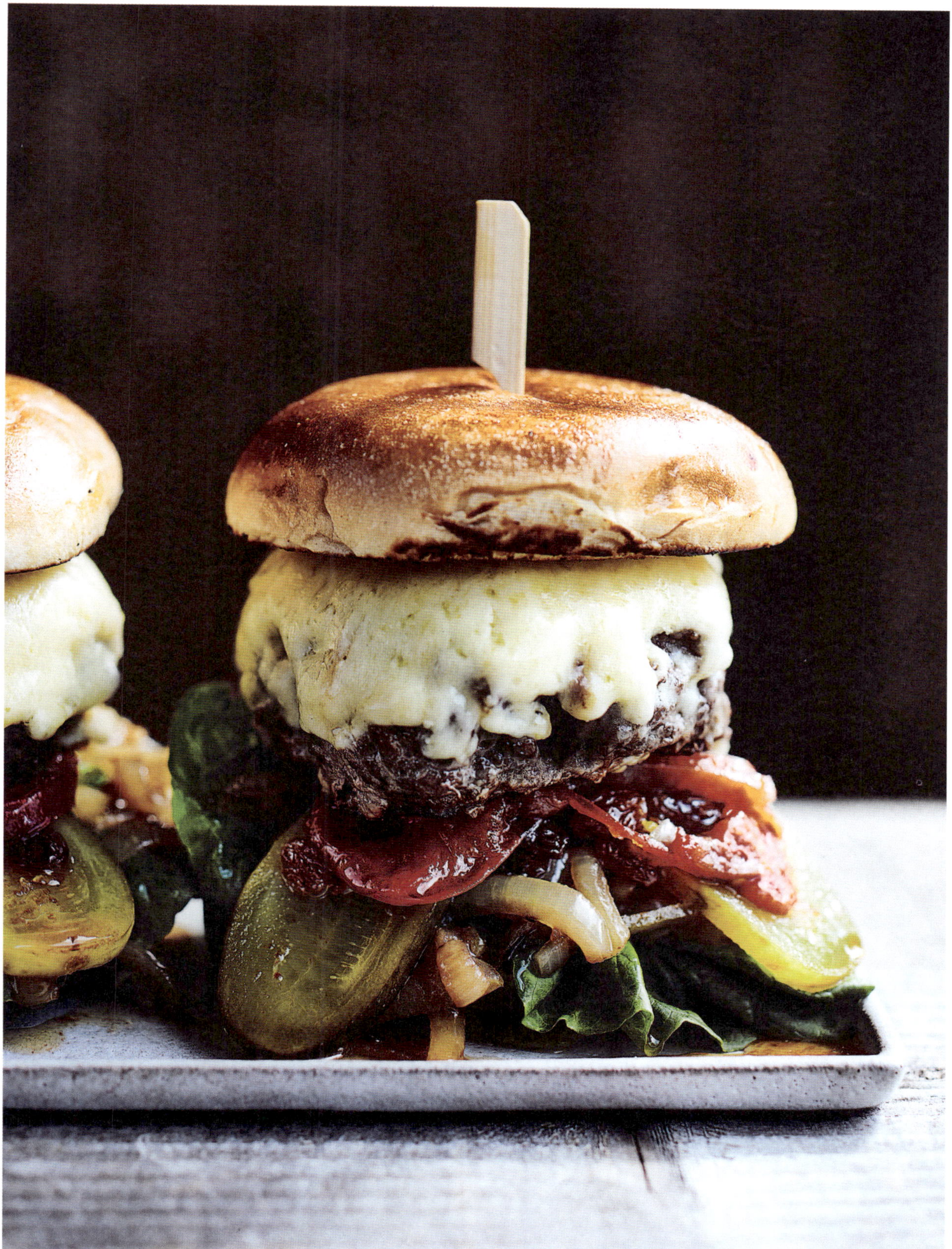

FILLET STEAK WITH TALEGGIO POTATOES AND LEEKS
\
SERVES 4

400g new potatoes
2 garlic cloves, sliced
2 sprigs of thyme, chopped
3 leeks, sliced
50g butter
200g Taleggio, chopped
100ml double cream
sea salt and freshly ground
　black pepper

FOR THE STEAK
25ml olive oil
600g fillet steak, cut into 4 pieces
25g butter

Taleggio is a great choice for melting onto or into dishes, thanks to its semi-soft texture. Here it's stirred into new potatoes and leeks to make an unctuous sauce, the perfect side to a simply grilled fillet steak.

Cook the potatoes in boiling salted water until just soft. Drain, leave to cool and then slice in half.

Preheat the grill to high.

In an ovenproof pan, fry the potatoes, garlic, thyme and leeks in the butter over a high heat until the leeks are just soft. Season, then add the cheese with the cream and stir together. Pop under the grill for 5 minutes.

Meanwhile, heat a frying pan until hot, then add the oil and the steaks. Cook on both sides for 2–3 minutes for medium-rare. Add the butter and spoon it over the steaks until foaming. Season, remove from the heat and leave to rest for 5 minutes.

Serve the steak with the cheesy potatoes and leeks alongside.

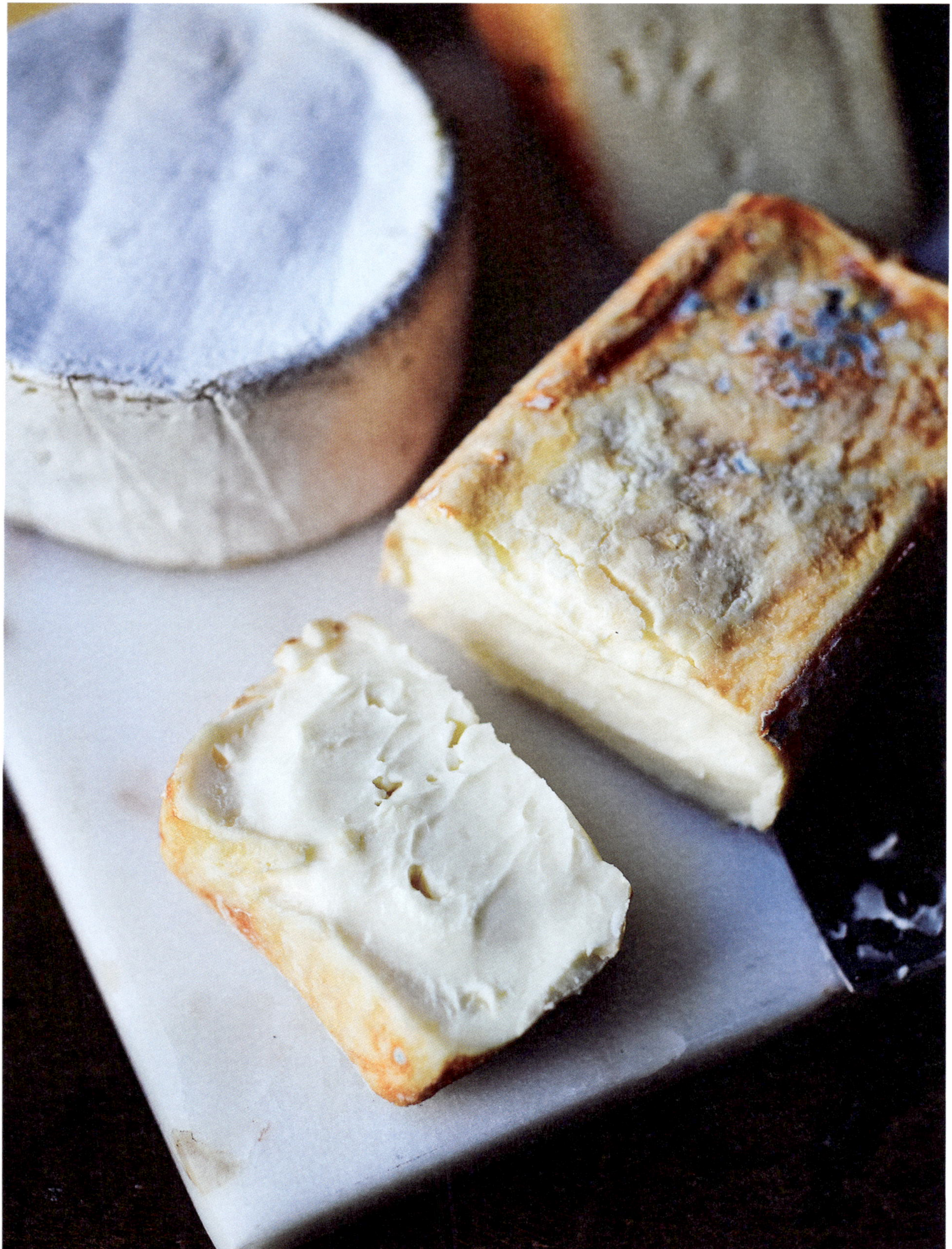

ARBROATH SMOKIE OMELETTE
\
SERVES 2

400ml full-fat milk
400g Arbroath smokies, flesh flaked and skin and bones reserved
6 eggs
50ml double cream
25g butter
sea salt and freshly ground black pepper
dressed watercress and radicchio, to serve

FOR THE SAUCE
½ onion
2 bay leaves
3 cloves
50g butter
25g plain flour
200ml milk (reserved from poaching, above)
50ml double cream
200g Cheddar, grated

Omelettes are an easy way to use all types of cheese, whether it's as a filling or in a sauce for coating, as in this recipe. I've used a classic Cheddar here to showcase another great British ingredient, the Arbroath smokie.

Warm the milk with the fish bones and skin, onion, bay and clove. Strain the milk, discarding the aromatics, and measure off 200ml.

To make the sauce, in a bowl, melt the butter over a medium heat and, when foaming, add the flour and cook out for a minute. Whisk in the strained milk, then the cream and season.

Preheat the grill to high.

To make the omelette, whisk together the eggs and cream and season. Heat a large non-stick frying pan over a low heat, add the butter and, when foaming, pour in the egg mixture. Reduce the heat to medium and, using a fork, bring the edges of the eggs in when starting to firm up. Keep cooking without colouring, then dot with the Arbroath smokies. Spoon over the sauce, sprinkle with the Cheddar and grill until golden and bubbling.

Serve with the dressed watercress and radicchio.

GOAT'S CHEESE AND RED ONION TART
\
SERVES 6

300g all-butter ready-rolled puff pastry
1 egg yolk, beaten
4 tablespoons red onion chutney
2 red onions, sliced
300g soft goat's cheese, crumbled
1 small bunch of basil, shredded
a few sprigs of thyme, leaves picked
1 tablespoon olive oil
sea salt and freshly ground black pepper
dressed green salad, to serve

Goat's cheese is a consistently popular tart filling and in this really easy recipe I've paired it with red onion for a classic version of that ever-present pairing. Just add some herbs, red onion chutney for another layer of onion flavour, and serve with a simple green salad.

Preheat the oven to 220°C (200°C fan)/425°F/gas 7. Line a baking sheet with baking parchment.

Cut the pastry into a 20cm square and pop onto the prepared baking sheet. Prick all over with a fork and brush with the egg yolk. Top with the chutney, onions, cheese and basil. Sprinkle over the thyme, season and drizzle with the olive oil. Bake in the oven for 15–20 minutes.

Slice and serve warm with a dressed green salad.

BURRATA-FILLED LAMB MEATBALLS WITH TOMATO SAUCE AND BASIL PESTO

SERVES 6

250g sourdough bread, cut into small pieces
300ml full-fat milk
500g minced lamb
80g Grana Padano
80g Pecorino Romano
30g flat-leaf parsley, chopped
2 eggs
250g burrata
sea salt and freshly ground black pepper
50g Parmesan, grated, to serve

FOR THE SAUCE
1 large onion, chopped
1 garlic clove, chopped
1 tablespoon extra virgin olive oil
1kg passata
1 small bunch of basil, leaves picked

FOR THE PESTO
1 large bunch of basil, leaves picked
80ml extra virgin olive oil
20g Pecorino Romano
20g Grana Padano
½ garlic clove
20g pine nuts

Burrata makes the perfect luxurious filling for these lamb meatballs, which are also flavoured with Grana Padano and Pecorino Romano.

First make the tomato sauce. In a saucepan over a medium heat, sweat the onion and garlic with the extra virgin olive oil for 10 minutes. Add the passata, season and add the basil leaves. Simmer for about 1 hour, adding some water if it gets too dry.

While the tomato sauce is simmering, cut the bread into small pieces and soak in the milk until all of it has been absorbed. Squeeze out any excess liquid and discard

Put the lamb in a bowl, add the bread and mix thoroughly. Add the Grana Padano, Pecorino Romano, parsley and eggs. Mix well and season to taste. Shape the mixture into about 12 meatballs. Make a small well in the centre of each one, then add a teaspoon of burrata and close them up again, being careful they are well sealed so the burrata won't leak out.

To make the pesto, quickly blanch the basil leaves in boiling water, then cool and halt the cooking in iced water. Drain and transfer to a blender. Add the remaining pesto ingredients and blitz until everything is well combined. Add salt to taste.

Add the meatballs to the tomato sauce and let them cook for 15 minutes. Transfer to a serving dish and finish with generous dollops of pesto and the grated Parmesan.

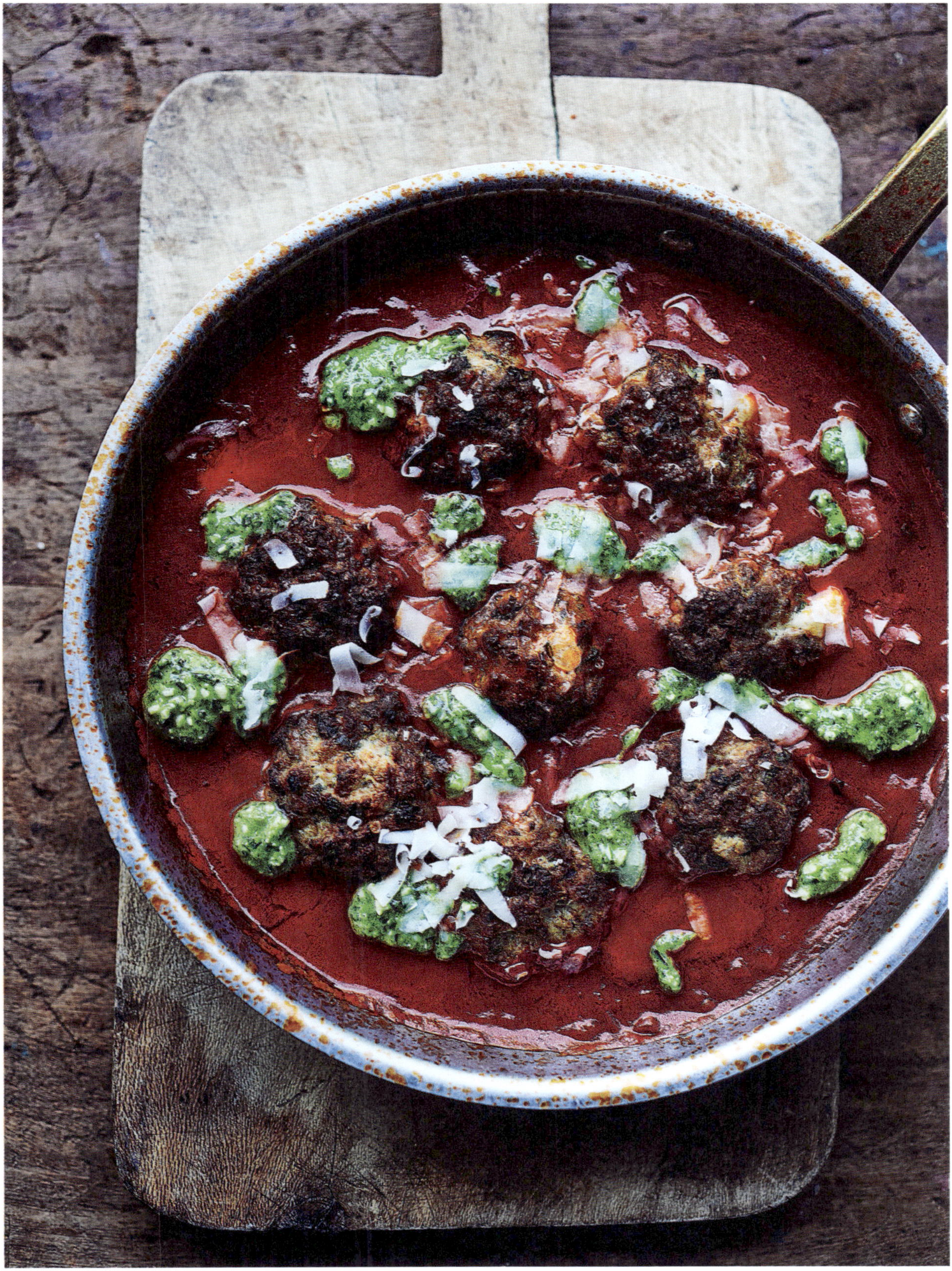

WILD GARLIC BARLEY RISOTTO WITH FILLET STEAK AND PICKLED KOHLRABI
\
SERVES 4

FOR THE RISOTTO
2 heads of garlic
1 tablespoon olive oil
2 shallots, diced
75g butter
100g pearl barley, cooked according to the packet instructions
600ml chicken stock
50ml white wine
2 bunches of wild garlic (or flat-leaf parsley when wild garlic is not in season)
75g Parmesan, grated
sea salt and freshly ground black pepper

FOR THE STEAK
25ml olive oil
4 x 200g fillet steaks
25g butter

FOR THE KOHLRABI
100g caster sugar
100ml white wine vinegar
1 kohlrabi, peeled and sliced

Parmesan is frequently used stirred through risotto, and this wild garlic pearl barley version offers a fresh twist on a classic dish. The fillet steak and pickled kohlrabi take it all up a gear.

Preheat the oven to 200°C (180°C fan)/400°F/gas 6.

To pickle the kohlrabi, put the sugar and vinegar into a pan and bring to the boil. Pour over the kohlrabi.

Cut the tops off the garlic, set the heads on a sheet of foil and drizzle with oil. Seal the parcel tightly, place on a baking sheet and roast for 30 minutes.

To make the risotto, in a large pan, gently fry the shallots in 50g of the butter until charred, then add the pearl barley and coat in the buttery shallots. Pour in the stock and wine and simmer for 5 minutes, stirring occasionally.

Meanwhile, cook the steaks. Heat a frying pan until hot, then add the oil and the steaks. Cook on each side for 2–3 minutes, then add the butter and cook until foaming, using it to the coat the steaks. Season, remove from the heat and leave to rest for 5 minutes.

To finish the risotto, squeeze out the roasted garlic cloves from their skins into the rice pan, stir through and add half the wild garlic. Sprinkle over the Parmesan, then season and set aside.

Heat the remaining 25g butter in a pan over a high heat, add the remaining wild garlic and cook until wilted.

To serve, spoon the risotto onto plates, top with the steak and spoon over the pickled kohlrabi with the wilted wild garlic.

WARM PASTA CAESAR SALAD
\
SERVES 2

120g pancetta, thinly sliced
80g Parmesan, finely grated
1 garlic clove
zest and juice of 1 unwaxed lemon
4 egg yolks
5g flat-leaf parsley, finely chopped
6 anchovies, chopped
1 tablespoon Worcestershire sauce
30g panko breadcrumbs
1 tablespoon sunflower oil
300g fresh malloreddus or gnocchi
4 leaves Romaine lettuce, finely shredded
sea salt and freshly ground black pepper

This Caesar salad recipe adds pasta but keeps it classic with the usual Parmesan, anchovies and bread elements.

In a large hot frying pan, sauté the pancetta until crisp. Set aside, keeping it in the pan with the fat.

Put the Parmesan in a bowl, grate in the garlic and add half the lemon zest, plus the egg yolks. Mix to a paste. Add the parsley and the anchovies and mix them in. Finish the paste with a small squeeze of lemon juice and the Worcestershire sauce to taste. Set aside.

In a frying pan over a medium heat, sauté the panko breadcrumbs in the sunflower oil until golden. Season, then drain on kitchen paper.

Bring a large pan of salted water to the boil and cook the malloreddus for 3–4 minutes until al dente (or the gnocchi until they rise to the surface). Use a strainer to remove the pasta from the pan, retaining some of the pasta water.

Add the pasta to the pancetta and return the pan to a low heat, adding a spoonful of the pasta water. Loosen the paste with a spoonful of the pasta water, then add to the pan. Stir over a very low heat for 5 minutes until the sauce thickens and coats the pasta. Take care not to scramble the egg.

When the sauce is glossy and has a coating consistency, fold in the lettuce, portion onto warm plates and top with the crunchy breadcrumbs. Serve immediately.

BUTTER PANEER CURRY
\
SERVES 4

600g paneer, cubed
2 litres vegetable oil, for frying

FOR THE SAUCE
125g butter
2 onions, sliced
2 tablespoons garam masala
1 teaspoon mild chilli powder
1 teaspoon ground cumin
2 garlic cloves, crushed
1 tablespoon ginger paste
400ml vegetable stock
5 tomatoes, chopped
1 green chilli, sliced
1 red chilli, sliced
12 curry leaves
100ml double cream
sea salt and freshly ground
    black pepper

TO SERVE
chopped coriander
basmati rice

Paneer is a cheese best enjoyed cooked and, like halloumi, its firm texture lends itself perfectly to frying. Firm, golden cubes are then smothered in a buttery tomato sauce for this delicious vegetarian curry.

In a deep-sided pan, heat the vegetable oil to 170°C (340°F). Deep-fry the paneer in the oil until golden – you will need to do this in batches.

Place a large pan over a medium heat, add 25g of the butter and then the onions and cook for 10 minutes until golden. Add the spices, garlic, ginger, stock and tomatoes and simmer for 5 minutes. Pop in the paneer, chillies and curry leaves and cook for a further 5 minutes.

Stir through the cream and remaining 100g butter to finish. Sprinkle with chopped coriander and serve alongside some basmati rice.

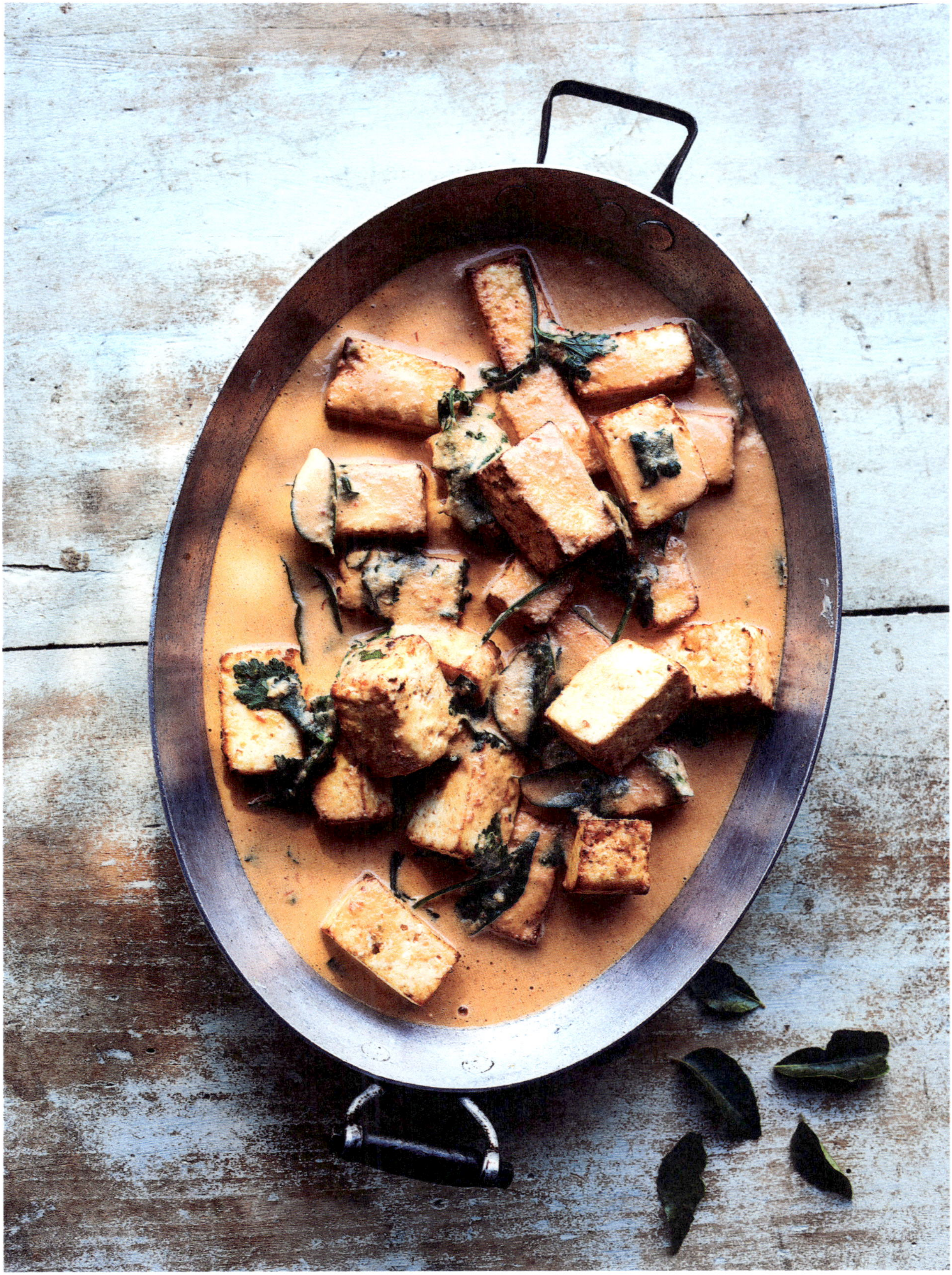

CHICKEN SCHNITZEL WITH HALLOUMI
\
SERVES 2

2 chicken breasts
100g halloumi, thinly sliced
2 thick slices of ham
100g plain flour, seasoned
2 eggs
100g panko breadcrumbs
75g butter
½ lemon

TO SERVE
lemon wedges
watercress

This German-inspired dish traditionally consists of thinly pounded chicken breast which is then breaded and fried for a wonderful crispy coating. However, I've decided to take things up a notch here by adding a creamy ham and halloumi filling.

Preheat the oven to 200°C (180°C fan)/400°F/gas 6.

Place the chicken breasts between two layers of clingfilm and bash them until they are 1cm thick. Lay the halloumi and ham on half of each chicken breast and then fold it over.

Put the flour in a bowl, the beaten eggs in another and the breadcrumbs in a third. Dip the folded chicken breasts into the flour, then the egg and finally in the breadcrumbs.

In a large faying pan over a low heat, fry the schnitzels in the butter for 3 minutes on each side until they are golden brown and crispy. Transfer to a tray (reserving the butter in the pan) and pop in the oven for 5–6 minutes.

Squeeze the juice from the half lemon into the butter in the pan and drizzle over the chicken. Serve with lemon wedges and watercress.

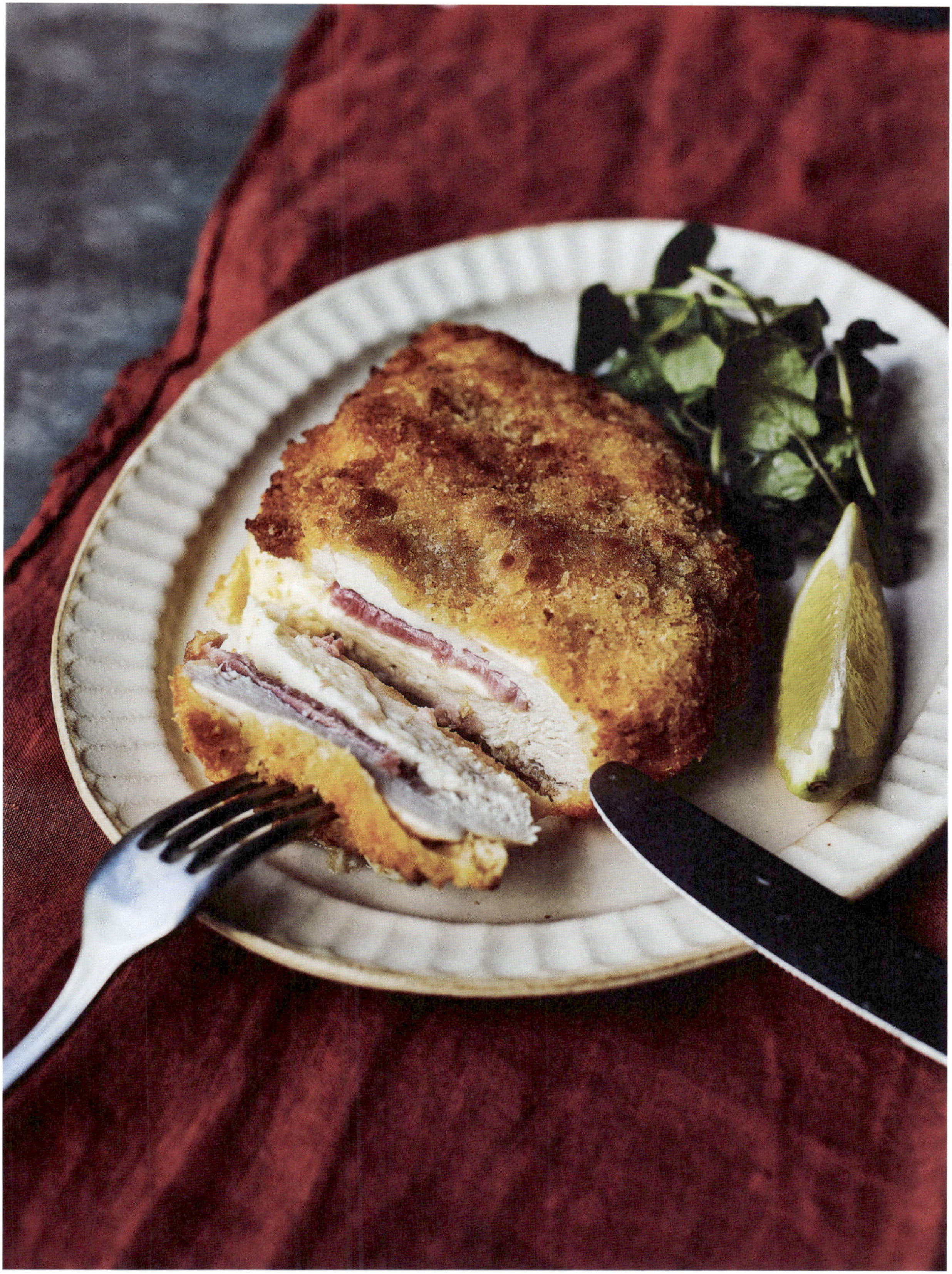

TENDERSTEM BROCCOLI QUICHE

SERVES 6

2 onions, sliced
a few sprigs of thyme, leaves picked
a knob of butter
200g Tenderstem broccoli, roasted for 5 minutes
8 eggs
300ml double cream
300g Comté, grated
sea salt and freshly ground black pepper

FOR THE PASTRY

200g plain flour, plus extra for dusting
100g butter, plus extra for greasing
pinch of salt
1 egg, plus extra for brushing

Quiche is a great vehicle for all varieties of cheese and here I've paired a nutty Comté with roasted Tenderstem broccoli. As in other Comté dishes, Gruyère would make an excellent substitute but you could also try another hard cheese such as Parmesan.

First make the pastry. Put the flour into a bowl, add the butter and salt, then rub between your fingers until the mixture looks like coarse breadcrumbs. Add the egg and mix with your fingers, adding a splash of water if needed to bring the dough together. Knead on a floured surface until smooth, wrap in clingfilm and chill in the fridge for 30 minutes.

Preheat the oven to 180°C (160°C fan)/350°F/gas 4. Grease a 24cm tart tin.

Roll out the pastry on a lightly floured work surface and use to line the tin, allowing it to overhang slightly. Wrap some flour in clingfilm and use to line the tin. Blind bake for 15–20 minutes. Remove the clingfilm and brush the pastry with a little egg.

Set a pan over a medium heat and sweat the onions and thyme in the butter until golden. Leave to cool, then spread over the bottom of the tart case. Top with the broccoli.

To make the filling, in a bowl, whisk together the eggs and cream, then season. Pour the custard into the tart tin and sprinkle the cheese over the top. Bake in the oven for 30–40 minutes – it should have a slight wobble in the middle.

Once cooked, let the quiche sit for 5 minutes and trim the edge of the pastry crust. Serve hot, or warm.

COQUILLES ST JACQUES
\
SERVES 4

4 large scallops, shells reserved
20ml vegetable oil
sea salt and freshly ground
　　black pepper

FOR THE SAUCE
50g butter
200g raw prawns, shelled, deveined
　　and chopped
½ leek, diced
50g plain flour
300ml full-fat milk
50ml white wine
1 small bunch of chervil, chopped

FOR THE TOPPING
400g potatoes, such as King Edward,
　　peeled and diced
50g butter
50g Gruyère, grated

This French dish is classically a simple scallop gratin with a buttery, herby breadcrumb topping. My version plays with tradition by adding prawns to the scallops and replacing the breadcrumbs with a cheesy mashed potato topping. Gruyère works well here as its mild flavour doesn't overpower the delicate seafood.

First make the white sauce. Melt the butter in a pan over a medium heat and sweat the prawns and leeks until the prawns turn pink. Whisk in the flour and cook out for 2 minutes. Add the milk and wine and stir to combine, then simmer until bubbling. Stir in the chervil.

In a frying pan over a high heat, pan-fry the scallops in the oil for 1 minute on each side. Season.

Put the scallops into their shells, pour over the sauce and leave to cool.

Cook the potatoes in boiling salted water for 20 minutes until soft. Drain, then pass through a ricer into a bowl. Mix with the butter. Transfer to a piping bag and snip the end off.

Preheat the grill to high.

Pipe the potato around the edges of the scallops, then sit them on a baking tray. Sprinkle over the cheese and grill for 5 minutes until golden and bubbling.

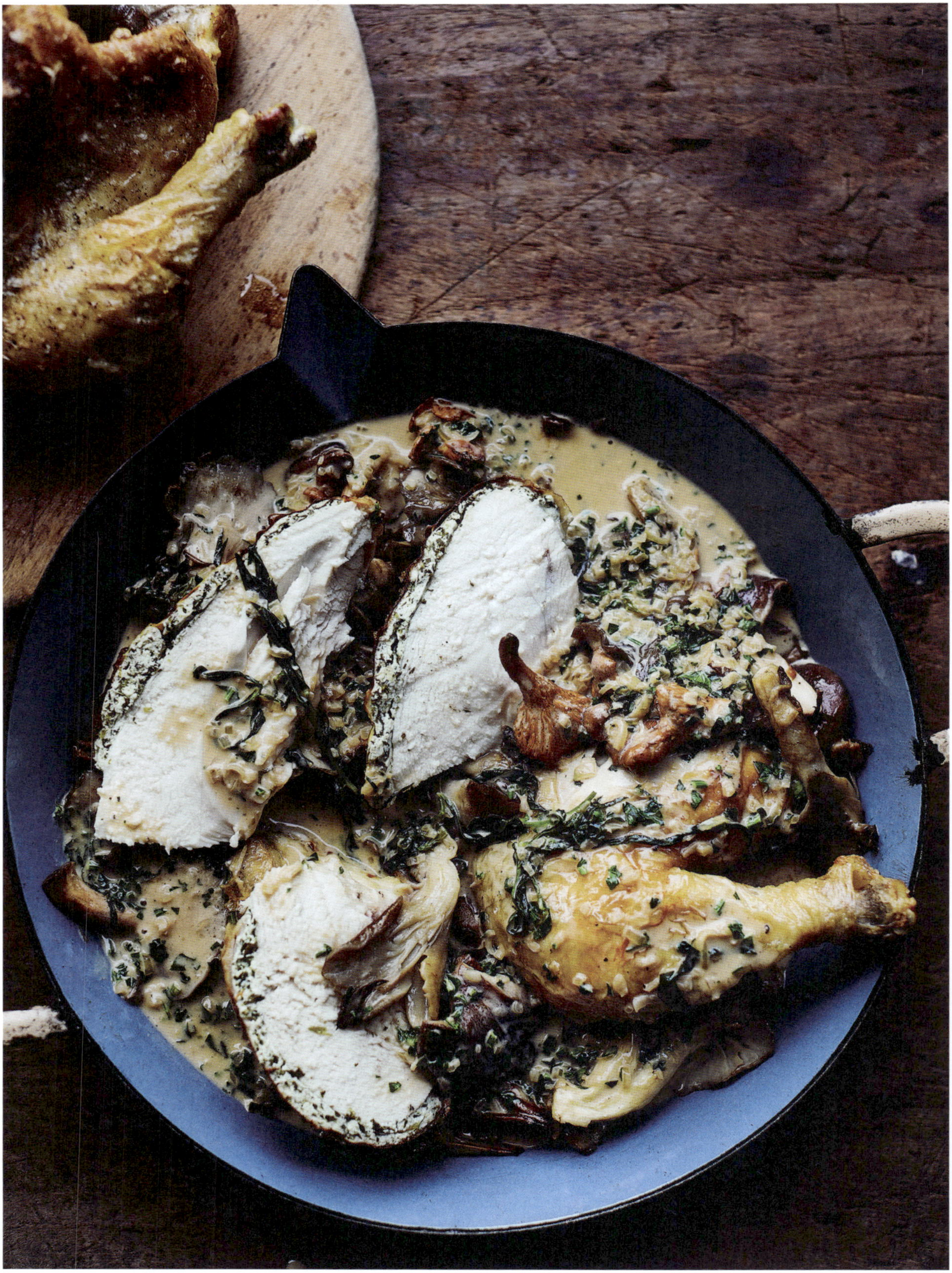

CHICKEN STUFFED WITH HERBS AND RICOTTA
\
SERVES 4

100g ricotta
a few sprigs of mint
1 small bunch of coriander
1 large (2kg) chicken
olive oil, for drizzling
sea salt and freshly ground black pepper

FOR THE SAUCE
1 tablespoon olive oil
1 shallot, diced
300g wild mushrooms, chopped
15g butter
300ml veal jus
50ml white wine
50ml double cream
a few sprigs of tarragon

Mild, creamy ricotta is the perfect cheese for stuffing dishes, whether it's cannelloni (see page 139), ravioli or chicken, as in this recipe. Switch it up for mascarpone or a full-fat cream cheese for simliar results.

Preheat the oven to 200°C (180°C fan)/400°F/gas 6.

Pop the ricotta and herbs into a food processor and blitz until smooth. Transfer to a piping bag and snip the end off.

Use your fingers to release the skin over the chicken breasts and create a pouch, then pipe the cheese and herb mixture under the skin. Put the chicken onto a roasting tray, then drizzle with olive oil and season. Roast for 1 hour 10 minutes, then remove from the oven and leave to rest for 20 minutes.

To make the sauce, heat a non-stick frying pan until very hot, add the oil, then the shallot and mushrooms. Add half the butter and fry for 2 minutes, then pour in the jus, wine and cream. Sprinkle over the tarragon, bring to the boil, then reduce by half. Add the remaining butter and season.

To serve, carve the chicken into eight pieces, pile onto a platter and spoon over the sauce.

FILLET STEAK WITH LOBSTER MAC AND CHEESE

SERVES 4

1 beef stock cube, crumbled
1 teaspoon salt
4 x 200g fillet steaks
a few sprigs of thyme
4 garlic cloves, unpeeled
50g butter

FOR THE MAC AND CHEESE
400g macaroni
100g butter
15g plain flour
300ml full-fat milk
50ml white wine
300ml double cream
600g Cheddar, grated
2 cooked lobsters, flesh removed
sea salt and freshly ground
    black pepper

Mac and cheese is classic comfort food, but this version really takes it to the next level. Adding lobster to the usual Cheddar sauce gives a real taste of luxury and, served alongside some fillet steak, there is no better dish than this with which to impress your friends and family.

Preheat the oven to 240°C (220°C fan)/475°F/gas 9.

To make the mac and cheese, cook the pasta according to the packet instructions.

Preheat the grill to high.

Melt the butter in a pan over a medium heat, then whisk in the flour and cook out for a couple of minutes. Whisk in the milk, wine and cream. Add half the cheese and stir through, then remove from the heat.

Drain the pasta and return to the pan. Season the sauce, pour onto the pasta and mix together. Pour into a 20 x 15cm ovenproof dish, top with the lobster and remaining cheese. Pop under the grill for 5 minutes.

Mix the stock cube with the salt and rub all over the steaks. Seal the steaks in a very hot ovenproof pan on both sides, add the thyme, garlic and butter, then transfer to the oven and roast for 5 minutes. Remove from the oven and leave to rest.

Pop the steaks onto a platter and serve with the mac and cheese alongside.

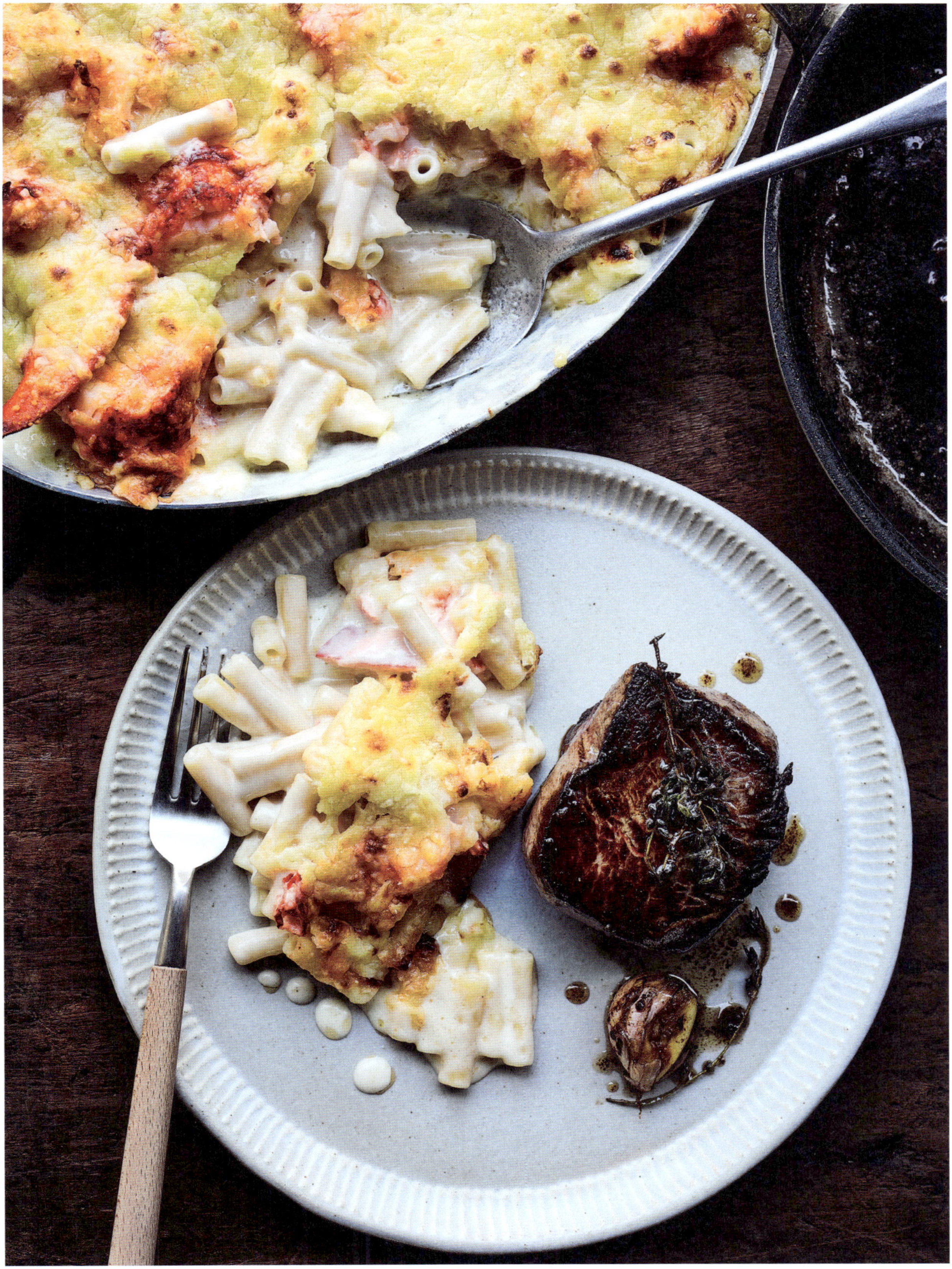

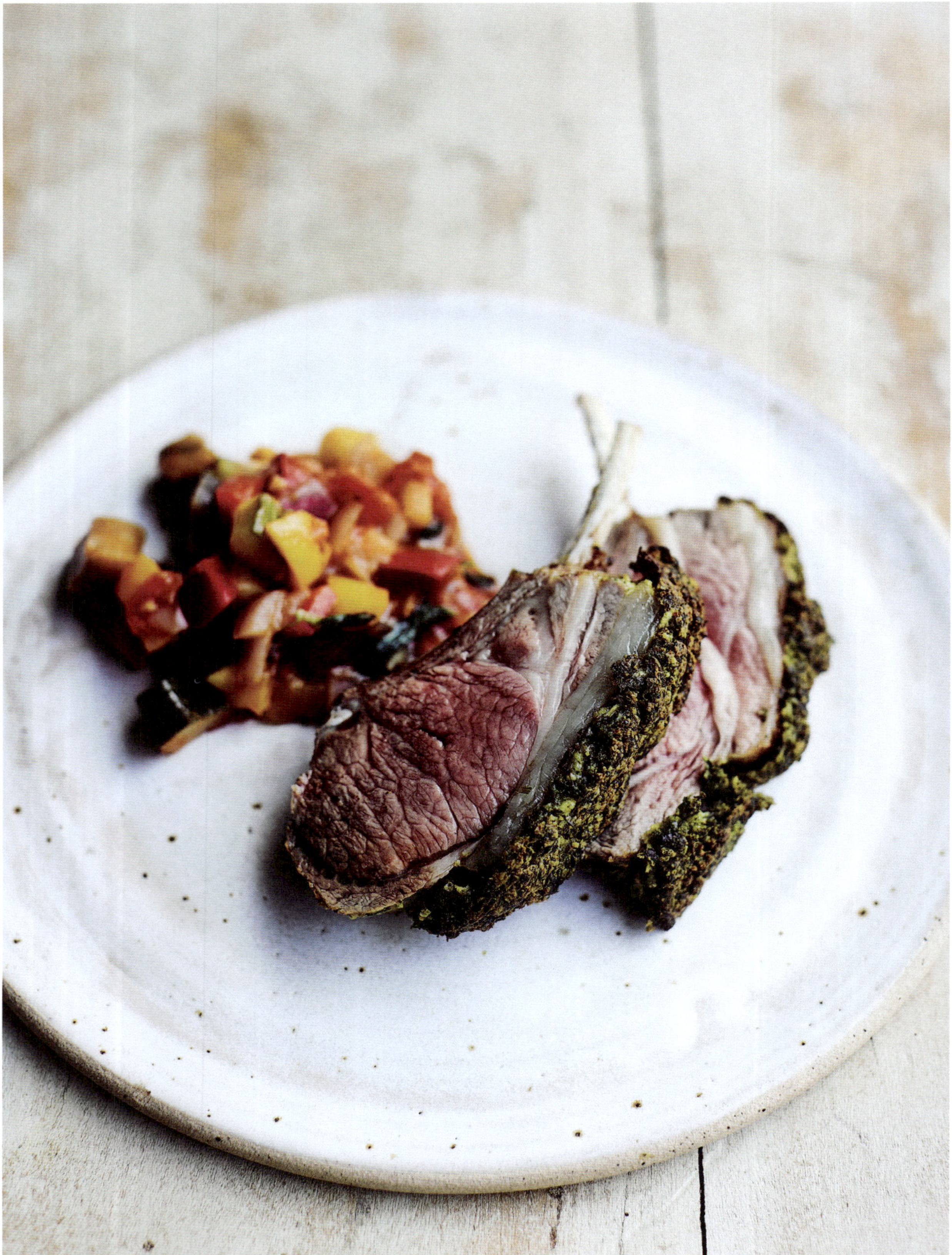

HERBED LAMB RACK WITH RATATOUILLE
\
SERVES 4

8 rib rack of lamb, trimmed and cleaned
1 tablespoon Dijon mustard

FOR THE HERB CRUST
1 small bunch of flat-leaf parsley
1 small bunch of mint
25g Parmesan, grated
1 thick slice of white bread
1 tablespoon full-fat cream cheese
zest of 1 unwaxed lemon

FOR THE RATATOUILLE
2 tablespoons olive oil
1 onion, diced
½ garlic clove, sliced
1 red pepper, diced
1 yellow pepper, diced
1 green pepper, diced
1 courgette, cut into 1cm cubes
1 aubergine, cut into 1cm cubes
3 large tomatoes, diced
1 small bunch of basil, torn
sea salt and freshly ground black pepper

Grated Parmesan adds an umami element to the wonderful herby crust on this lamb, which is held together by the cream cheese. You can swap the Parmesan for Grana Padano or Pecorino Romano, while ricotta or mascarpone would work well in place of the cream cheese.

Preheat the oven to 200°C (180°C fan)/400°F/gas 6.

Heat a large frying pan until hot, then fry the lamb, fat-side down, for 2 minutes.

To make the herb crust, blitz all the ingredients to a fine paste in a food processor or blender. Brush the fat on the lamb with the mustard, then top with the herb paste. Transfer to a roasting tray and roast for 15–18 minutes. Remove from the oven and leave to rest for 10 minutes. Slice.

Meanwhile, for the ratatouille, heat a large non-stick pan over a medium heat, add the oil, then add the onion and fry for 1 minute. Add the garlic, then the peppers and cook for 30 seconds, then add the courgette and cook for another 30 seconds. Finally, add the aubergine and tomatoes, season and cook over a gentle heat for 5 minutes or until cooked. Finish by stirring through the basil.

Serve the ratatouille with the lamb.

ITALIAN SAUSAGE GNOCCHI WITH FRISÉE
\
SERVES 4

50g butter
8 Italian sausages, sliced
2 frisée (curly endive), sliced
sea salt and freshly ground black pepper

FOR THE GNOCCHI
400g cooked baking potatoes, riced and cooled
50g Parmesan, grated
125g plain flour, plus extra for rolling
2 egg yolks

FOR THE SAUCE
15g butter
15g plain flour
400ml full-fat milk
100g Parmesan, grated

TO SERVE
1 small bunch of flat-leaf parsley
2 tablespoons small capers
zest of 1 unwaxed lemon

In this recipe Parmesan plays a dual role, flavouring both the gnocchi itself as well as the sauce for a double hit of cheese flavour. As with other pasta dishes, you could try replacing it with Grana Padano or Pecorino Romano if you want to change things up.

To make the gnocchi, mix the potato, Parmesan, flour and egg yolks together in a bowl and season. Then roll into 20cm long sausages, 2cm thick, using a little extra flour. Cut the gnocchi sausages into 3cm pieces, plunge into boiling water and cook for 1 minute. Drain and set aside.

To make the sauce, melt the butter in a pan over a medium heat. Whisk in the flour and cook out for a minute. Then whisk in the milk and, when bubbling, add the cheese and season.

Preheat the grill to high.

Heat a large ovenproof frying pan until hot, add the butter and fry the sausage pieces until crisp. Add the gnocchi and frisée, stir through and season. Cover in the sauce. Grill for 2–3 minutes.

Meanwhile, chop the parsley, capers and lemon together. Sprinkle on top of the gnocchi bake and serve.

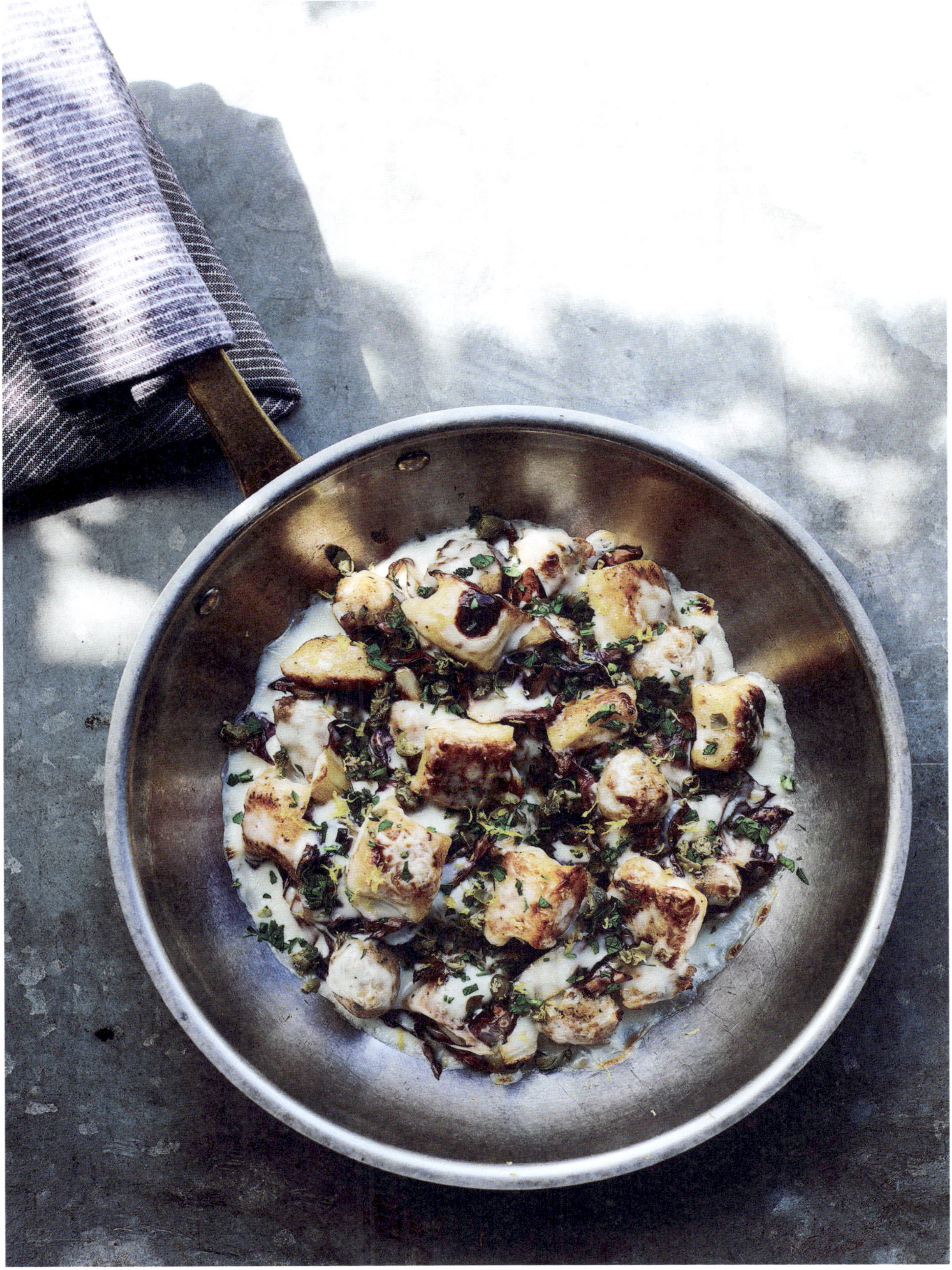

BAKED POTATOES WITH SAUSAGES AND SLOPPY JOE SAUCE

SERVES 4

4 baking potatoes
8 pork sausages
25ml olive oil

FOR THE SAUCE
400g minced pork
1 onion, diced
1 garlic clove, sliced
1 green chilli, diced
200g dark brown soft sugar
100ml ketchup
50ml dark soy sauce
50ml white wine vinegar
2 tablespoons chipotle paste
1 small bunch of coriander, chopped
1 small bunch of mint, chopped

TO SERVE
100g butter
300g firm mozzarella, grated
2 tablespoons kibbled (chopped, dried) onions
1 small bunch of coriander, chopped
1 small bunch of mint, chopped

This dish uses firm mozzarella, which you can grate but still melts wonderfully into the other ingredients. Here it's topping some baked potatoes with a meaty sloppy joe sauce, complemented by freshness from the herbs and crunch from the kibbled onions.

Preheat the oven to 200°C (180°C fan)/400°F/gas 6.

Prick the potatoes all over with a fork, pop on a baking tray and bake for 1¼ hours.

Heat a non-stick frying pan until hot, then add all the sauce ingredients and bring to the boil. Reduce the heat and simmer for 10 minutes, stirring occasionally. Set aside.

Drizzle the sausages in the oil and fry them in a non-stick ovenproof pan over a medium heat until crisp and cooked through. Pop in the oven for 10 minutes.

To serve, pop the potatoes onto plates and cut a cross in the top of each one. Squeeze up the cooked potato flesh and dot with butter and cheese. Pile the sausages on top, then spoon over the sauce. Sprinkle with the kibbled onions and herbs.

LAMB CHOPS WITH GREEN OLIVE TAPENADE, ARTICHOKES, ALMONDS AND GOAT'S CHEESE
\
SERVES 4

12 lamb chops
400g jar baby artichoke hearts, drained
sea salt and freshly ground
   black pepper

FOR THE MARINADE
50ml olive oil
2 garlic cloves, crushed
2 sprigs of rosemary, chopped
a few sprigs of thyme

FOR THE TAPENADE
200g pitted green olives
50ml extra virgin olive oil
2 tablespoons minced anchovies in oil
3 tablespoons capers
juice of 1 lemon
½ bunch of flat-leaf parsley, chopped

TO SERVE
50g skinned almonds, toasted
200g soft goat's cheese, crumbled

Soft goat's cheese is a great final addition to dishes to provide that extra layer of flavour and here it's used to perfection, scattered around the lamb chops with the almonds and artichokes. Its mild creaminess works fantastically alongside the punchy green olive tapenade.

Put all the marinade ingredients into a large bowl and mix together. Then use to coat all the lamb chops, cover the bowl and pop in the fridge for 2 hours.

To make the tapenade, add all the ingredients to a small food processor. Blend to a rough purée.

Preheat the grill to high.

Transfer the lamb chops onto a large tray and grill for 8–10 minutes. Leave to rest for 3–4 minutes.

Pop the artichoke hearts into a small pan and gently warm through. Season.

Serve the lamb with a dollop of tapenade, dot around the artichokes and sprinkle over the almonds and goat's cheese.

Pictured overleaf

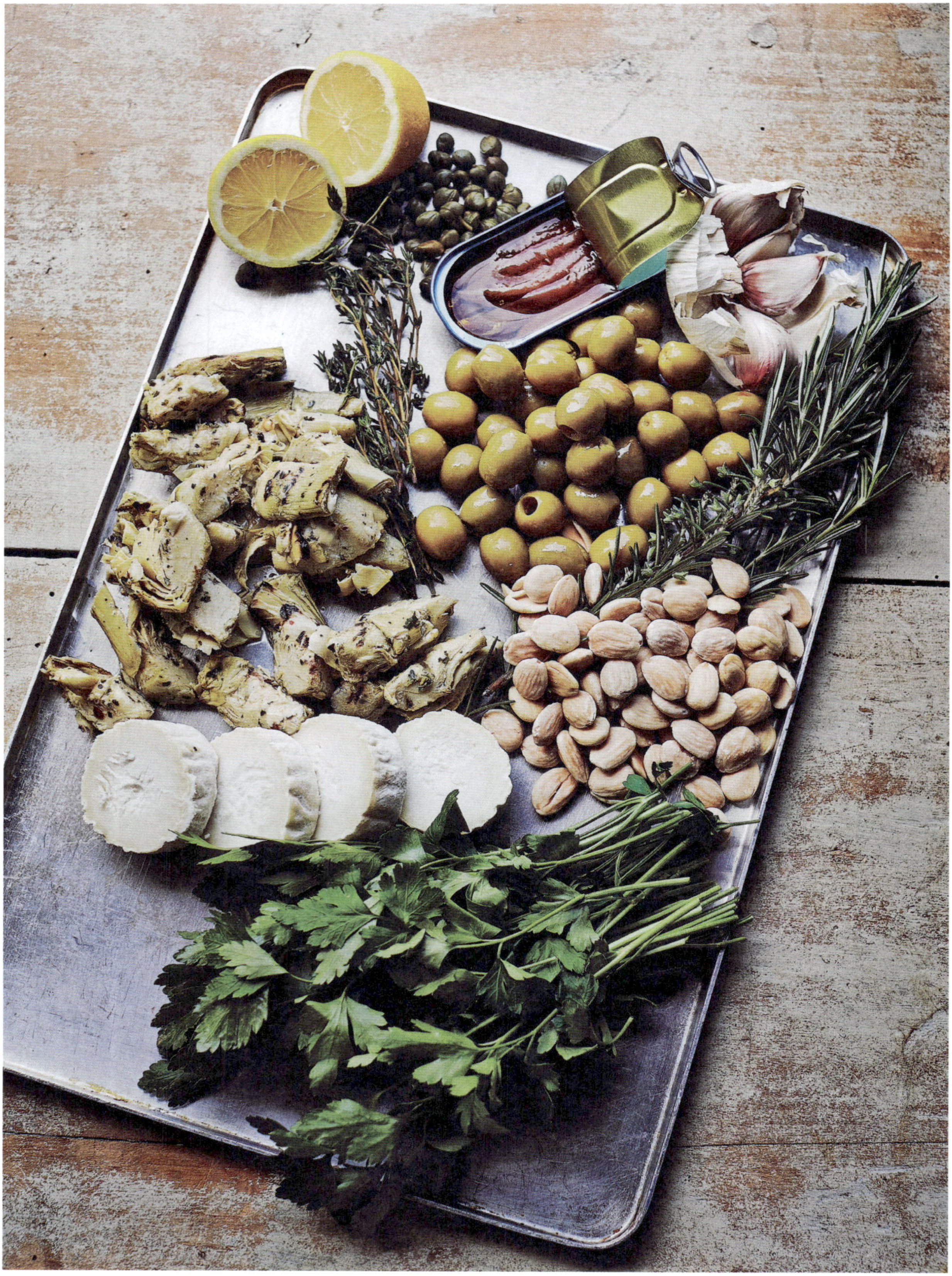

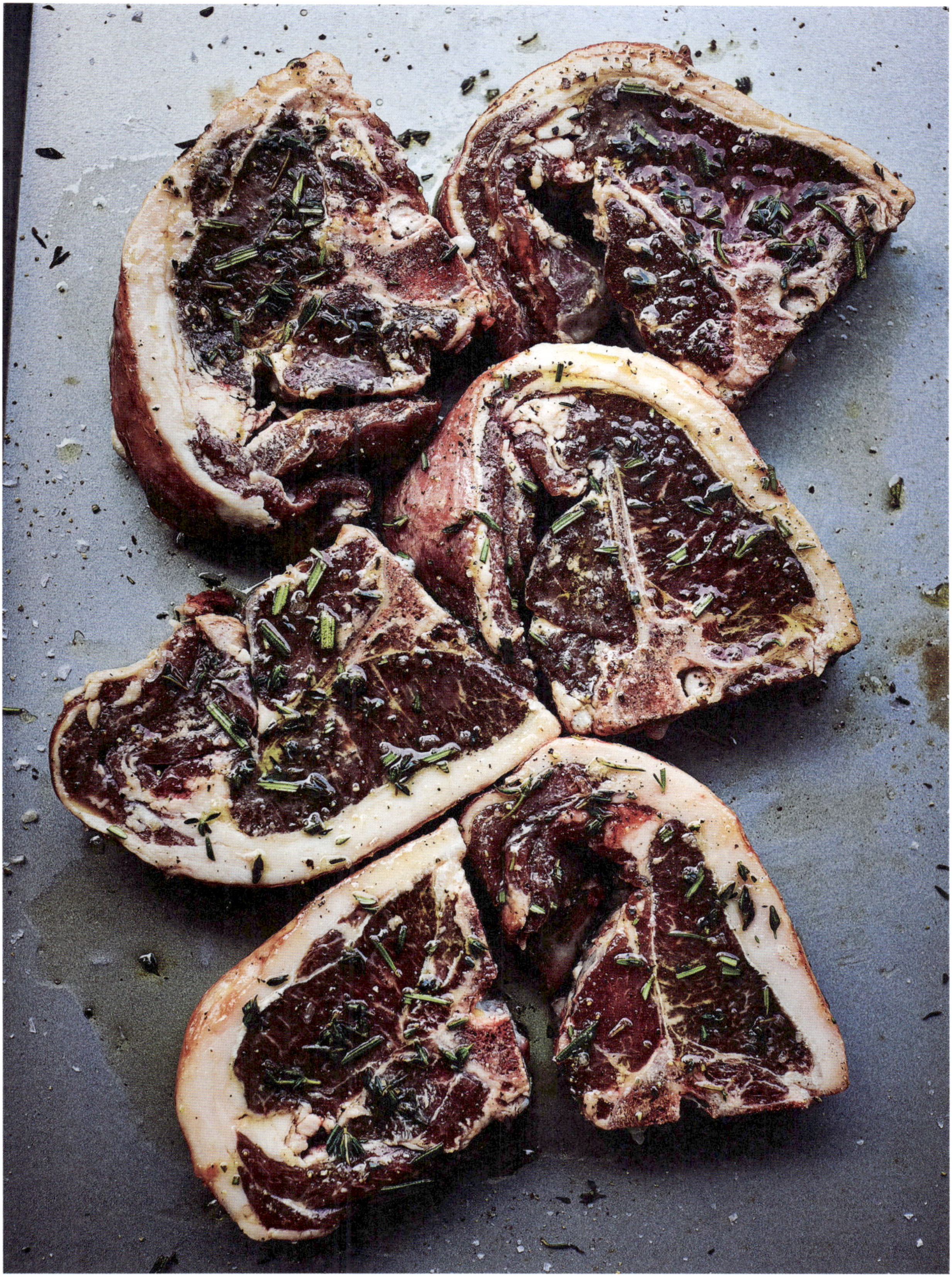

LASAGNE
\
SERVES 4-6

500g minced beef
1 onion, diced
3 garlic cloves, minced
a few sprigs of thyme
200ml beef stock
100ml red wine
400g can chopped tomatoes
2 tablespoons tomato purée
12 lasagne sheets
200g firm mozzarella, grated
50g Pecorino Romano, grated
50g Parmesan, grated

FOR THE SAUCE
½ onion
1 bay leaf
2 cloves
300ml full-fat milk
200ml double cream
25g butter
1½ tablespoons plain flour

Lasagne can be the vehicle for a variety of cheeses, though a classic Italian version, originating from Emilia-Romagna, would usually just contain Parmigiano Reggiano (aged Parmesan). In other regions of Italy, the dish might feature ricotta or mozzarella, so I've gone for a cheese trio here: Parmesan, Pecorino Romano and firm mozzarella.

Preheat the oven to 200°C (180°C fan)/400°F/gas 6.

Set a large frying pan over a medium heat and fry the beef, onion, garlic and thyme for 20 minutes until browned. Top with the stock, wine, tomatoes and tomato purée and gently bubble for 30 minutes.

To make the white sauce, stud the onion with the bay leaf and cloves and place in a small pan with the milk and cream. Gently simmer but do not boil. In a separate pan, melt the butter over a medium heat, then whisk in the flour and cook out for 2 minutes. Remove the onion from the milk, then whisk into the flour, mix and simmer until bubbling.

Place one-third of the meat in the bottom of a large ovenproof dish. Top with four lasagne sheets and repeat twice more, finishing with a final layer of pasta. Then pour over the sauce and top with all the grated cheeses. Bake in the oven for 30 minutes.

Remove from the oven and serve immediately.

MUSHROOM AND RICOTTA CANNELLONI
\
SERVES 4-6

Not one but four cheeses star in this dish – as well as ricotta to make the creamy mushroom filling, it's topped with a holy trinity of mozzarella, Parmesan and Gruyère. Cheese heaven.

1 onion, diced
3 garlic cloves, crushed
50ml olive oil, plus extra (optional) for drizzling
1kg chestnut mushrooms, blitzed in a food processor
1 small bunch of tarragon, chopped
300g ricotta
18 dried cannelloni
sea salt and freshly ground black pepper

FOR THE SAUCE
300ml double cream
pinch of grated nutmeg
1 small bunch of tarragon, torn

FOR THE TOPPING
2 balls of mozzarella, sliced
50g Parmesan, grated
150g Gruyère, grated

Preheat the oven to 180°C (160°C fan)/350°F/gas 4.

Set a pan over a medium heat and fry the onion and garlic in the oil for 5 minutes. Then add the mushrooms and tarragon and bring to the boil. Reduce the heat, then simmer for 5 minutes. Remove from the heat and leave to cool. Season and beat in the ricotta, then transfer to a piping bag and snip the end off.

Meanwhile, make the sauce. Set a pan over a low heat and bring the cream to the boil with the nutmeg and tarragon. Remove from the heat.

Fill each tube of cannelloni with the ricotta mixture and place into a large ovenproof dish. Top with sauce, dot with mozzarella and sprinkle over the Parmesan and Gruyère. Bake in the oven for 45 minutes.

To serve, drizzle with extra olive oil if desired.

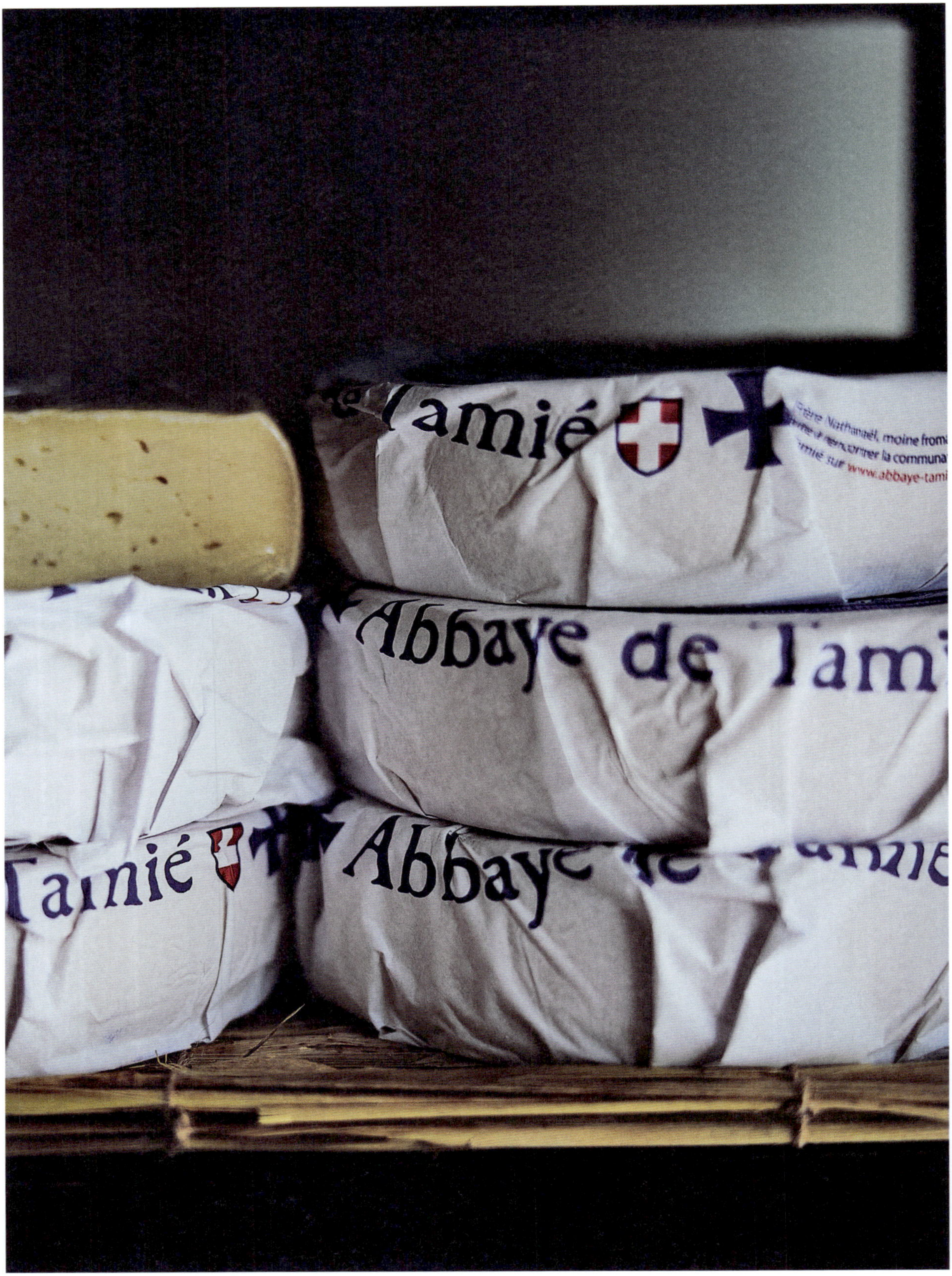
Abbaye de
Abbaye
Tamié

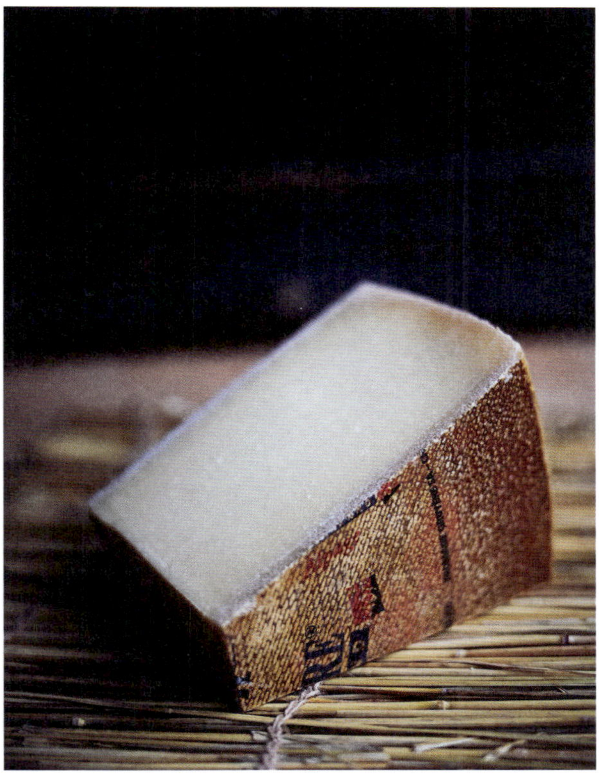
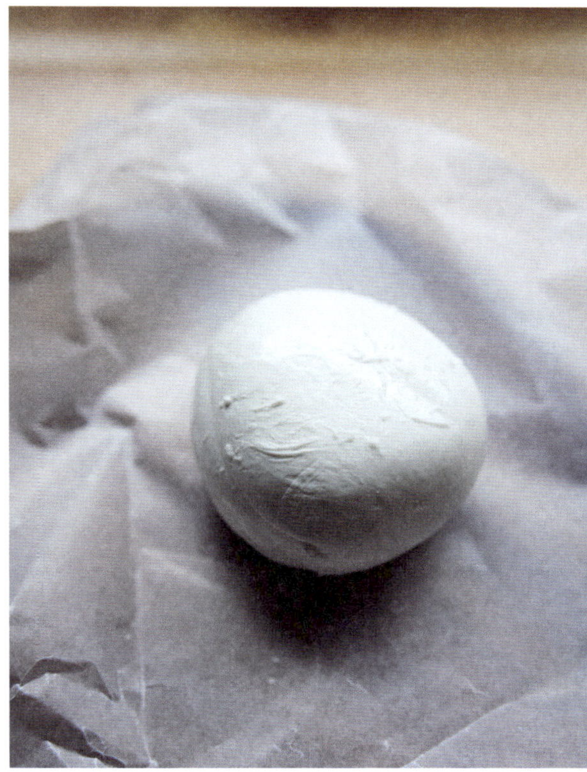

LAMB FILLET, FIG AND FETA SALAD
\
SERVES 4

600g lamb fillet, cut into 1cm slices
12 thin slices of baguette
100ml olive oil
12 figs, halved
50ml champagne vinegar
  (or white wine vinegar)
1 tablespoon water
50ml maple syrup
1 small radicchio, cut into wedges
4 Little Gem lettuces, cut into wedges
100g feta

Feta and lamb make a brilliant culinary combination and in this dish they're paired with sweet seared figs, bitter radicchio and crunchy Little Gem and croutons. An impressive salad fit to feed a crowd.

Dry-fry the lamb in a hot frying pan for 10 minutes until crispy, then spoon into a bowl. Fry the baguette slices in the same pan with half the olive oil until golden, then add to the bowl.

In the same pan, sear the figs, cut-side down, for a few seconds and add to the bowl.

Pour the remaining olive oil, the vinegar, water and maple syrup into the pan and warm through.

Arrange the radicchio and Little Gem wedges on a large platter, then spoon over the figs, croutons and lamb.

Pour the lamb fat from the bowl into the dressing and drizzle over the salad.

Crumble over the feta and serve.

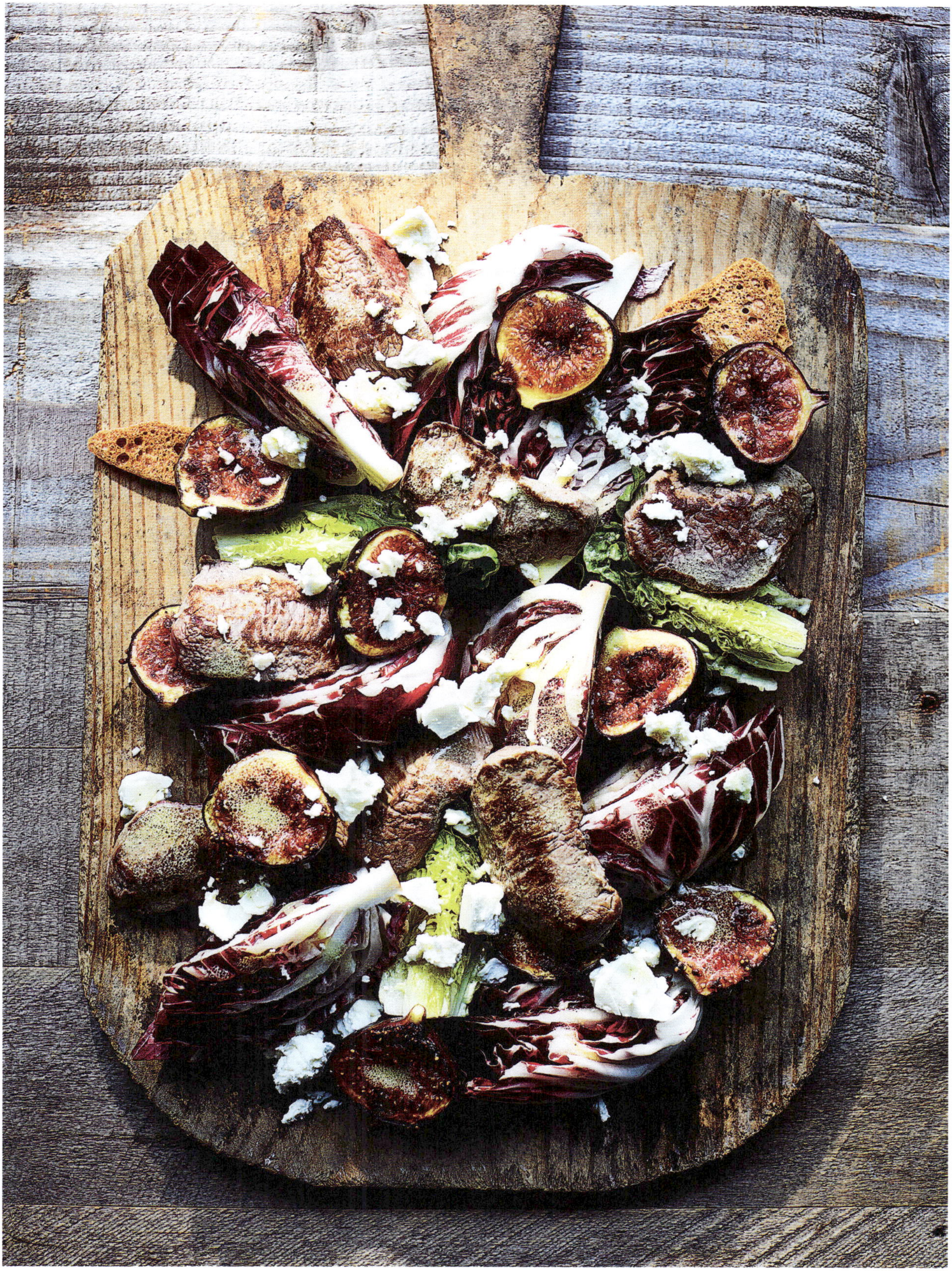

LAMB WITH STILTON GNOCCHI

SERVES 4

1 small bunch of flat-leaf parsley, chopped
25g flaked almonds, chopped
zest of 1 unwaxed lemon
2 garlic cloves, chopped
2 lamb loins (about 600g)
sea salt and freshly ground black pepper

FOR THE GNOCCHI
500g cooked potato, riced
125g plain flour, plus extra for dusting
75g Stilton, crumbled
2 egg yolks

FOR THE SAUCE
25g butter
1 garlic clove, crushed
1 small bunch of mint, chopped
1 small bunch of flat-leaf parsley, chopped
1 tablespoon capers

TO GARNISH
1 small bunch of mint, chopped
1 tablespoon small capers

Adding cheese to gnocchi is a great way to bring another layer of flavour to a dish and, instead of the more usual Parmesan, I've gone for a punchier Stilton. This stands up well to the herb-crusted lamb and it's all brought together with a buttery, herb sauce.

Preheat the oven to 220°C (200°C fan)/425°F/gas 7.

Mix the parsley, almonds, lemon and garlic together and spread all over the centre of the lamb loin. Season. Place on a baking sheet and roast for 15–20 minutes. Remove from the oven and leave to rest for 5–10 minutes.

Meanwhile, to make the gnocchi, mix all the ingredients together and season. Then roll into 20cm long sausages, 2cm thick, using a little extra flour. Cut into 3cm pieces, then plunge into boiling water and cook for 2 minutes. Drain.

To make the sauce, heat a large frying pan until hot, then add the butter and, when foaming, add the garlic, mint, parsley, capers and gnocchi and stir through. Season.

To serve, spoon the gnocchi and sauce onto four plates. Slice the lamb and serve alongside.

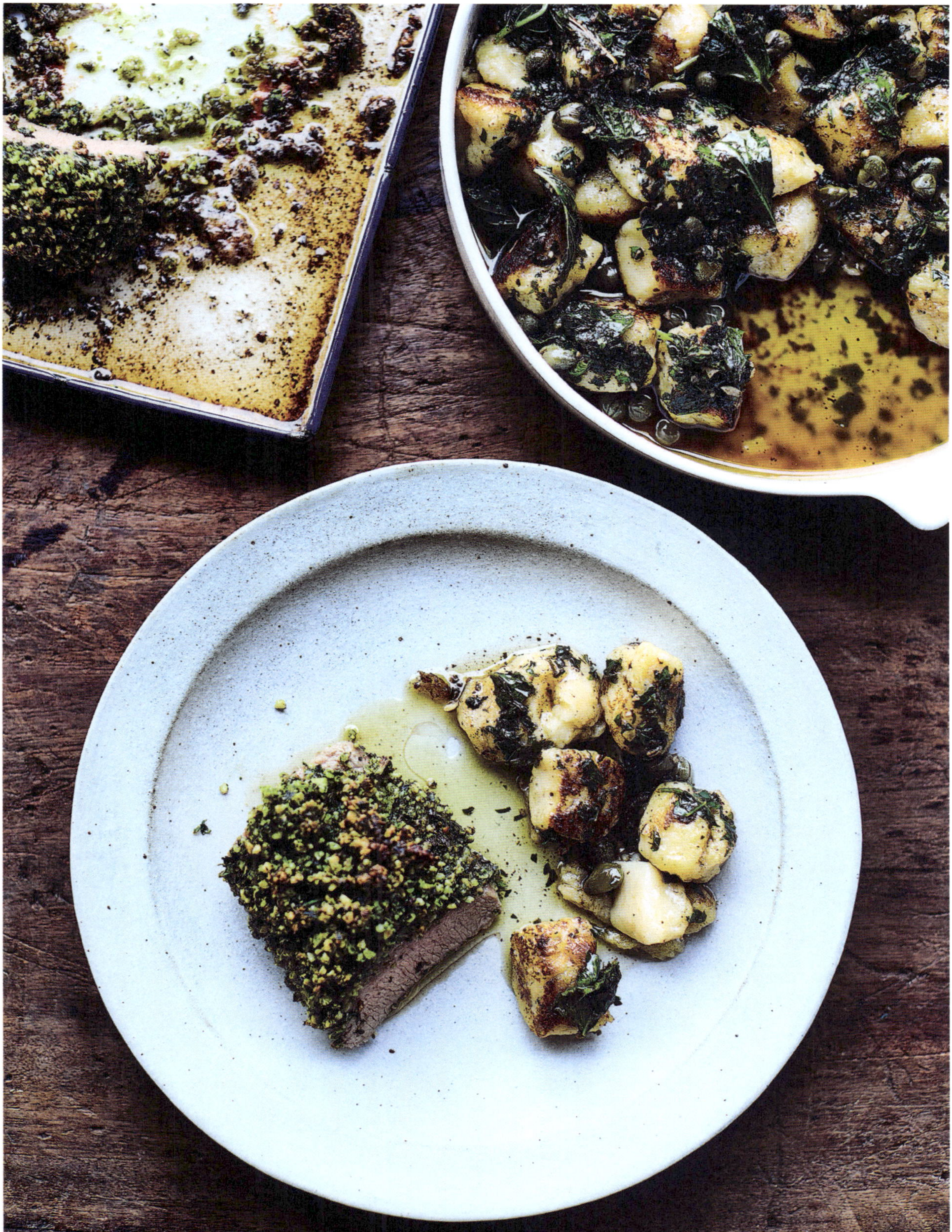

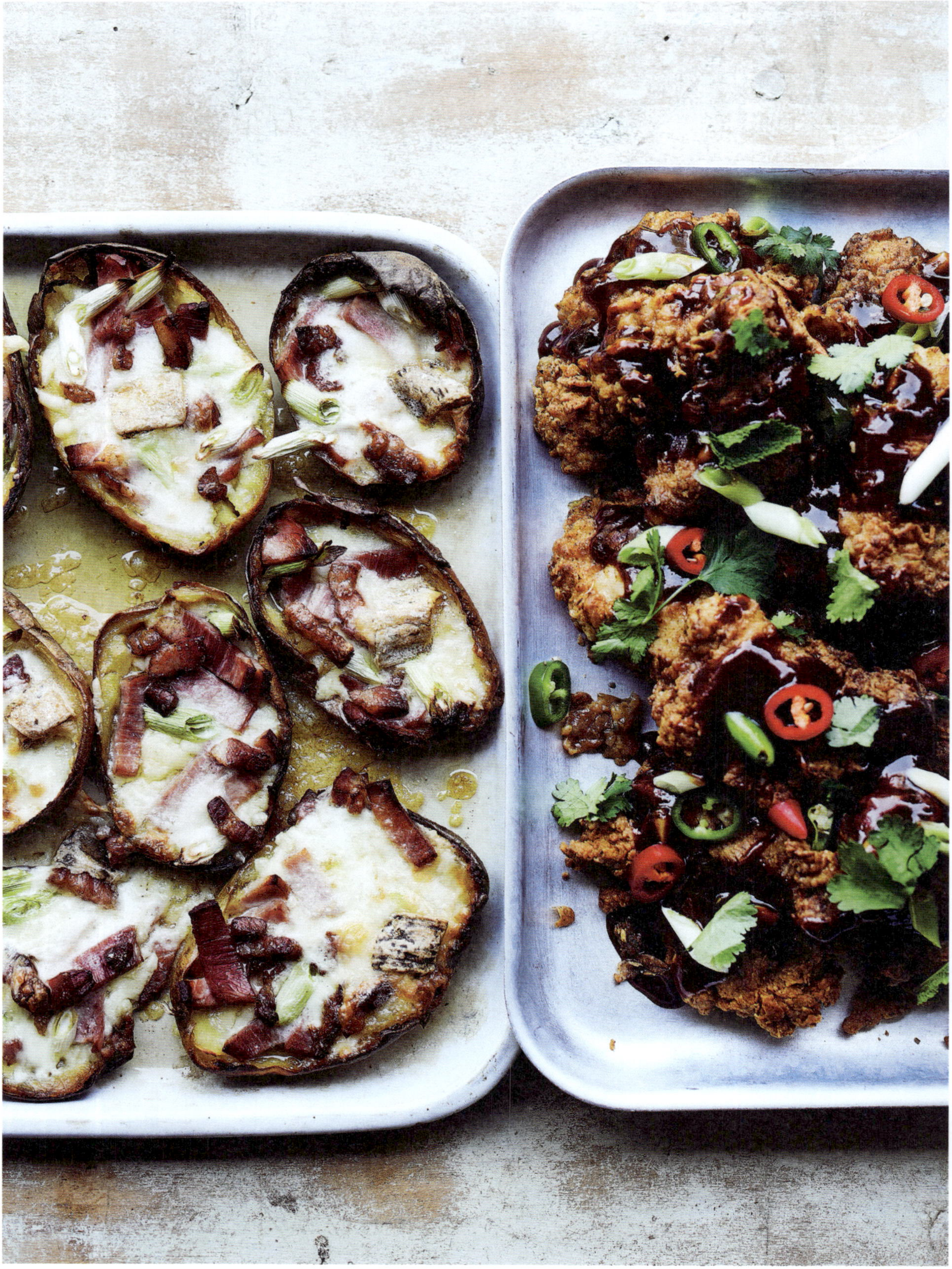

LOADED POTATO SKINS WITH FRIED CHICKEN
\
SERVES 4-6

600g boneless, skinless chicken thighs
300ml buttermilk
4 large baking potatoes
6 spring onions, sliced
100g butter
200g cooked ham, diced
200g Taleggio, sliced
2 litres vegetable oil
1 tablespoon paprika
2 teaspoons onion salt
1 teaspoon black pepper
½ teaspoon celery salt
½ teaspoon dried sage
½ teaspoon garlic powder
½ teaspoon ground allspice
1 teaspoon dried oregano
1 teaspoon dried marjoram
200g plain flour

FOR THE SAUCE
2 garlic cloves, crushed
100g dark brown soft sugar
1 teaspoon smoked paprika
1 teaspoon celery salt
50ml cherry cola
1 tablespoon Worcestershire sauce
25ml black treacle
300ml ketchup
½ red chilli, diced

TO SERVE
1 small bunch of mint, chopped
1 small bunch of coriander, chopped
4 spring onions, sliced
1 red and 1 green chilli, sliced

Taleggio melts wonderfully into these loaded potato skins, which are the perfect side to crispy fried chicken.

Put the chicken into a bowl, pour over the buttermilk, cover and refrigerate overnight.

When you're ready to cook, preheat the oven to 180°C (160°C fan)/350°F/gas 4.

Prick the potatoes all over with a fork, place on a baking tray and bake for 1½ hours. Once cooked, cut them in half and scoop out the flesh. Return the skins to the baking tray.

Preheat the grill to high.

To make the sauce, put all the ingredients in a non-stick pan and bring to the boil. Reduce the heat, then simmer for 4–5 minutes.

In a pan over a medium heat, fry the spring onions in the butter for 3 minutes. Remove from the heat and mix in the potato flesh and ham. Spoon into the skins, top with the cheese and grill for 5 minutes. Set aside and keep warm.

In a deep-fat fryer or deep-sided saucepan, heat the oil to 170°C (340°F). Mix all the dried spices and herbs with the flour. Dip the chicken into the spiced flour, then deep-fry in batches for 5–6 minutes. Drain on kitchen paper.

To serve, pile the chicken onto a platter and spoon over some of the sauce. Pour the remaining sauce into a dipping bowl. Sprinkle over the herbs, spring onions and chillies. Serve the loaded potato skins alongside.

PORK CHOPS WITH GORGONZOLA MAÎTRE D'HÔTEL BUTTER

SERVES 4

150g unsalted butter
150g Gorgonzola
20g flat-leaf parsley, finely chopped
zest of 1 unwaxed lemon and juice of ½
1 teaspoon sea salt
1½ teaspoons black pepper
½ teaspoon Worcestershire sauce (optional)
pinch of cayenne pepper (optional)
4 pork chops
steaming-hot Jersey Royals, to serve

Gorgonzola is the hero ingredient in this maître d'hôtel butter, which is traditionally just made with butter, parsley, lemon juice and salt and pepper. The addition of the blue cheese really kicks things up a gear and it's wonderful melted over succulent pork chops and served alongside seasonal Jersey Royals.

Mix the butter, Gorgonzola, parsley, lemon zest and juice, salt, pepper and Worcestershire sauce and cayenne, if using, until combined. Place on a sheet of clingfilm and roll into a sausage shape. Wrap tightly, then pop in the fridge to chill.

Preheat the grill to high.

Put the pork chops on a baking tray and grill for 8–10 minutes.

Slice the maître d'hôtel butter and slather onto the pork chops to melt. Serve with some steaming-hot Jersey Royals.

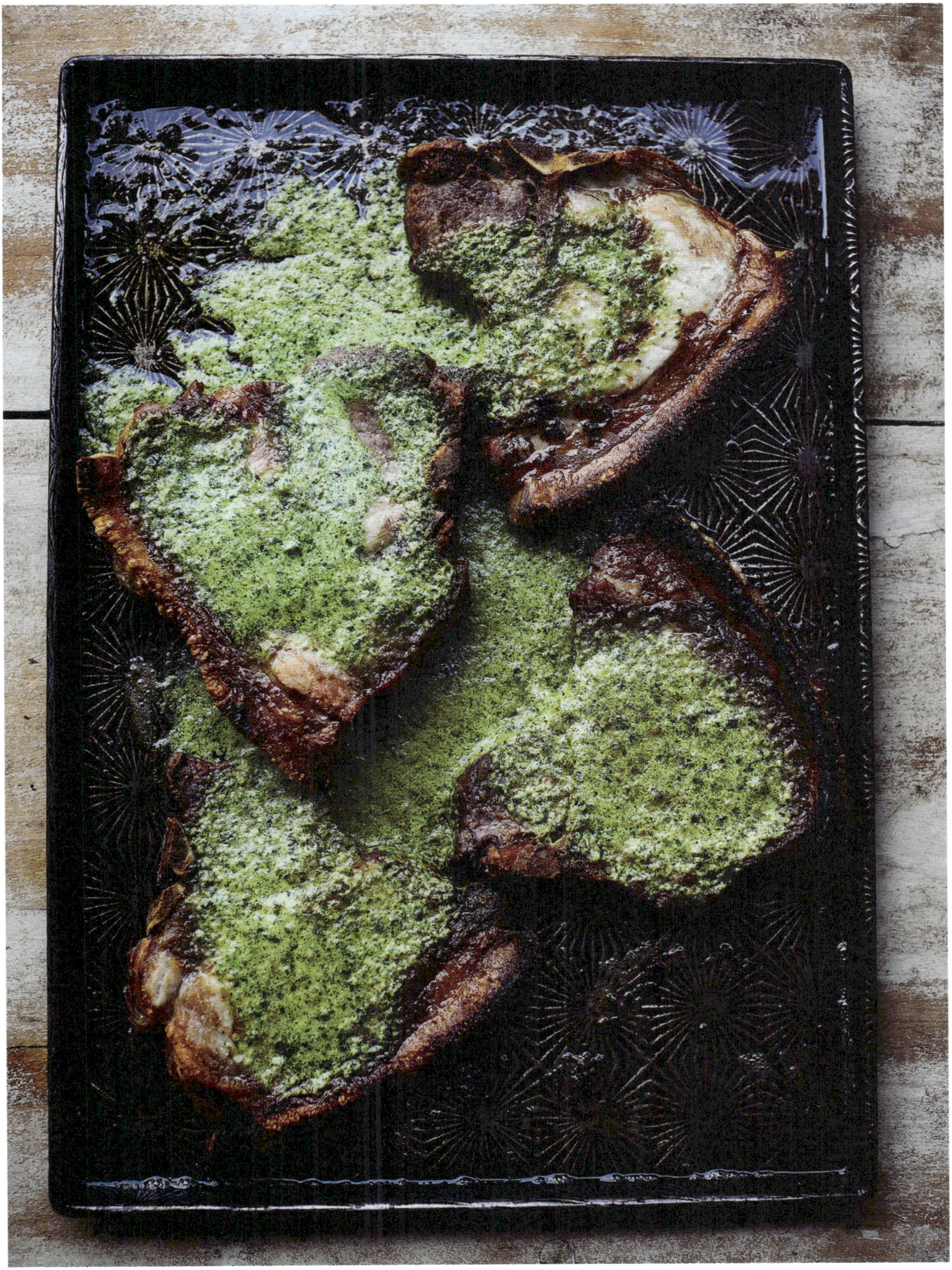

MARGHERITA PIZZA
\
SERVES 10

1kg strong bread flour
20g fresh or 2 x 7g sachets dried yeast
50g semolina, plus extra for dusting
100ml olive oil
650ml water
20g salt

FOR THE TOPPINGS
400g can San Marzano tomatoes, blitzed
400g mozzarella (about 3 balls, drained weight)
100g Pecorino Romano, grated
a few basil leaves
olive oil, for drizzling

An Italian classic which makes the most of a few simple but great-quality ingredients. At its heart is the ever-popular pairing of cheese and tomato with mozzarella melted into the tomato sauce until bubbling.

Put all the ingredients for the dough into the bowl of a stand mixer fitted with a dough hook and mix on a slow speed for 4 minutes. Increase the speed to medium for 12 minutes. Tip the dough onto a surface dusted in semolina and shape into ten even balls. Leave to prove at room temperature for 15 minutes, or cover and pop in the fridge overnight.

When ready to cook, heat a pizza oven to 500°C (932°F) or alternatively preheat the oven to 200°C (180°C fan)/400°F/gas 6 and put in a pizza stone for 30 minutes.

Using more semolina flour, roll out the dough balls as thinly as you dare. Top with the tomato, cheeses and basil, then drizzle with olive oil. Slide the first pizza into the pizza oven, or onto the pizza stone. Bake, one at a time, for 3–4 minutes until crisp and bubbling in the centre.

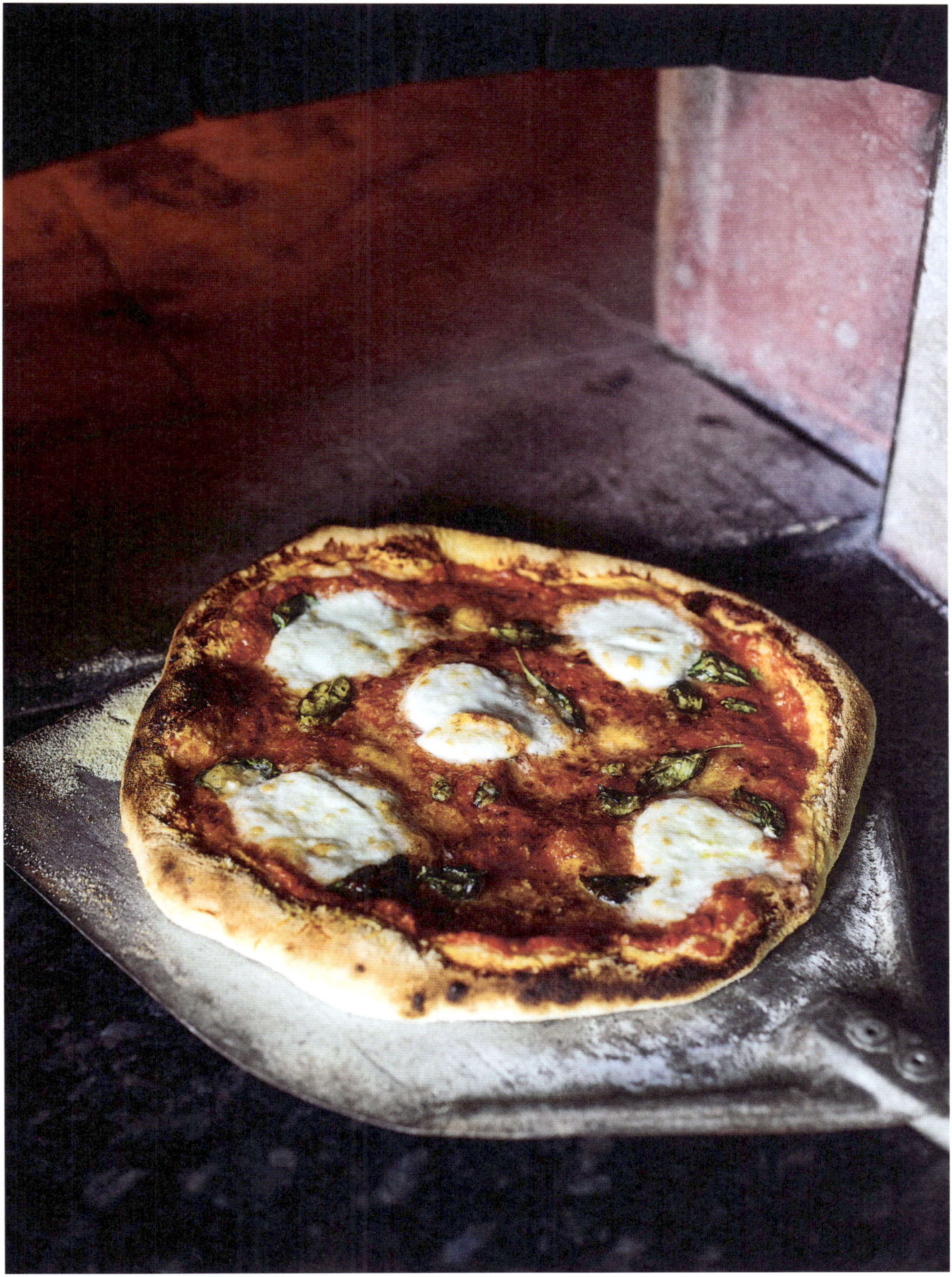

PASTA RAGOUT
\
SERVES 6

250g '00' flour
250g semolina
5 eggs

FOR THE RAGOUT
1 onion, diced
3 garlic cloves, crushed
1 carrot, peeled and diced
1 leek, diced
2 celery sticks, diced
25ml olive oil
3 bay leaves
2 tablespoons tomato purée
500g minced beef
8 pork sausages, chopped
75ml red wine
2 x 400g cans chopped tomatoes
1 bunch of basil, chopped
grated Pecorino Romano, to serve

This classic ragout is lifted by a final grating of Pecorino Romano cheese, a small but nonetheless essential element which brings the pasta and sauce together. You could also use Parmesan or Grana Padano here if that's what you've got in the fridge.

To make the pasta, add the flour and semolina to a food processor and, with the motor on low speed, slowly add the eggs until it forms a dough. Cover the dough in clingfilm and let it rest in the fridge for 30 minutes.

Wipe clean the food processor bowl, then blitz the onion, garlic, carrot, leek and celery.

To make the ragout, heat a large pan over a high heat and drizzle in the oil. Add the blitzed vegetables, bay leaves and tomato purée. Cook out for a few minutes. Add the beef and sausages, then pour in the wine and tomatoes. Gently simmer for 2–3 hours. Sprinkle in the basil.

Pass the pasta through a pasta machine until it is at the thinnest setting, then cut into tagliatelle. Cook the pasta in boiling salted water for 2–3 minutes, then spoon into the ragout.

Sprinkle with grated cheese and serve.

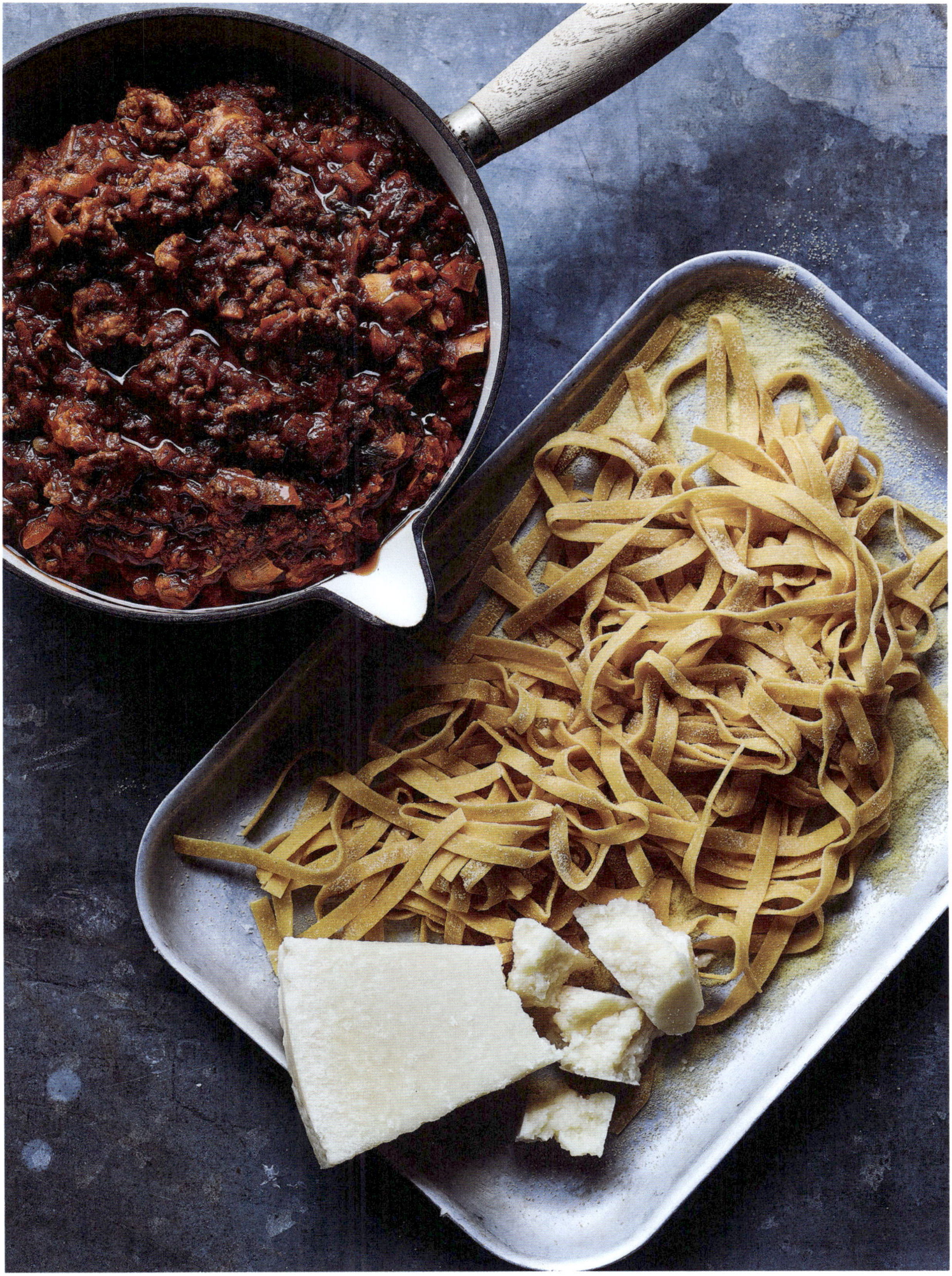

SPANAKOPITA
\
SERVES 6

2 x 250g packs filo pastry
250g butter, melted
Greek salad, to serve

FOR THE FILLING
400g baby spinach, washed
olive oil (ideally Greek)
4 spring onions, chopped
400g feta, crumbled
200g mascarpone
4 tablespoons grated Parmesan
2 tablespoons chopped dill
2 tablespoons chopped mint
2 large eggs, beaten
1 nutmeg, grated
sea salt and freshly ground
　　black pepper

One of Greece's most famous dishes, the key to this filo pie is the feta and spinach filling but my twist also uses mascarpone and Parmesan for extra cheesiness. Serve with a Greek salad.

Preheat the oven to 160°C (140°C fan)/325°F/gas 3.

In a large pan over a medium heat, wilt the spinach with a little olive oil and seasoning. Then allow to cool and drain well. Extra squeezing may be necessary when cool.

Mix the remaining ingredients for the filling together with the spinach in a large bowl. Season with a little salt and pepper.

Unroll the filo sheets and place them between two lightly damp tea towels. (This stops the pastry drying out.) Brush a deepish baking tray with some of the melted butter and cover the bottom with two or three sheets of filo, overhanging the edges of the tray.

Brush with more butter and place two more sheets on top. Brush with butter and repeat with two more sheets.

Now evenly spread the spinach and feta filling on top of the pastry. Continue to add more sheets and butter, two sheets at a time, until all the pastry is used up.

Fold in the pastry flaps and brush with a final topping of butter. Using a sharp knife, cut the spanakopita into squares, cutting only halfway through the depth (marking it, really).

Bake in the oven for 1 hour until crispy and golden brown. Remove from the oven and finish cutting all the way through the square cuts. Allow to cool slightly and serve with some lovely fresh Greek salad.

RACK OF LAMB WITH ASPARAGUS AND SHEEP'S CHEESE
\
SERVES 4

olive oil, for drizzling
8-rib rack of lamb, French trimmed
pinch of salt
pinch of sugar
400g asparagus stalks, woody ends snapped off and peeled

FOR THE GREMOLATA
30g wild garlic leaves, chopped (or 10g garlic, chopped, when wild garlic is not in season)
10g picked flat-leaf parsley
40g picked chervil
50g spinach
200ml grapeseed oil
zest of 1 unwaxed lemon
salt, to taste

FOR THE DRESSING
150g crème fraîche
150g buttermilk
10g roast garlic
1 teaspoon lemon juice
100g soft sheep's cheese

Here the soft sheep's cheese creates a wonderful tangy dressing to complement the lamb, asparagus and gremolata.

To make the gremolata, blitz all the ingredients in a blender for 3–4 minutes until smooth. Remove and chill immediately.

To make the sheep's cheese dressing, blitz all the ingredients in the clean blender until smooth. Pass the dressing through a fine sieve and refrigerate.

Preheat the oven to 160°C (140°C fan)/325°F/gas 3.

To cook the lamb, place a heavy-based frying pan over a high heat. Rub a little oil over the meat and season with the salt. Place in the hot pan and seal until golden on all sides. Transfer the lamb to a tray with a wire rack and roast in the oven for 12–15 minutes. Remove the lamb from the oven and leave to rest for 5 minutes.

Fill a medium pan with water, add a pinch of sugar and salt, then bring to the boil. Once boiling, add the asparagus and cook for 40 seconds, then remove from the pan and plunge straight into a bowl of iced water.

When ready to serve, heat a griddle pan and, once hot, remove the asparagus from the water and dry on a cloth. Slightly oil the asparagus and place in the griddle pan to get a nice char. Use a small paring knife to test the stalks, there should still be a light bite. Remove from the griddle, then season with a small amount of salt.

Slice the lamb, sit on top of the asparagus and spoon over the dressing and gremolata.

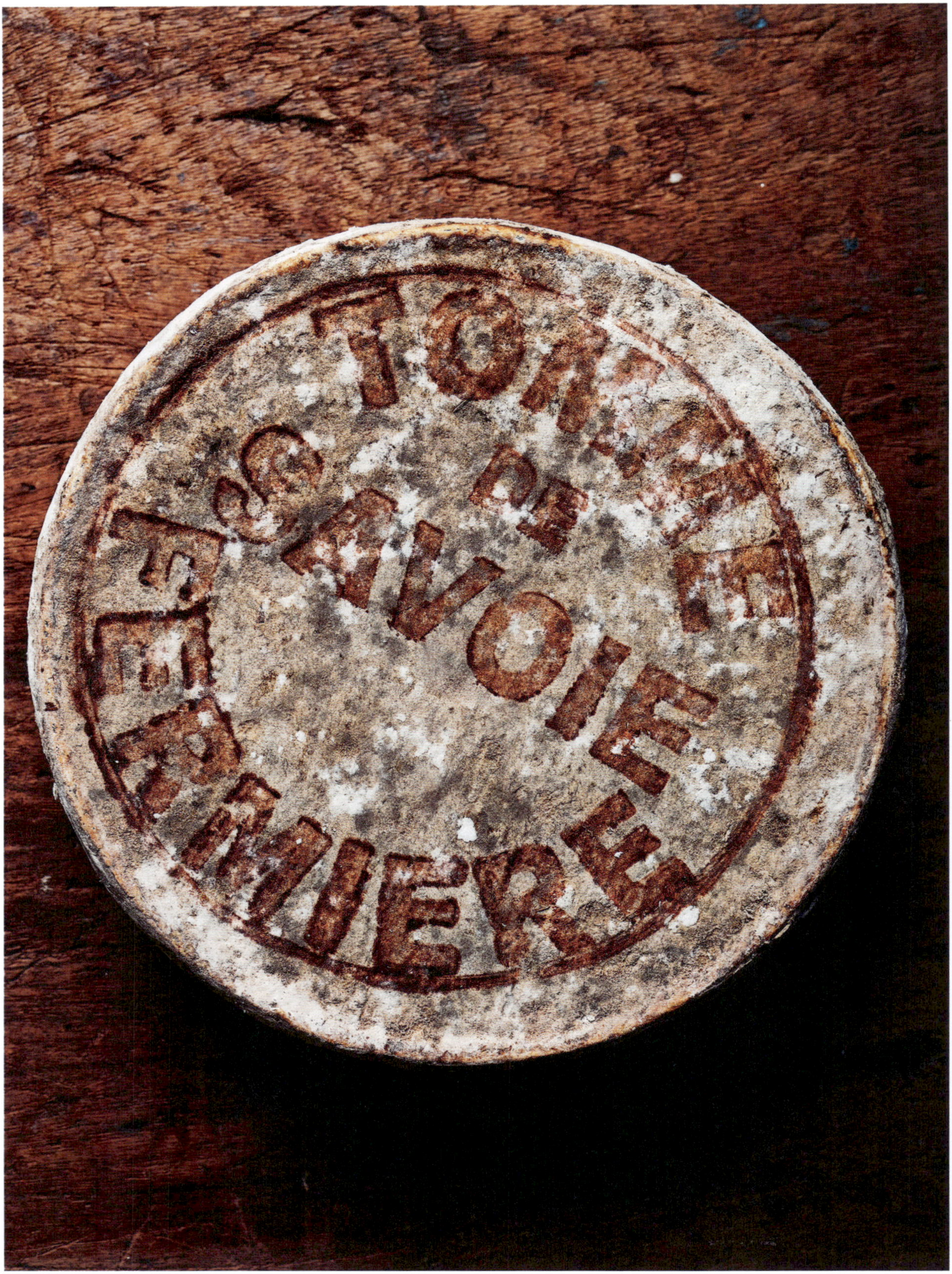
TOMME
DE
SAVOIE
FERMIER

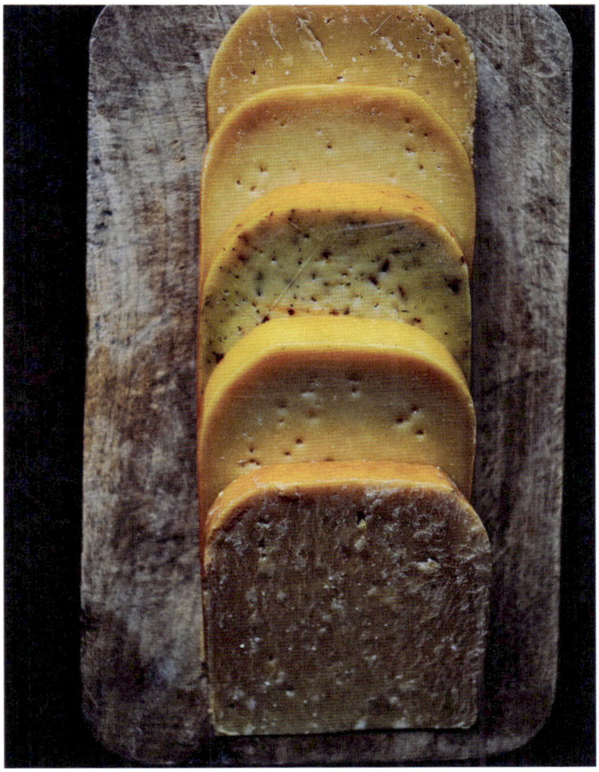

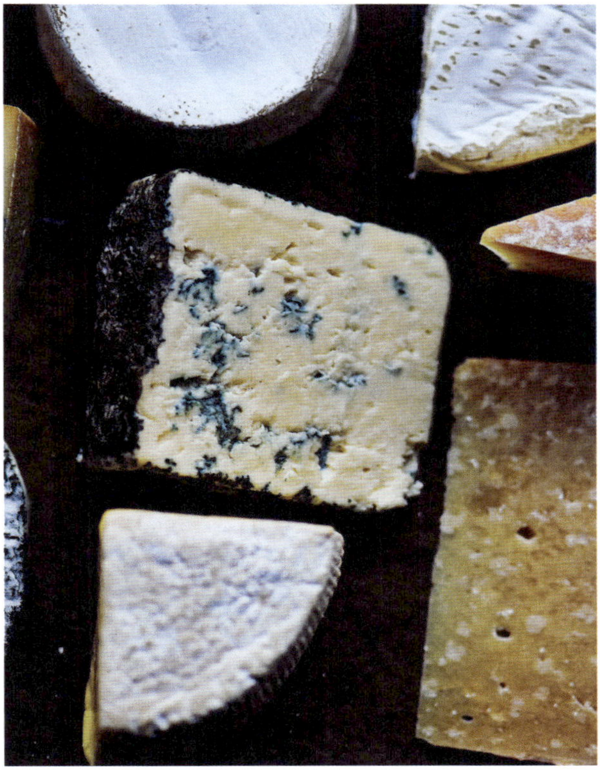

PEA RISOTTO
\
SERVES 4

50g butter
1 garlic clove, chopped
1 shallot, diced
200g arborio or carnaroli rice
100ml white wine
500ml chicken stock
1 small bunch of flat-leaf parsley
200g petits pois
50g mascarpone
25g Parmesan, grated, plus extra to serve
sea salt and freshly ground black pepper

TO SERVE
herb oil, for drizzling
a few sprigs of mint (optional)
200g feta, crumbled

Cheese is often an essential ingredient in a risotto and in this beautiful summery dish the usual Parmesan is joined by creamy mascarpone and a crumbling of feta to finish. You could try switching the mascarpone for ricotta or, to add a different, stronger flavour, a soft goat's or sheep's cheese would take it in a different direction.

Melt the butter in a pan over a medium heat, then add the garlic, shallot and rice and cook for a couple of minutes. Add the wine and three-quarters of the stock. Bring to the boil, then allow it to simmer gently for 15 minutes, stirring regularly. Season.

Meanwhile, blitz the parsley with half the petits pois in a food processor.

To finish the risotto, add the pea purée, the remaining petits pois, mascarpone and Parmesan. The texture should be slightly wet but add some of the remaining stock if needed.

To serve, spoon the risotto into bowls and finish with a drizzle of herb oil and a few sprigs of mint, if desired. Finally, dot with the feta and scatter with Parmesan.

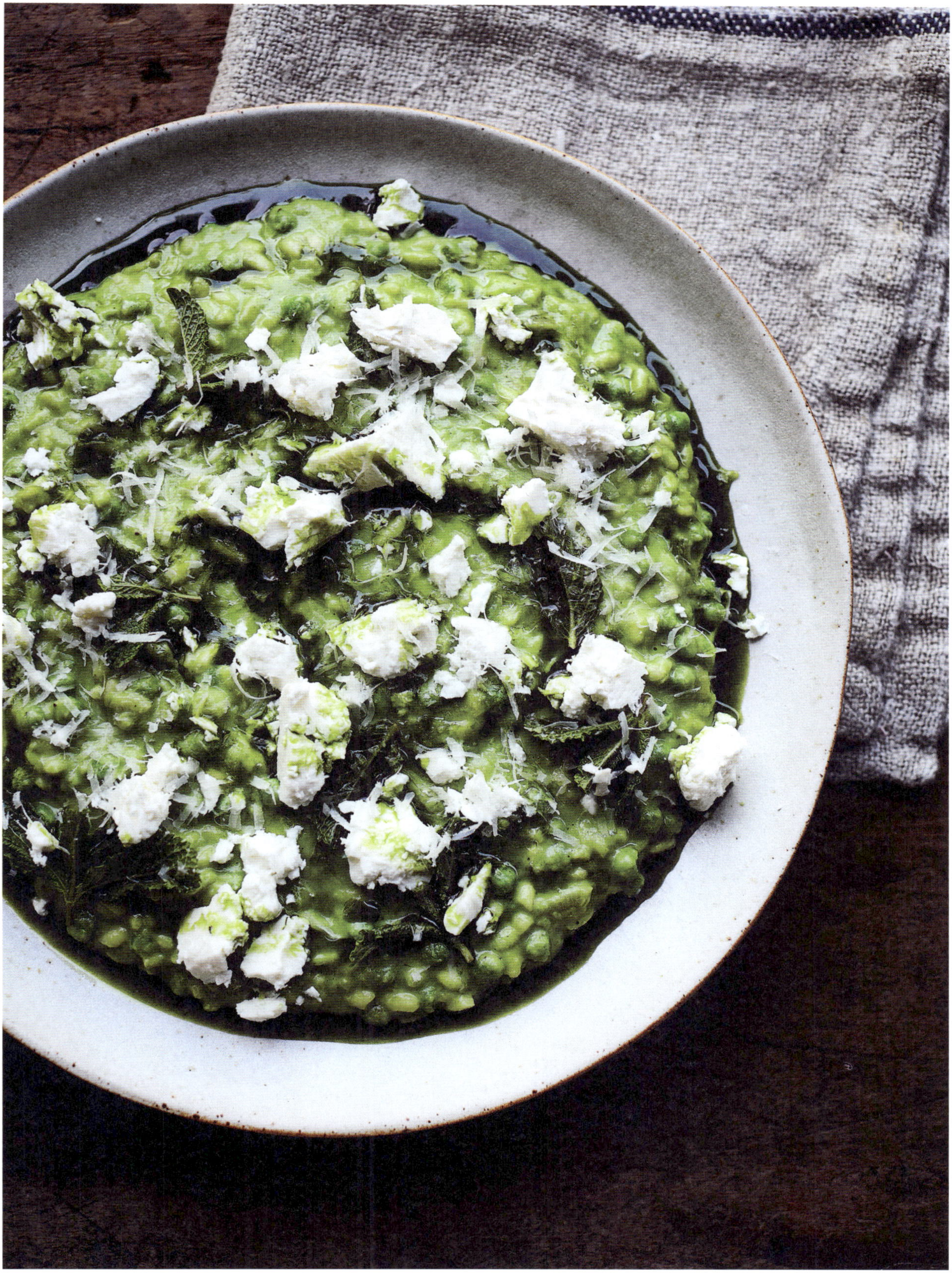

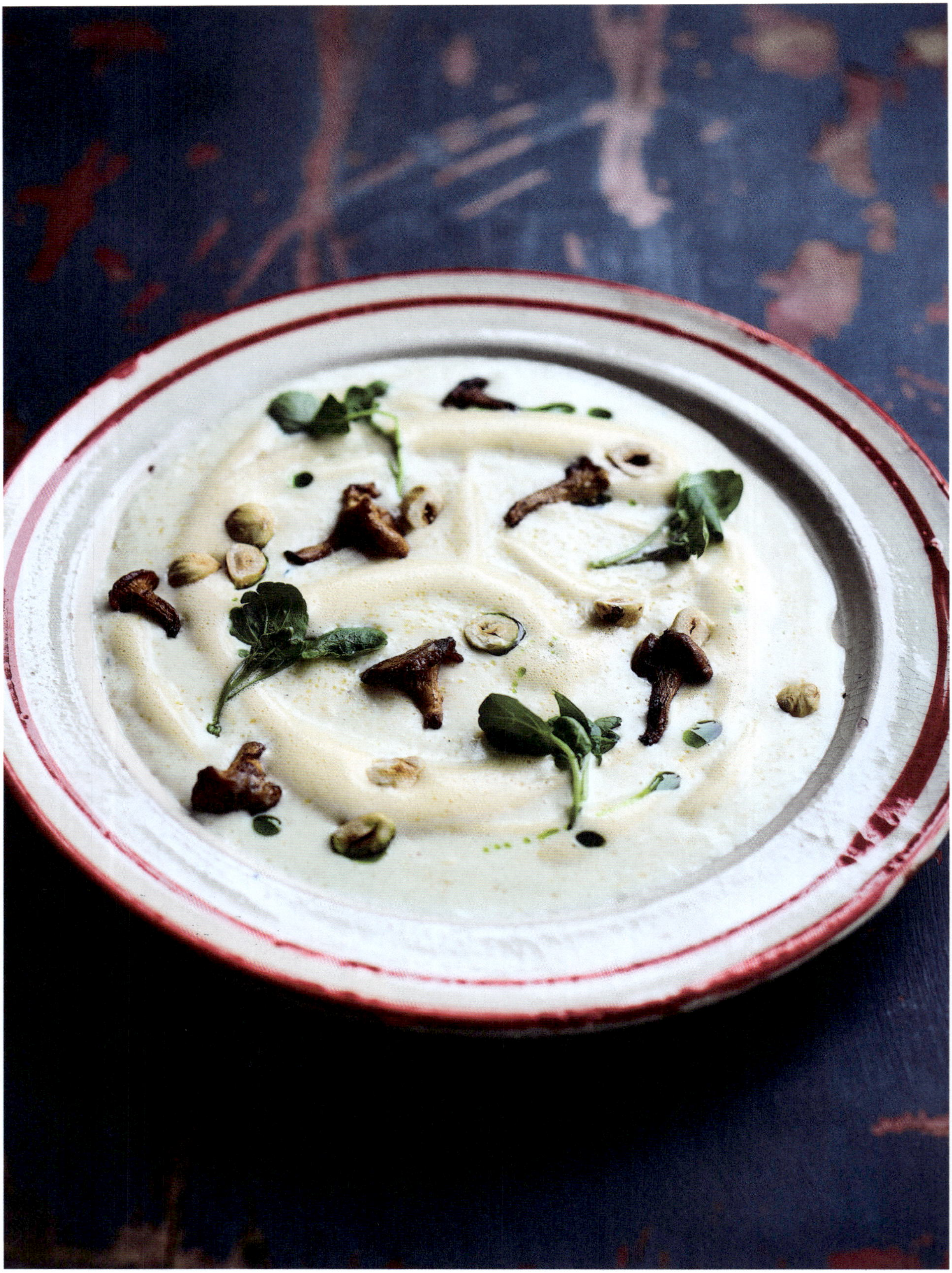

POLENTA WITH SAUTÉED MUSHROOMS AND HAZELNUTS
\
SERVES 4

1 litre full-fat milk
1 garlic clove, minced
1 sprig of thyme, leaves picked
200g polenta
50g Parmesan, grated
50ml double cream
50g butter

FOR THE BOUILLON
100ml chicken stock
2 garlic cloves, crushed
6 sage leaves
2 tablespoons hazelnut oil
2 egg yolks
sea salt and freshly ground
    black pepper

FOR THE MUSHROOMS
300g girolles
50g butter

TO SERVE
herb oil, for drizzling
watercress
100g toasted hazelnuts, crushed

Parmesan is a great addition to this creamy polenta, which serves as the base for girolle mushrooms and a hazelnut bouillon. Grana Padano or Pecorino Romano would also work well here.

To cook the polenta, in a pan, bring the milk, garlic and thyme to the boil. Then whisk in the polenta and cook gently for 30 minutes, stirring occasionally. Finish by stirring through the cheese, cream and butter.

When the polenta is cooked, set a small pan over a medium heat and warm the stock, garlic and sage. Pass through a sieve into a jug. Pour into a small food processor and blend with the oil and egg yolks. Season and transfer back to the pan to keep warm.

In a frying pan over a high heat, sweat the mushrooms in the butter for 5 minutes until just soft. Season.

To serve, spoon the polenta into bowls, top with the hazelnut bouillon and sprinkle over the mushrooms. Drizzle with herb oil and dot with watercress and the hazelnuts.

ROAST CHICKEN WITH PARMESAN BABY LEEKS
\
SERVES 4

1 large (1.8kg) corn-fed chicken
175g butter, softened
400g baby leeks
100g fresh breadcrumbs
a few sprigs of tarragon, chopped
25g Parmesan, grated
sea salt and freshly ground black pepper

These Parmesan-breadcrumbed baby leeks are the ideal side for a simple roast chicken, but versatile enough to work alongside other roasts or meat dishes. Swap the Parmesan for Grana Padano or Pecorino Romano, or vary things a little more with Comté or Gruyère.

Place the chicken in a large bowl, cover with water and add a small handful of salt. Pop in the fridge overnight.

Preheat the oven to 200°C (180°C fan)/400°F/gas 6.

Remove the chicken from the fridge and pat dry. Place the chicken on a roasting tray, season generously and smother in 150g of the butter. Roast for 1 hour. Then remove from the oven and leave to rest for 20 minutes.

Blanch the leeks for 5 minutes until soft, then drain.

Meanwhile, melt the remaining 25g butter in a large frying pan over a medium heat. Stir through the breadcrumbs and season. Pop the leeks into an ovenproof dish, top with the breadcrumbs, tarragon and Parmesan and roast for 10 minutes.

Carve the chicken and serve alongside the Parmesan baby leeks.

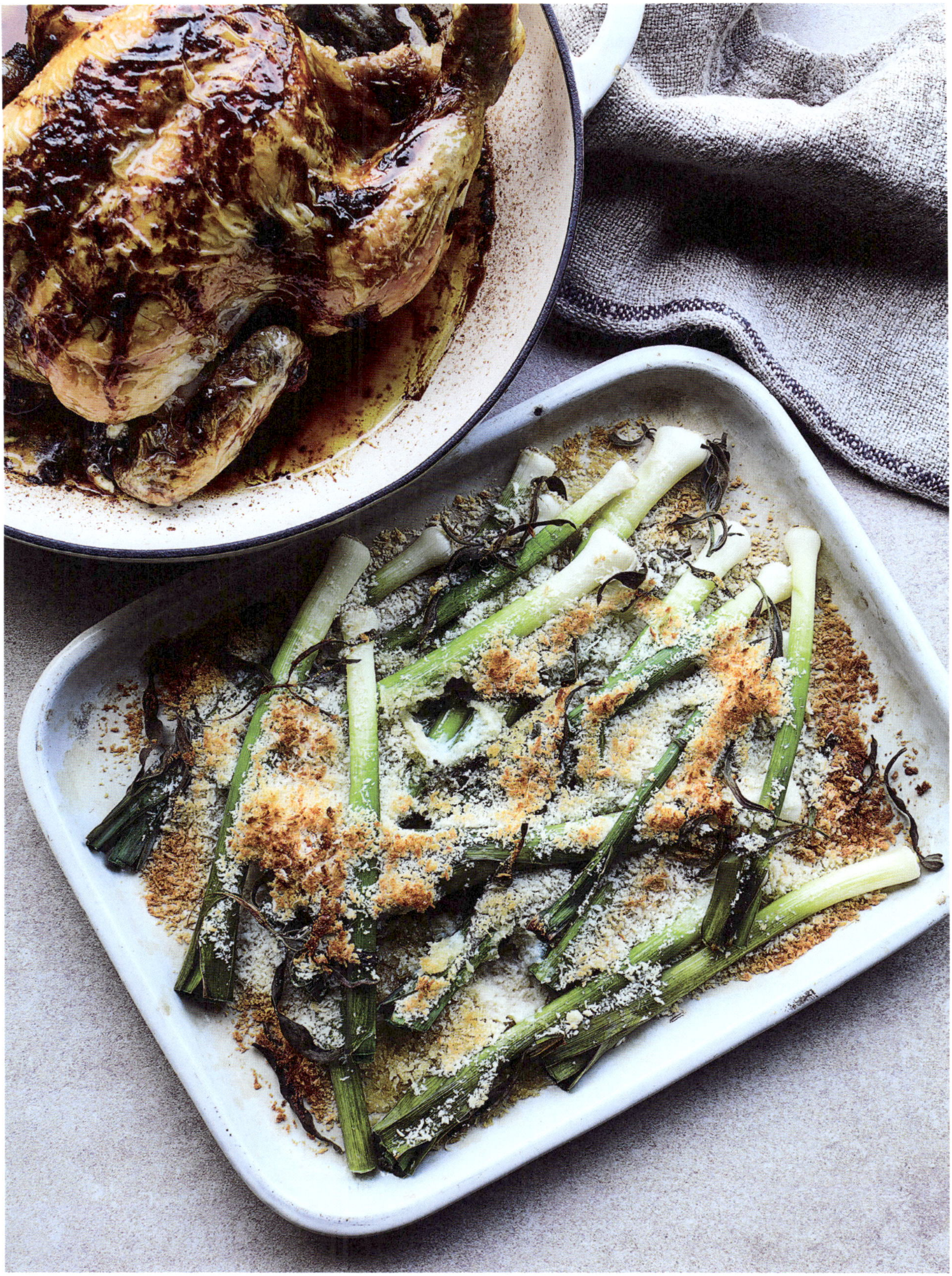

PUMPKIN RAVIOLI

SERVES 4-6

250g '00' flour
250g semolina, plus extra for dusting
5 eggs
200g pumpkin purée
75g mascarpone
50g amaretti biscuits, crushed
juice of ½ lemon
sea salt and freshly ground
   black pepper

FOR THE SAUCE
250g butter
juice of 1 lemon

TO SERVE
deep-fried sage leaves
grated Pecorino Romano

Mascarpone makes a brilliant filling, especially for pasta, and here I've combined it with a delicious pumpkin purée, encased in a ravioli wrapper. Serve with a simple buttery sauce and some crispy sage leaves.

To make the pasta, add the flour and semolina to a food processor and, with the motor running on low speed, slowly add the eggs until it forms a dough. Cover the dough in clingfilm and let it rest in the fridge for 30 minutes.

Mix the pumpkin purée and mascarpone together, season and mix again. Stir through the crushed amaretti and finish by squeezing in the lemon juice.

Put the pasta through a pasta machine until it is at its thinnest setting, then cut out 7cm circles on a dusted board. Add a spoonful of the pumpkin mixture to half the circles, top with the remaining circles and seal the edges of each ravioli using water. Press the edges all around to ensure they are sealed.

To make the sauce, heat the butter in a saucepan until it is nut brown in colour, then finish with the lemon juice.

Pop the ravioli into a large pan of boiling salted water and cook for 1 minute. Drain.

Divide the ravioli between plates. Spoon the sauce over the pasta. Scatter over some deep-fried sage leaves, sprinkle with Pecorino Romano and serve.

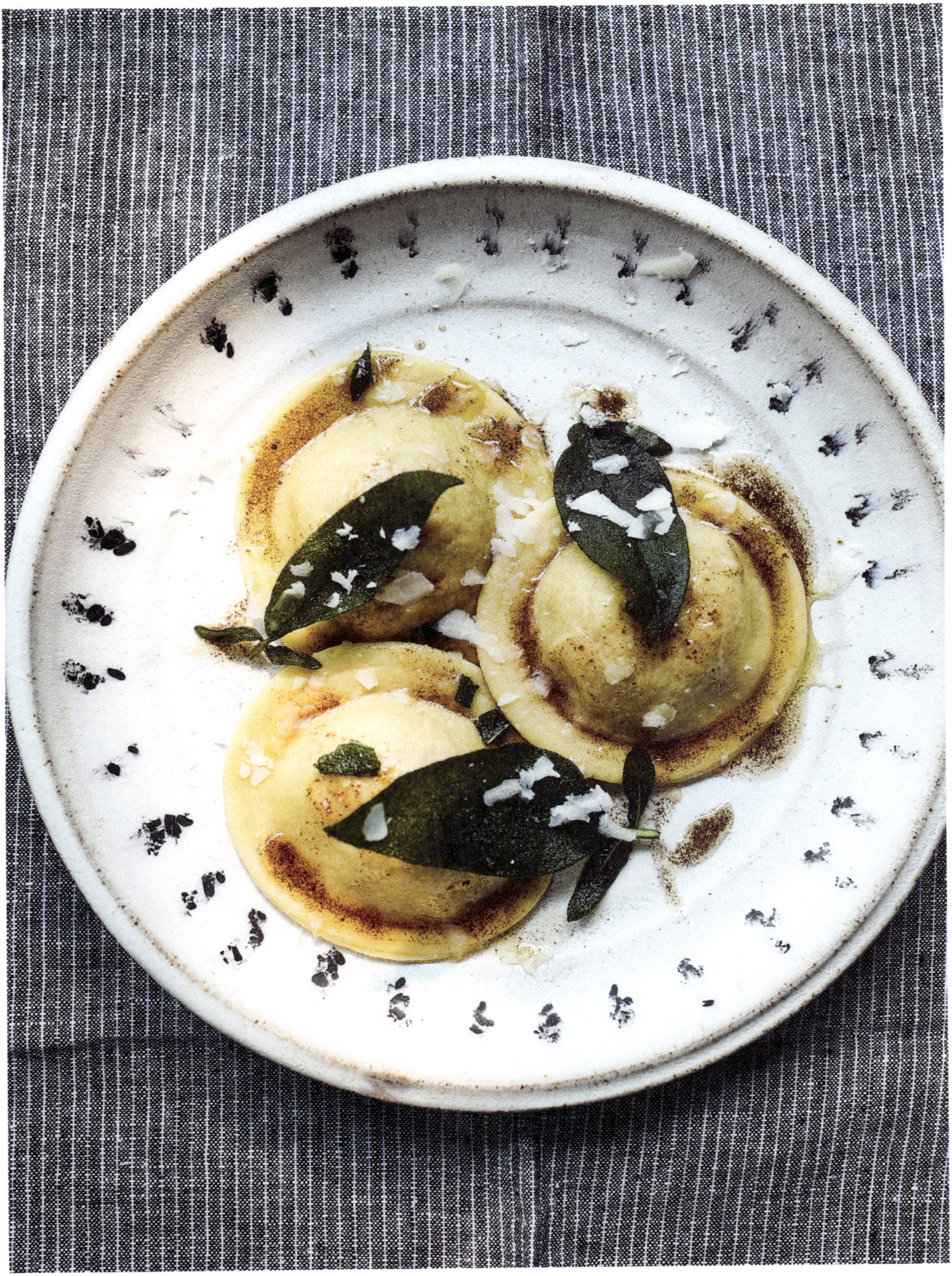

SHALLOT TARTE TATIN WITH SHEEP'S CURD
\
SERVES 4

6 shallots, peeled and halved
225g caster sugar
100ml red wine vinegar
15g butter
200g all-butter ready-rolled puff pastry
150g sheep's curd, to serve

This savoury take on the French dessert replaces the usual apples with shallots, while the sheep's curd is a wonderful topping to this stunning tart. If you don't have sheep's curd, try goat's curd or a soft goat's cheese instead.

Put the shallots in a frying pan over a high heat with enough water to cover, then add 25g of the sugar and all of the vinegar and cook until the shallots are just cooked. Remove from the heat and leave to cool, then drain.

Preheat the oven to 200°C (180°C fan)/400°F/gas 6.

Heat a large, non-stick ovenproof frying pan over a medium heat and, when hot, add the remaining sugar. Do not stir but carefully swirl in the pan until the sugar is brown and caramelised. This should take about 3–4 minutes. Once the sugar has caramelised, add the butter and sit the shallots flat-side down. Unroll the pastry and cover the shallots, making sure to tuck in the edges. Bake in the oven for 20 minutes.

To serve, carefully invert the tart onto a plate and top with the sheep's curd.

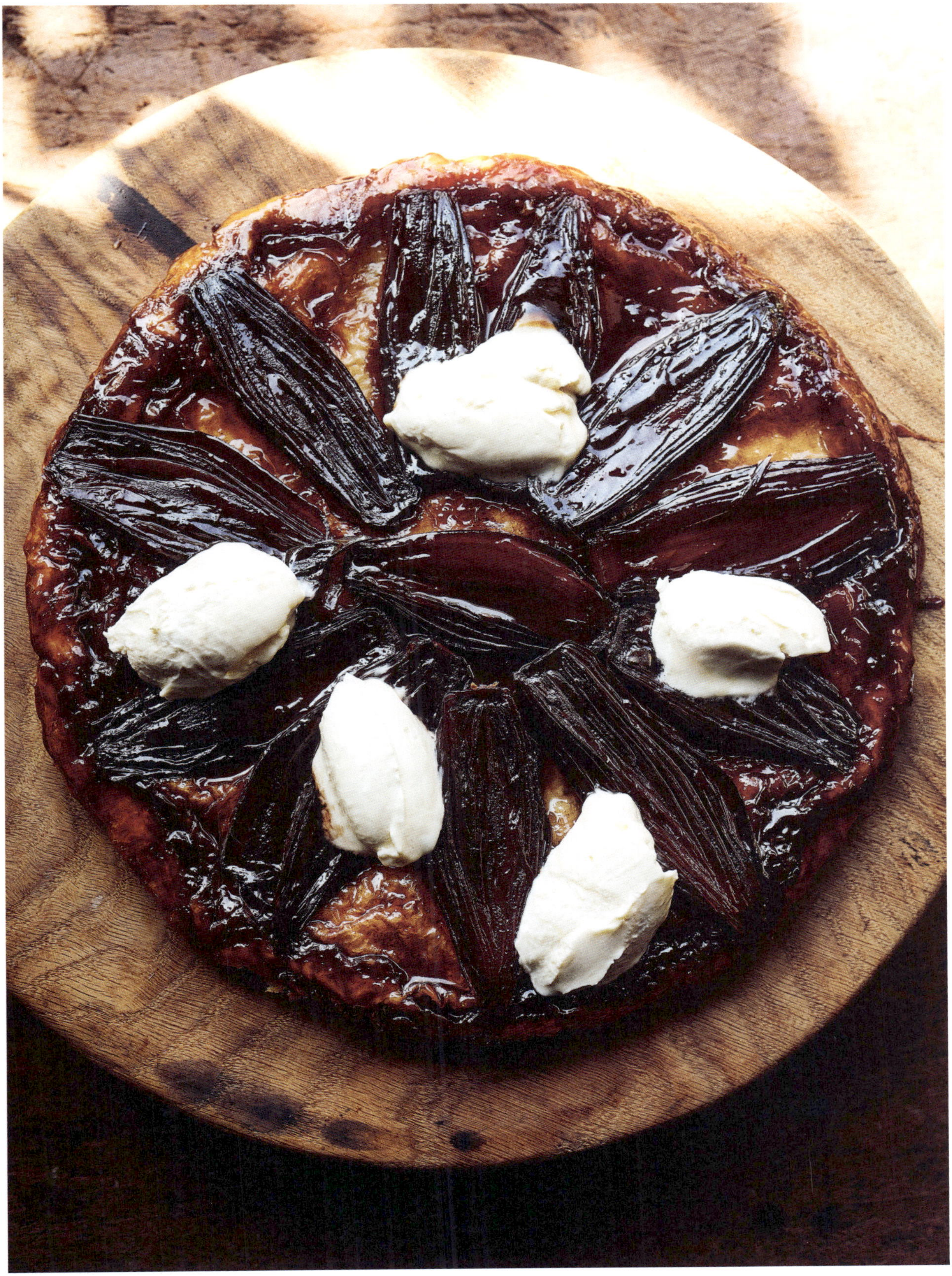

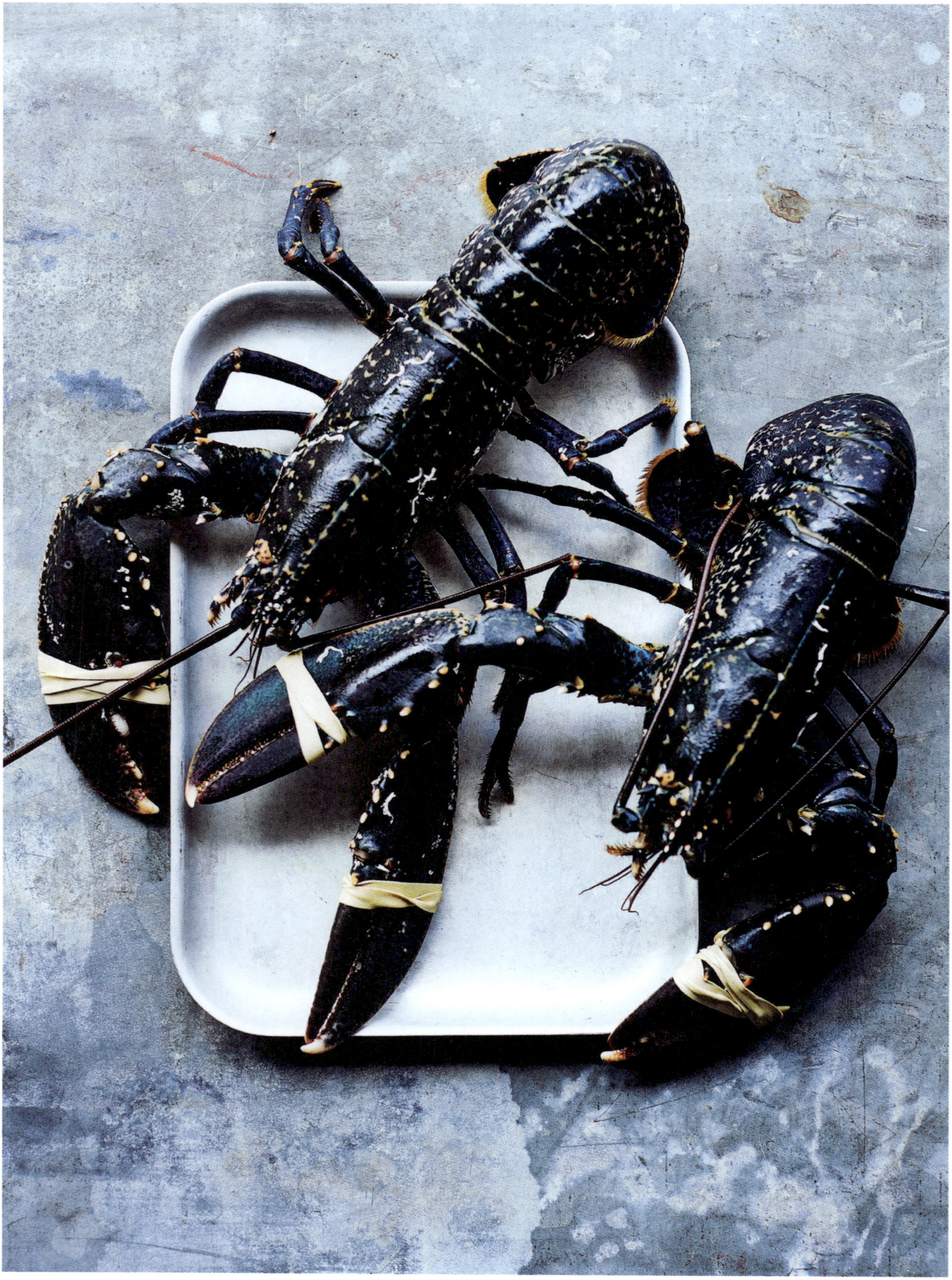

GRILLED LOBSTER THERMIDOR
\
SERVES 2

2 lobster tails
300ml chicken stock
100ml double cream
25ml brandy
1 teaspoon Dijon mustard
2 egg yolks
150g Gruyère, grated
sea salt and freshly ground black pepper
dressed green salad, to serve

An absolute French classic, lobster thermidor consists of lobster cooked in a rich, boozy sauce, then stuffed back into the shells and finished with a cheesy crust, most often using Gruyère as I've done here. However, some recipes feature Parmesan instead, or you could also try Comté too.

Split the lobster tails from top to bottom and pop onto a baking tray, shell-side down.

In a pan, bring the chicken stock to the boil, then reduce by half. Whisk in the cream, brandy and Dijon mustard. Remove from the heat and leave to cool slightly.

Preheat the grill to high.

Whisk the egg yolks into the sauce, season and spoon over the lobster tails. Sprinkle over the cheese. Grill for 5 minutes until golden and bubbling.

Serve with a dressed green salad.

STROGANOFF STEAK WITH BLUE CHEESE
\
SERVES 4

rapeseed oil, for frying
4 thick slices of sourdough
30g butter
500g sirloin or rump steak, cut into finger width strips
2 banana shallots, finely chopped
400g mixed field and chestnut mushrooms, sliced
1 garlic clove, crushed
1 tablespoon thyme leaves
1 tablespoon plain flour
200ml beer
200ml beef stock
pinch of sugar
150g Stilton, crumbled
1 small bunch of watercress, picked

A crumbling of Stilton is the ideal finishing touch to perfectly cooked steak, served with a simple watercress side.

Heat a few drizzles of rapeseed oil in a non-stick frying pan over a high heat. Lay in the sourdough slices, in batches if necessary. Cook for a minute on each side or until golden and crispy. Place on a baking sheet and keep warm in a low oven.

Add half the butter to the pan and return to a high heat. Season the beef well and add to the pan in two batches. Cook for 1 minute until golden and just sealed. Remove from pan and set to one side. Place the pan back over the heat and add the remaining butter. Stir in the shallots and gently cook for 5 minutes until softened.

Turn up the heat, add the mushrooms and cook for 3–4 minutes or until golden and the liquid has evaporated. Stir in the garlic, thyme and flour and cook for 1 minute, stirring well.

Pour in the beer and stock and add the sugar, stir well and bring to the boil. Reduce the heat and simmer for 2–3 minutes or until syrupy. Return the beef and any juices to the pan and stir through. Season to taste.

To serve, arrange the toast on warm plates. Top each with the beef and Stilton. Finish with watercress and serve straight away.

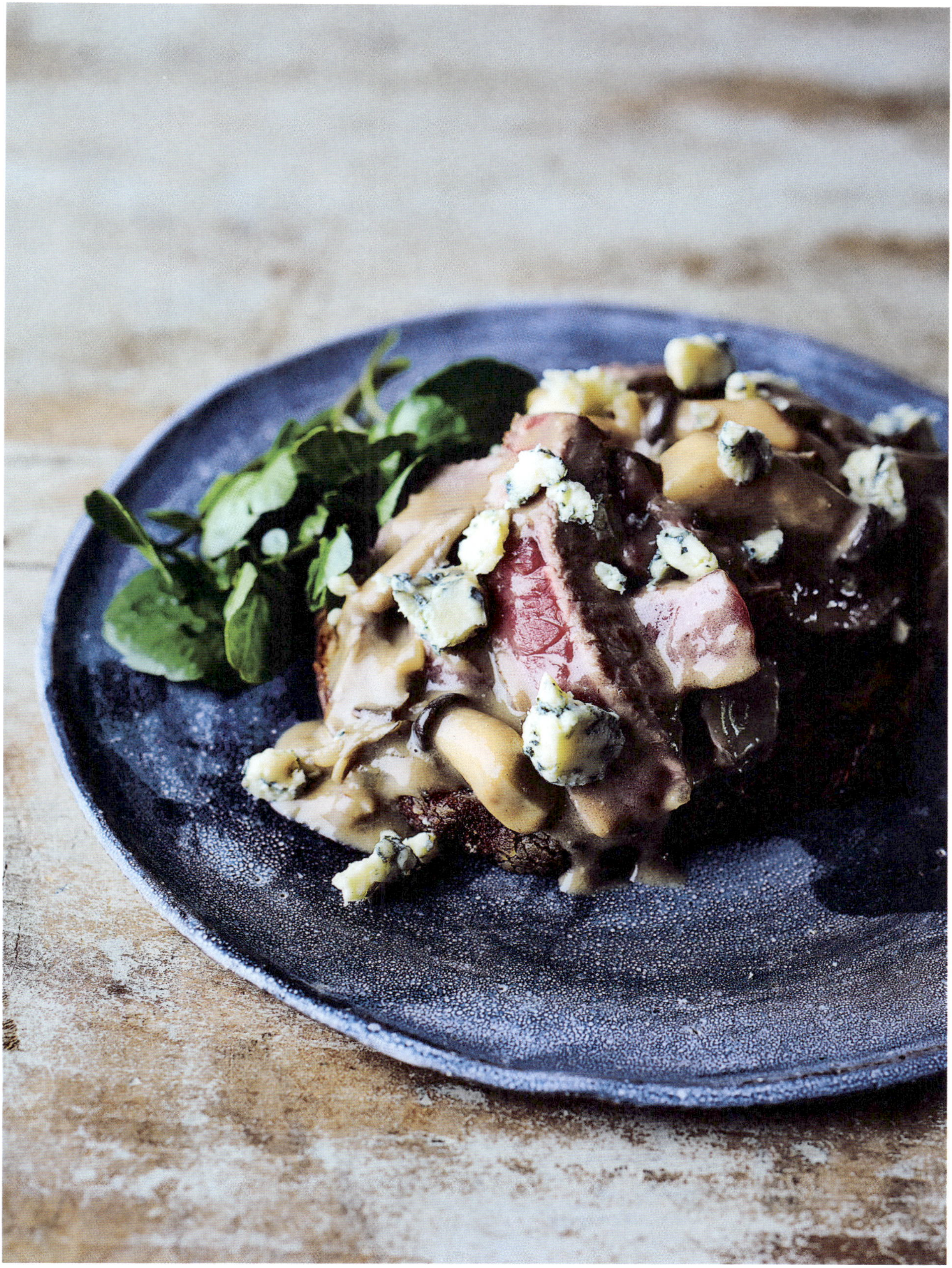

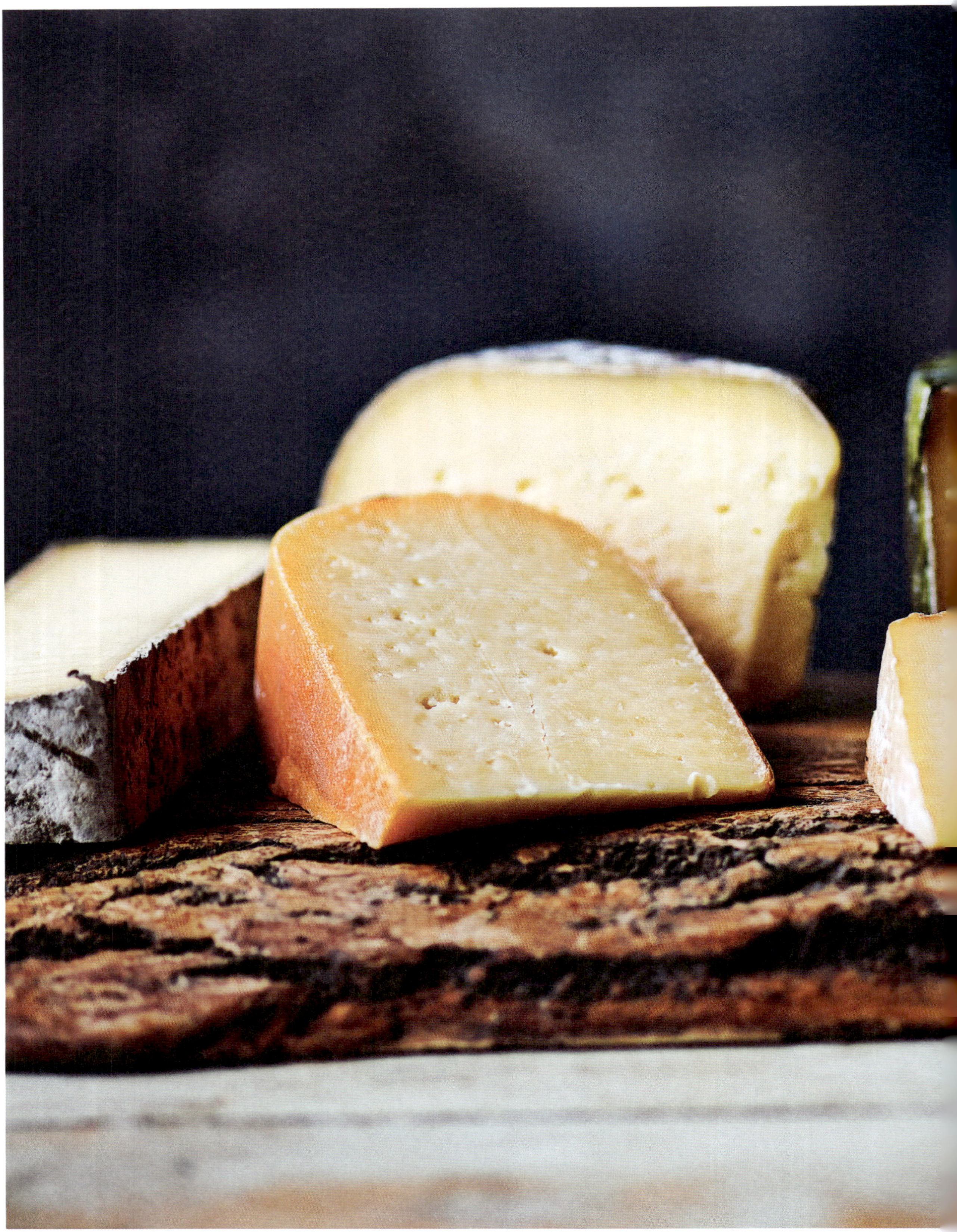

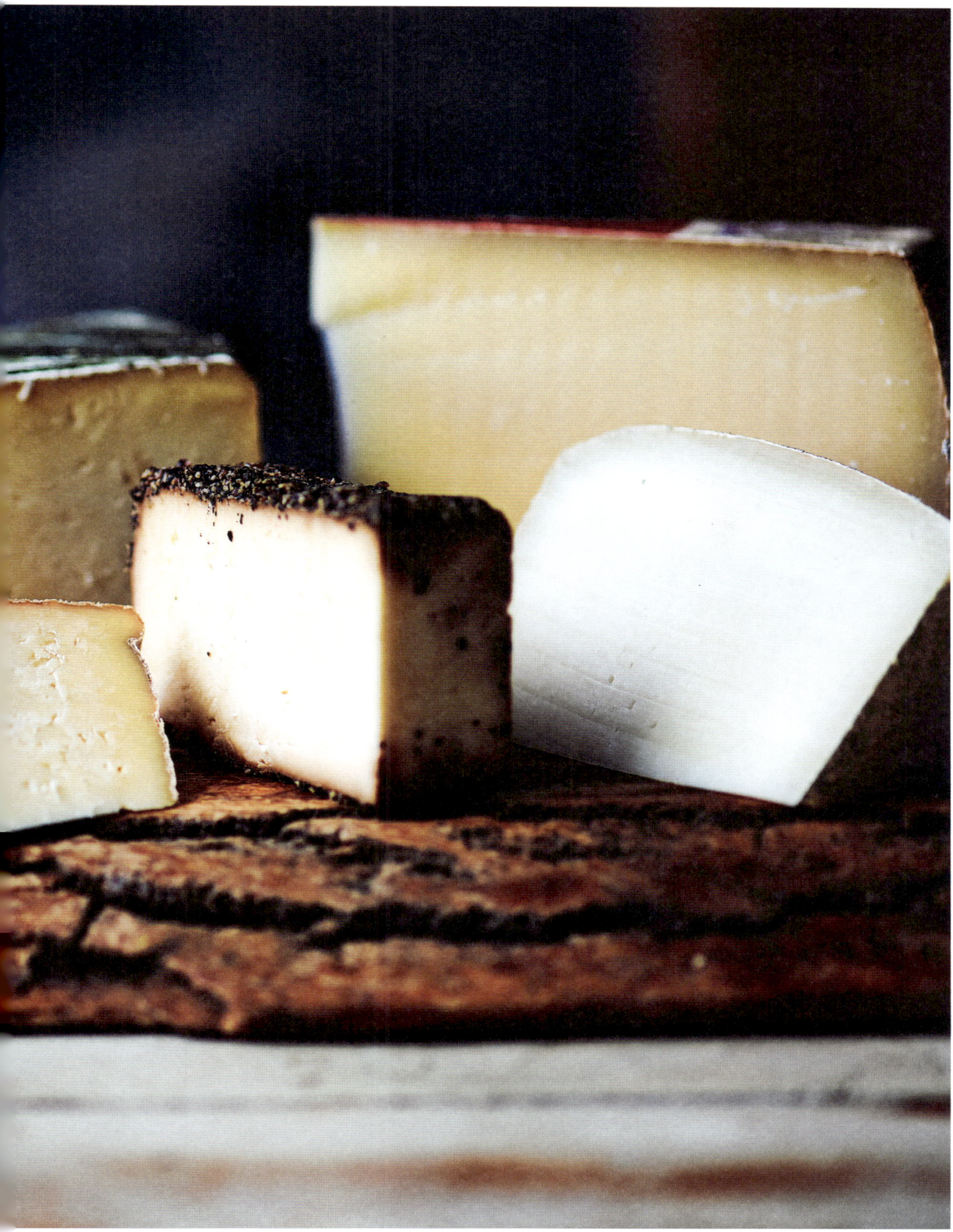

SUMMER VEGETABLE TARTS
\
SERVES 2

2 x 10cm baked pastry cases
150g mascarpone
2 x 50g goat's cheese rounds
sea salt and freshly ground
    black pepper
fennel fronds, pea shoots and
    edible pansies, to garnish

FOR THE PEA PURÉE
300g frozen peas
50g butter

FOR THE VEG
100g broad beans
100g fresh peas
2 spring onions, sliced
½ garlic clove
25g butter
a few chives, chopped

Goat's cheese is often used in tarts or to finish off dishes, and here I've combined the two approaches, using a whole round of goat's cheese to crown these delicate summer tarts.

First make the purée. Put the frozen peas in a pan with the butter, cover with 100ml water and bring to the boil. Remove from the heat and purée until smooth. Season and set aside to cool.

Put the broad beans, peas, spring onions, garlic and butter in a pan with a splash of water and cook over a high heat for 2 minutes until most of the water has evaporated. Season and finish with the chives.

Fill the base of each tart case with pea purée. Cover in vegetables, then dot with the mascarpone and more pea purée. Finish with a layer of vegetables, then sit the goat's cheese on top and garnish with fennel fronds, pea shoots and flowers.

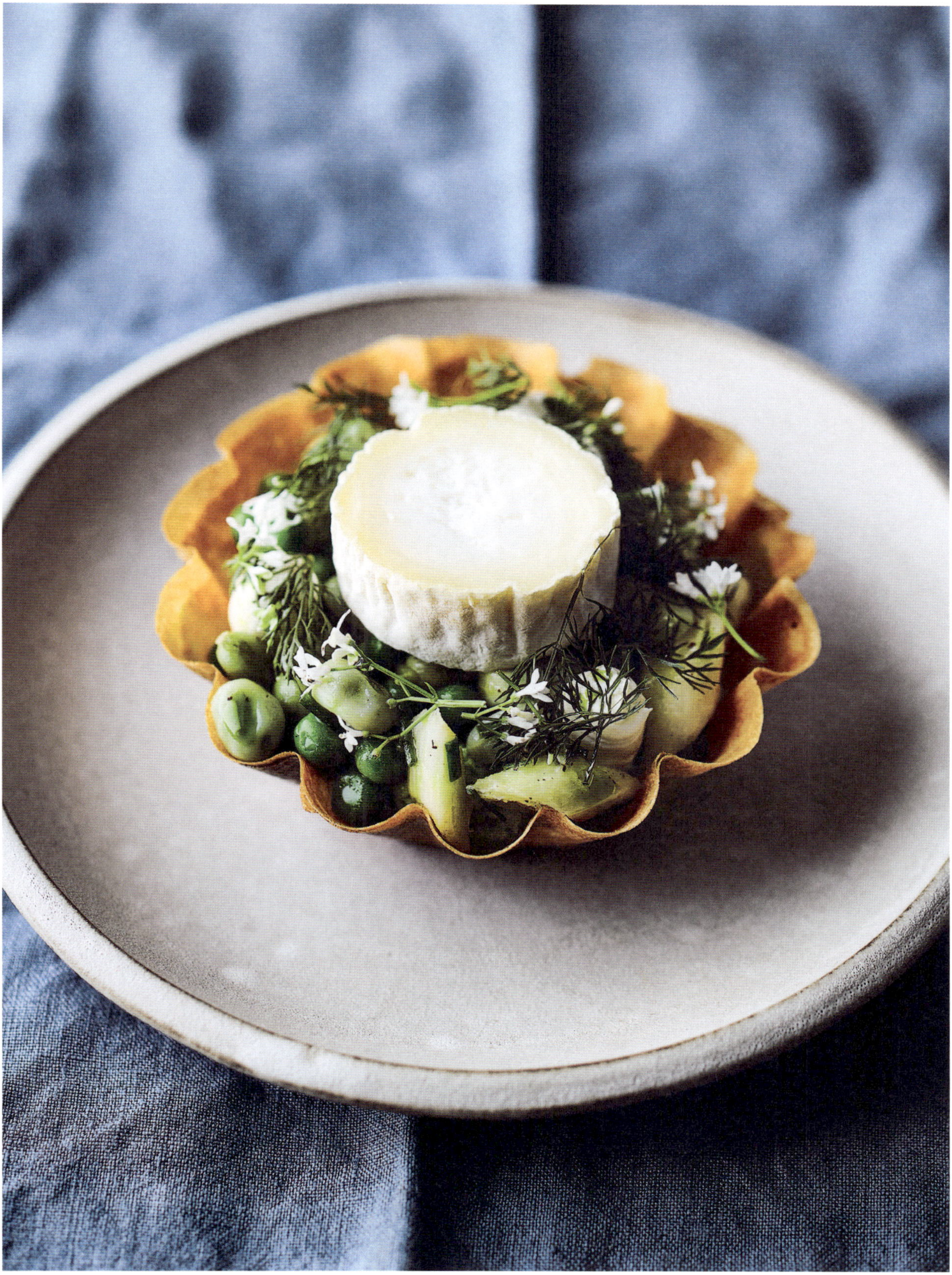

TARTIFLETTE WITH TOMME
\
SERVES 6

500g new potatoes
splash of vegetable oil
2 red onions, finely sliced
3 garlic cloves, crushed
125g bacon lardons
a few sprigs of thyme, chopped
250ml double cream
500g Tomme de Savoie, or
  Tomme d'Auvergne or
  Tomme de l'Aubrac, sliced
sea salt and freshly ground
  black pepper

Tomme is a type of cheese produced mainly in the French Alps and Switzerland, so it's the perfect choice to use in another Alpine favourite: tartiflette. Similar in both texture and flavour to the Reblochon most often used in this potato dish, Tomme melts perfectly to form the distinctive bubbling, golden topping. Serve with cornichons, small pickled onions and crusty bread.

Preheat the oven to 200°C (180°C fan)/400°F/gas 6.

Cook the potatoes in boiling salted water until just soft. Drain, leave to cool and then slice in half.

Set an ovenproof pan over a high heat, add the vegetable oil and sauté the onions, garlic and lardons with the thyme until the lardons are crisp. Season, add the cream and potatoes, then give it a big stir and top with the cheese.

Bake in the oven for 45 minutes–1 hour. Remove from the oven and leave to cool for 5 minutes, then serve straight from the pan.

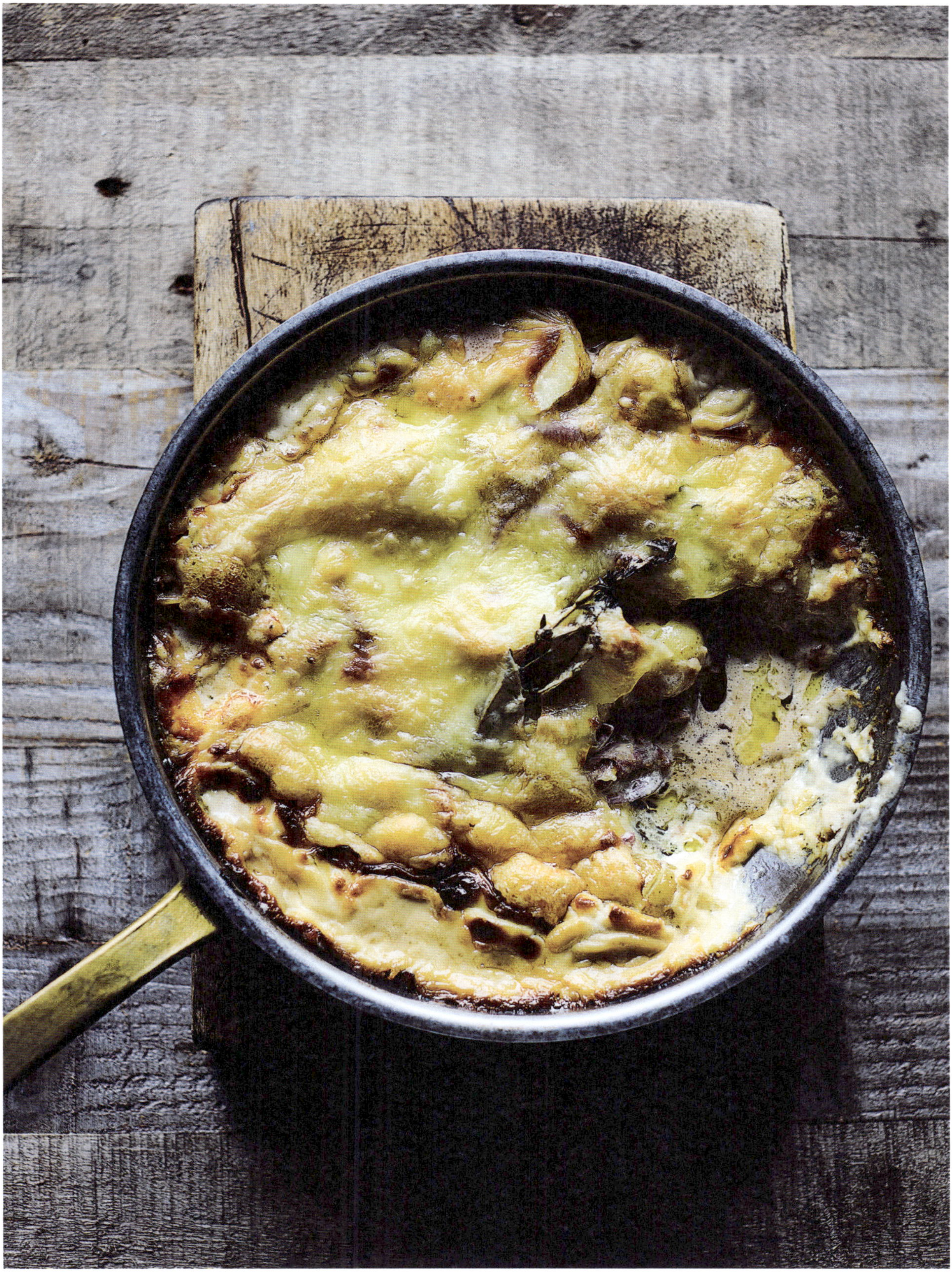

WILD MUSHROOM TART
\
SERVES 6

4 eggs
4 egg yolks
300ml double cream
300ml full-fat milk
2 shallots, diced
400g wild mushrooms, chopped
25g butter
200g Comté, grated
sea salt and freshly ground
    black pepper
green salad, to serve

FOR THE PASTRY
400g plain flour, plus extra for dusting
200g butter, plus extra for greasing
pinch of salt
3 sprigs of thyme, leaves picked
    (optional)
1 egg

This tart uses a nutty Comté to partner the wild mushrooms but feel free to substitute it for Gruyère or Manchego. Serve with a crispy green salad.

Preheat the oven to 150°C (130°C fan)/300°F/gas 2. Grease a 27cm tart tin.

To make the pastry, place the flour into a bowl, add the butter, salt and thyme, if using, then rub between your fingers until the mixture looks like coarse breadcrumbs. Add the egg and mix with your fingers, adding a splash of water if needed to bring the dough together. Knead on a floured surface until smooth, then wrap in clingfilm and chill in the fridge for 30 minutes.

Roll out the pastry on a lightly floured surface and use to line the prepared tart tin, allowing it to overhang slightly.

To make the custard filling, in a bowl, whisk together the eggs, egg yolks, cream and milk, then season.

Set a frying pan over a high heat and cook the shallots and mushrooms in the butter for 5 minutes. Remove from the heat and leave to cool. Spread over the base of the tart.

Pour the custard into the tart tin and sprinkle the cheese over the top. Bake in the oven for 30–40 minutes.

Once cooked, let the tart sit for 5 minutes and then trim the edge of the pastry crust.

Serve hot, warm or cold with a green salad.

TOMATO TART WITH DOLCELATTE
\
SERVES 6

300g all-butter ready-rolled puff pastry
3 teaspoons wholegrain mustard
500g tomatoes (a mixture of colours and sizes looks good), sliced or quartered; smaller ones left whole
a few sprigs of thyme, leaves picked
1 egg yolk, beaten
freshly ground black pepper

TO SERVE
200g Dolcelatte
dressed mixed salad leaves

Tomato and cheese are a perfect flavour pairing, whether it's a hard cheese like Cheddar, a soft goat's cheese or a melting ball of burrata. Here I've chosen a perhaps more unusual partner for this tomato tart, a blue cheese in the form of the creamy Dolcelatte.

Preheat the oven to 200°C (180°C fan)/400°F/gas 6. Line a large baking tray with baking parchment.

Pop the pastry onto the prepared tray. Using a butter knife, mark a border all the way around, about 1cm from the edges. Prick the centre all over with a fork.

Spread the mustard over the pastry and evenly top with the tomatoes. Sprinkle over the thyme, season with black pepper and brush the edges with the egg yolk. Bake in the oven for 20–25 minutes.

Serve dotted with pieces of Dolcelatte and the dressed salad leaves alongside.

Pictured overleaf

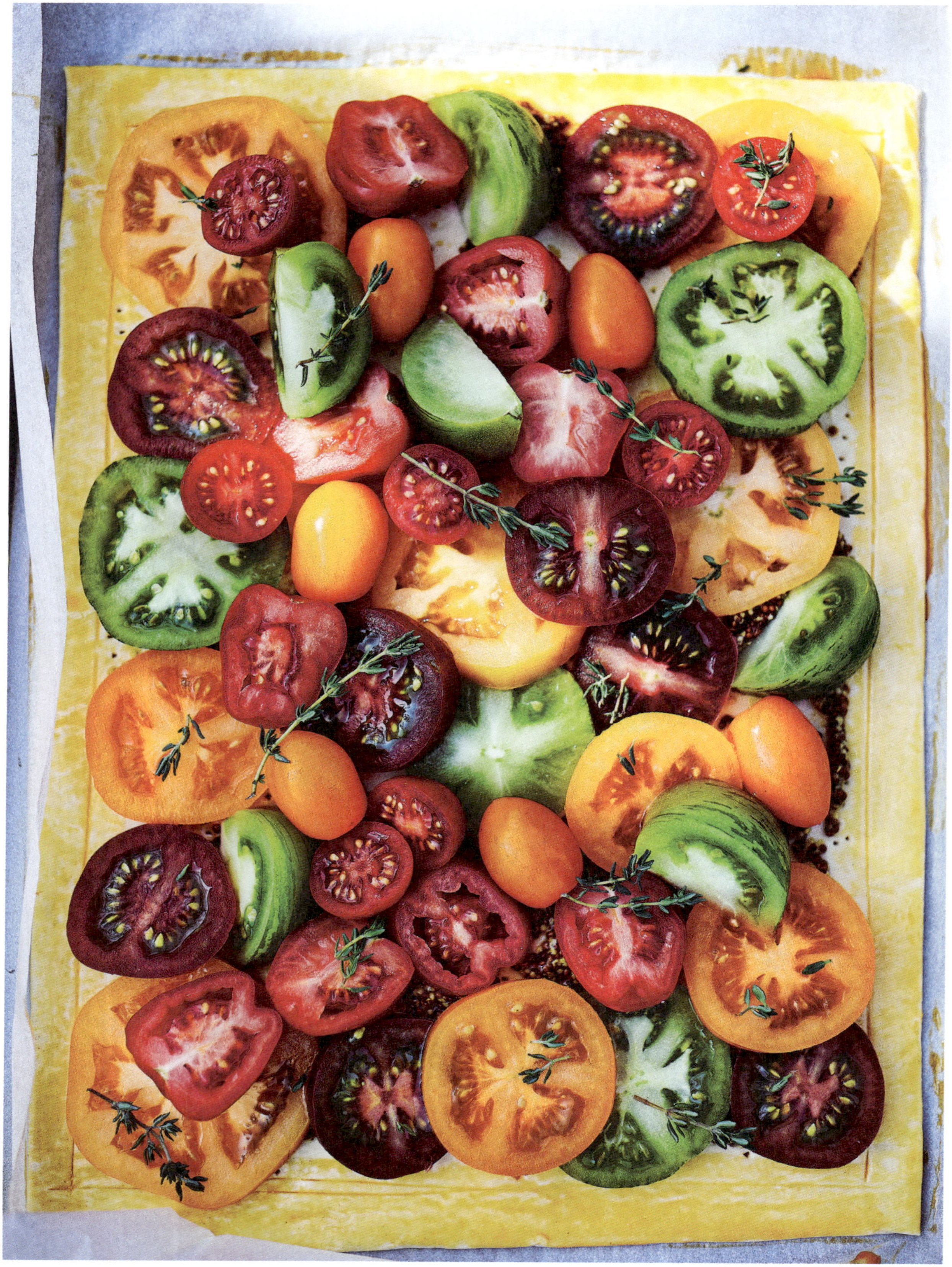

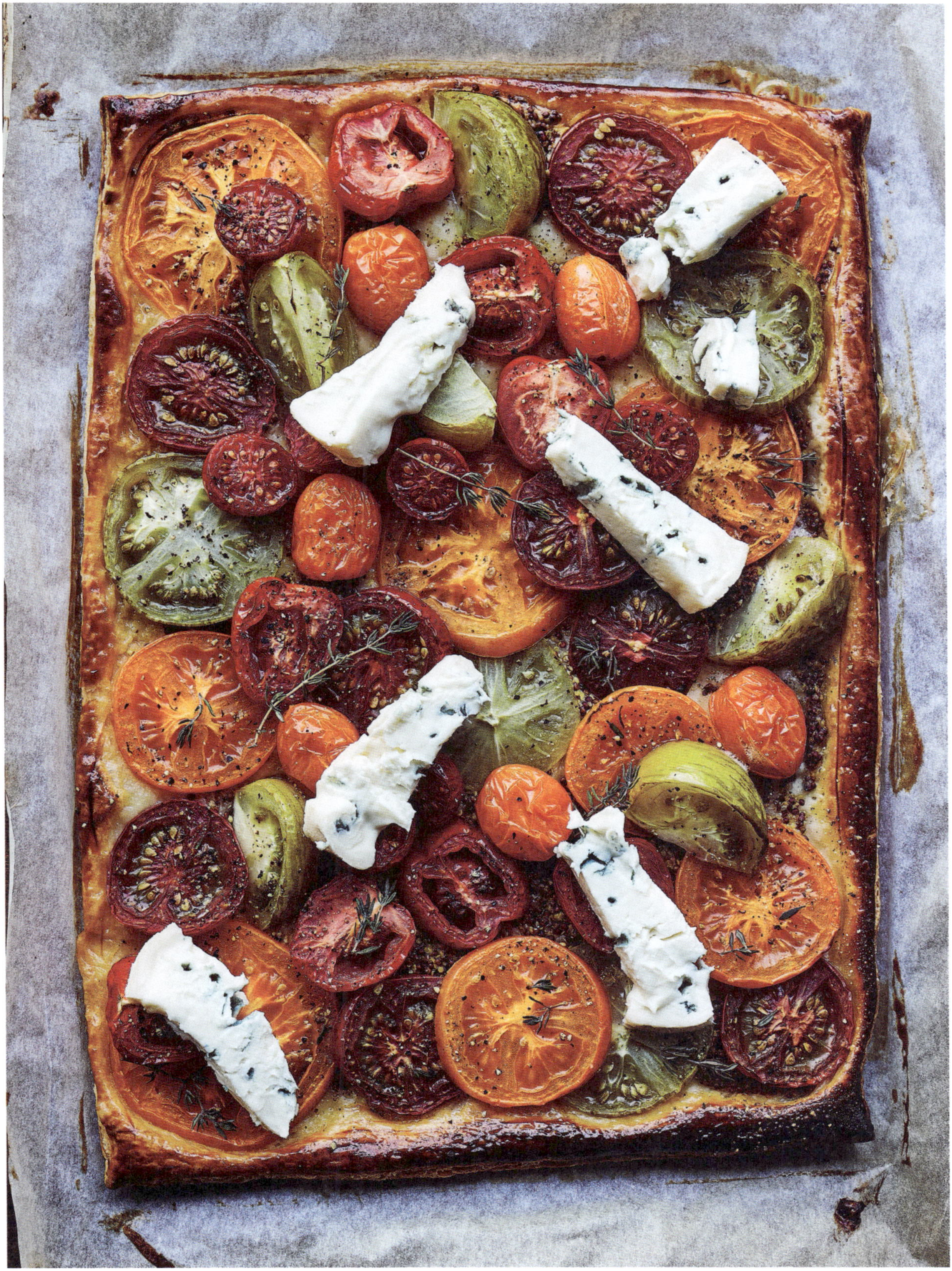

ON THE SIDE

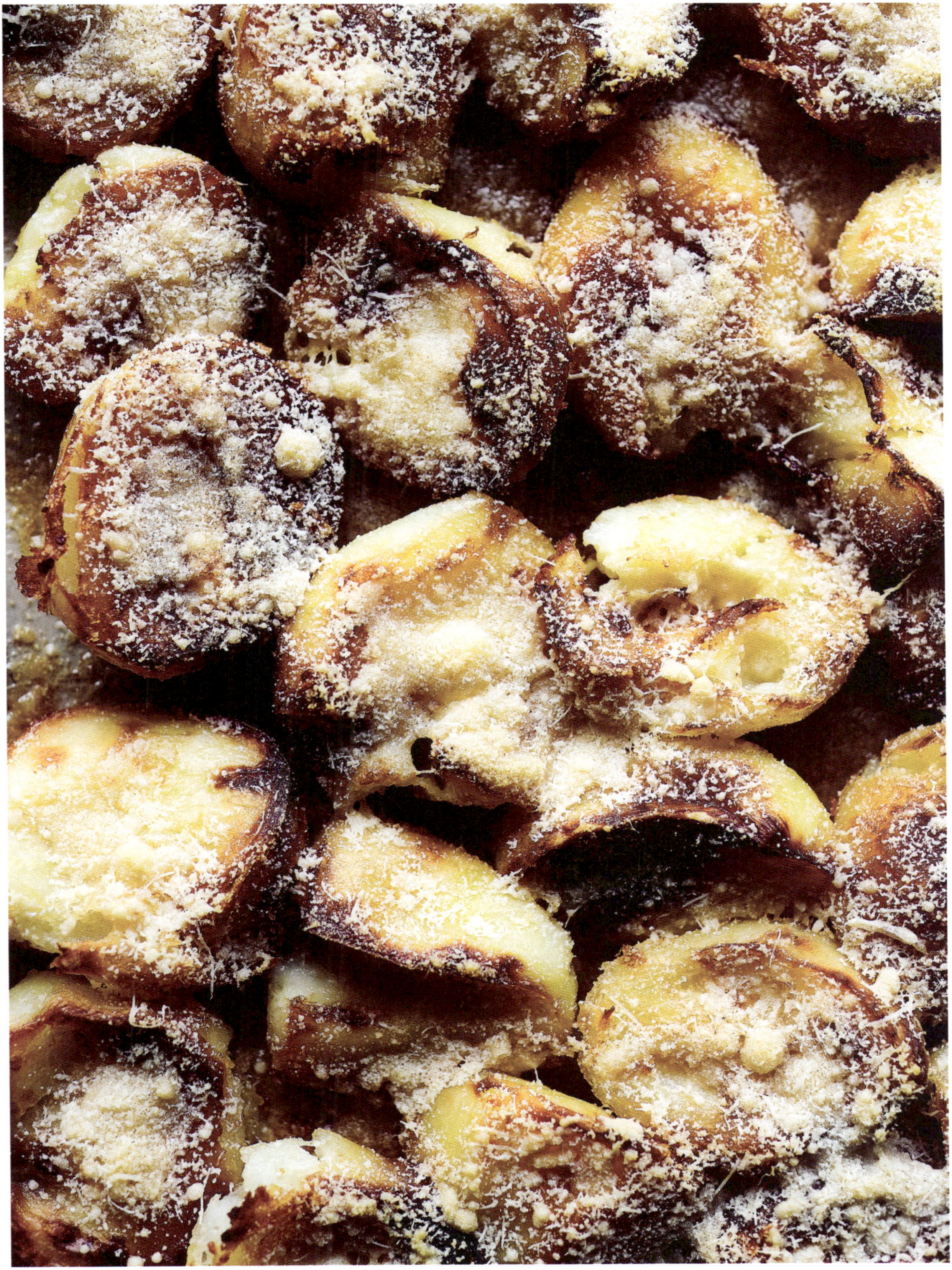

CAULIFLOWER CHEESE
\
SERVES 6

1 cauliflower, cut into florets and leaves reserved
olive oil, for drizzling
1 litre full-fat milk
½ onion
1 bay leaf
1 clove
100g butter
50g plain flour
400g Cheddar, grated
1 tablespoon Dijon mustard
sea salt and freshly ground black pepper

Perhaps the ultimate comfort food, cauliflower cheese is the perfect accompaniment to a winter roast dinner but works just as well as a lighter bite for lunch. You could try changing things up by switching the Cheddar for another hard cheese that melts well – Gruyère or Comté would be good options.

Preheat the oven to 200°C (180°C fan)/400°F/gas 6.

Place the cauliflower florets and leaves on a roasting tray, drizzle with olive oil and season. Roast for 10 minutes until lightly charred.

Warm the milk in a saucepan over a medium heat. Stud the onion with the bay leaf and clove and add to the milk to infuse for 10 minutes. Remove from the heat.

To make the sauce, melt the butter in a pan over a medium heat, whisk in the flour and then add the milk gradually, discarding the onion.

Add half the Cheddar to the sauce, then take off the heat and add the mustard and season.

Put the roasted cauliflower into an ovenproof dish. Pour over the sauce and top with the remaining cheese. Pop under the grill for 8–10 minutes.

Serve with pork chops, steak or a roast dinner.

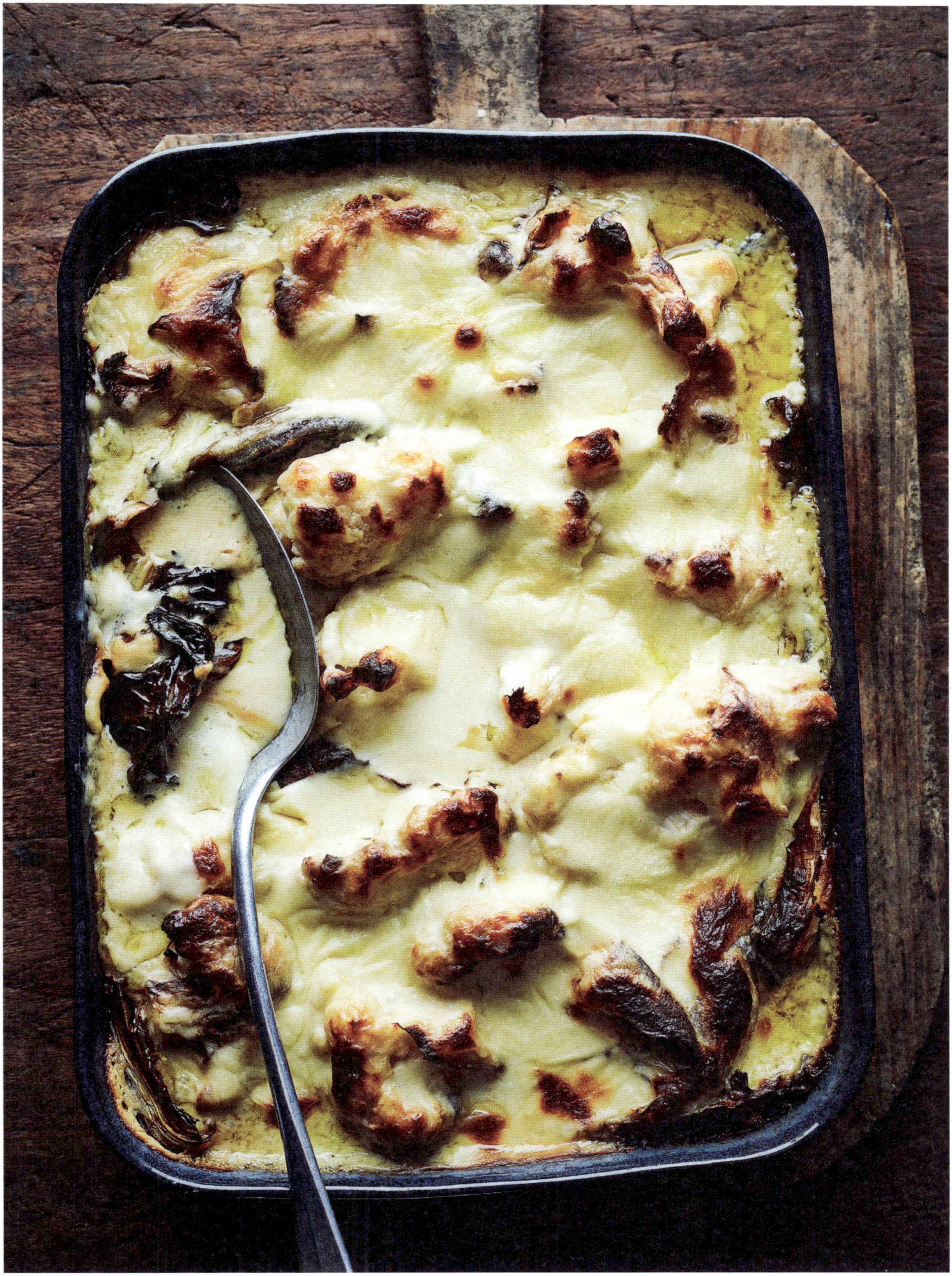

CHEESY MASHED POTATOES

\
SERVES 6

1kg Yukon Gold potatoes, or other floury potatoes, such as Maris Piper, peeled
2 garlic cloves, minced
100g butter
100ml double cream
250g firm mozzarella, grated
250g Cheddar, grated
sea salt

Cook the potatoes in lots of boiling salted water until you can pierce them easily with a knife. Drain and pass through a ricer. Return to the pan and beat in the garlic, butter and cream, then half of both cheeses. When fully mixed in, add the remaining cheese and beat in again.

Serve with sausages, chicken or lamb chops.

DAUPHINOISE POTATOES

\
SERVES 6–8

butter, for greasing
3 garlic cloves, chopped
10 Maris Piper potatoes, peeled and very thinly sliced
200ml full-fat milk
200ml double cream
½ nutmeg, grated
175g Gruyère, grated
sea salt and freshly ground black pepper

Preheat the oven to 180°C (160°C fan)/350°F/gas 4.

Grease a 28cm round ovenproof dish with butter and rub the garlic all over the dish. Layer up the potatoes, cover in the milk and cream and season well. Sprinkle over the nutmeg and cheese and bake for 1 hour.

Serve with roast chicken or beef, or a rack of lamb.

LOADED FRIES
\
SERVES 4–6

vegetable oil, for deep-frying
1kg frozen skinny fries
12 slices of streaky bacon
1 bunch of spring onions, sliced
2 red peppers, cored and sliced
2 tablespoons Cajun seasoning
400g Cheddar, grated

In a deep-fat fryer or deep-sided saucpean, heat the enough oil for deep-frying to 170°C (340°F). Preheat the oven to 200°C (180°C fan)/400°F/gas 6.

Fry the skinny fries for 8 minutes until golden and crisp, then drain on kitchen paper.

Meanwhile, in a frying pan, fry the bacon until crisp, then add the spring onions and peppers and cook for 3–4 minutes, adding the Cajun seasoning for the final 2 minutes.

Spoon the fries onto a baking tray, scatter over the bacon and spicy vegetables, top with the cheese, then bake for 10 minutes until hot and bubbling.

CHEESY POTATO WAFFLES
\
SERVES 6

1 large potato, diced and blanched
3 cabbage leaves, blanched and diced
4 spring onions, sliced
4 slices of bacon, cooked and diced
300g Cheddar, grated

FOR THE WAFFLE BATTER
250g plain flour
1 teaspoon baking powder
1 teaspoon caster sugar
3 eggs
200ml full-fat milk
2 tablespoons chopped flat-leaf parsley
15g butter, melted

Preheat the grill to high. Heat a waffle machine to high.

To make the waffles, whisk all the batter ingredients together in a large bowl. Then fold through the potato, cabbage, spring onions and bacon.

Ladle into the waffle machine and cook for 2 minutes until golden. You should have enough batter to make six waffles, so you will need to cook them in batches. Then transfer the waffles to a baking tray, top with the grated cheese and grill for 2 minutes until bubbling.

FOCACCIA WITH PARMESAN, TALEGGIO AND ROSEMARY
\
SERVES 8

500g strong bread flour
7g sachet fast action yeast
1 tablespoon salt
100ml olive oil
350–400ml lukewarm water
300g Taleggio, cubed
50g Parmesan, grated
a few sprigs of rosemary, chopped

I've taken things up a notch here by adding two classic Italian cheeses to complement this iconic Italian bake: Parmesan and Taleggio. The Taleggio is a great melting cheese, providing an oozy filling to contrast the salty rosemary bread.

Use a stand mixer fitted with a dough hook to mix the flour, yeast and salt with half the oil and the lukewarm water (start with 350ml). Knead for 5–10 minutes until you have a sticky dough.

Oil a shallow rectangular baking tray, drop the dough in and stretch out to the corners, dimpling as you go. Cover and leave to prove at room temperature for 1 hour.

Preheat the oven to 220°C (220°C fan)/425°F/gas 7.

Dimple the dough and dot with the cheeses and rosemary, then drizzle over the last of the oil. Bake for 20 minutes until golden.

Serve alongside cold meats and salads.

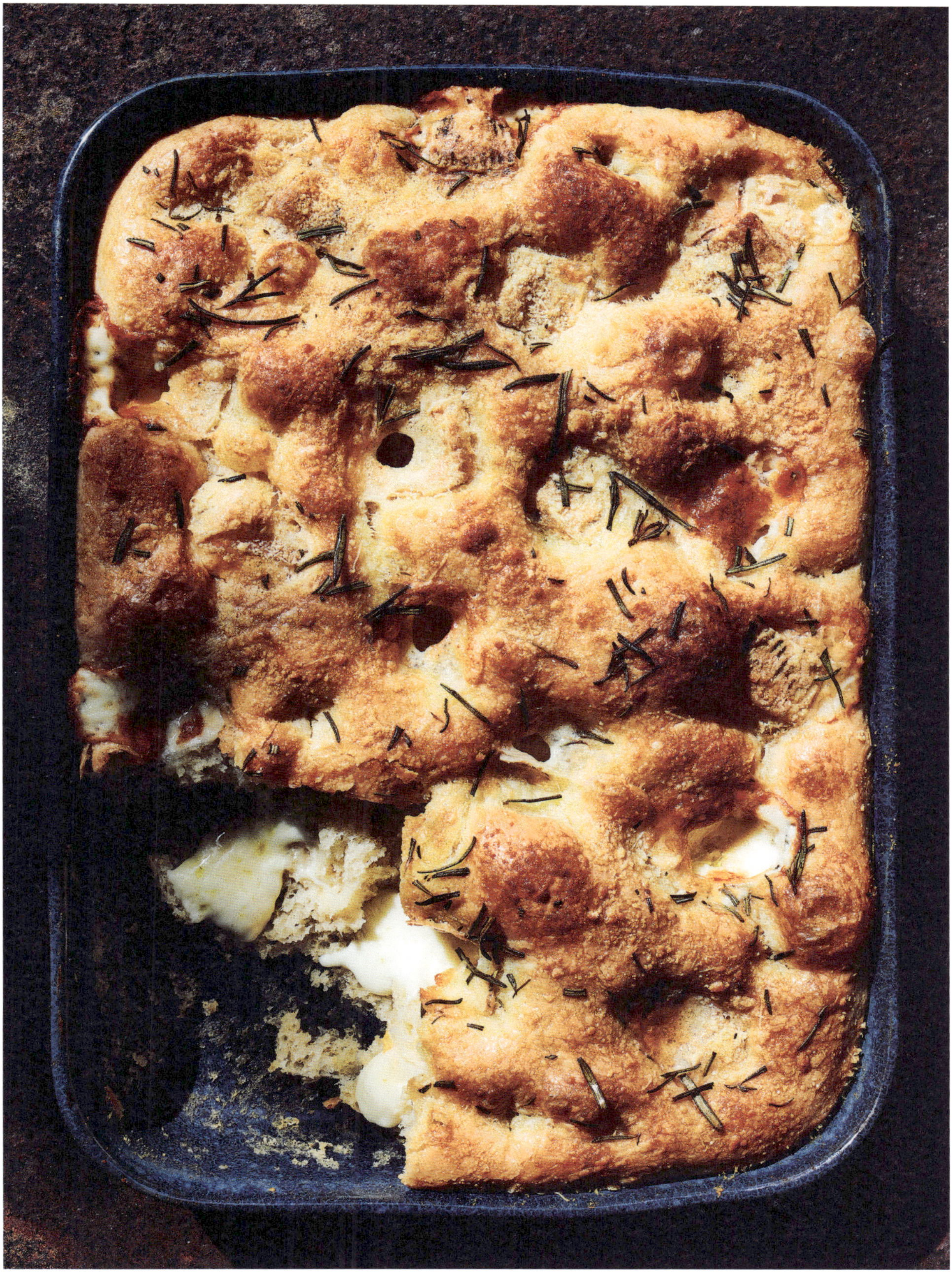

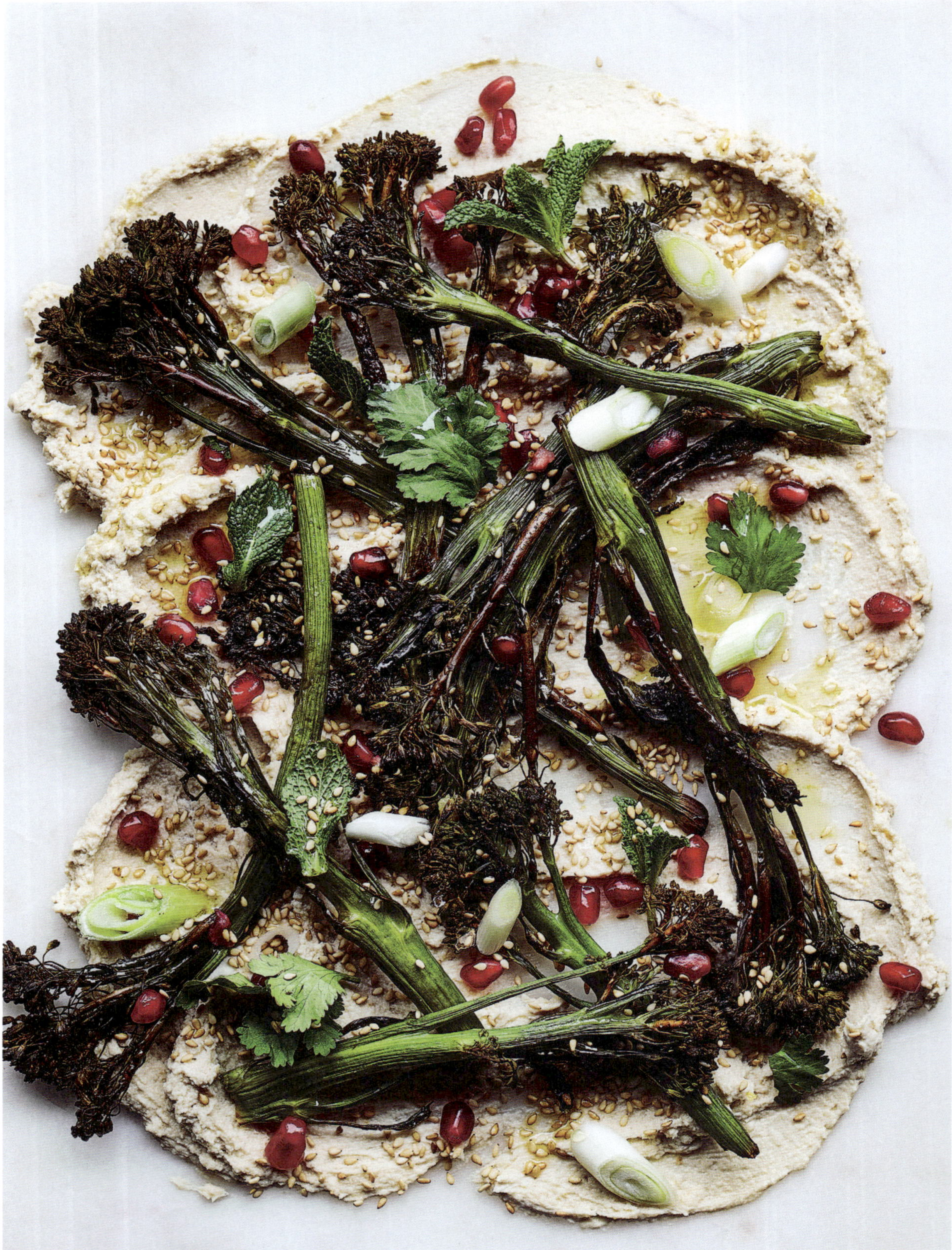

PURPLE SPROUTING BROCCOLI WITH TAHINI DRESSING
\
SERVES 4

400g purple sprouting broccoli
50ml olive oil, plus extra for drizzling
sea salt and freshly ground black pepper

FOR THE DRESSING
5 tablespoons tahini
300g full-fat cream cheese
zest and juice of 1 unwaxed lemon

TO SERVE
2 tablespoons white sesame seeds, toasted
100g pomegranate seeds
1 small bunch of coriander, chopped
1 small bunch of mint, chopped
a few spring onions, sliced

Here cream cheese is mixed with tahini and lemon to form the ultimate backdrop to chargrilled purple sprouting broccoli. The pale sauce contrasts wonderfully with the colourful veg and pomegranate seeds. This is a great accompaniment to fish dishes.

Preheat the grill to high.

To make the dressing, in a bowl, whisk all the ingredients together. Set aside.

Place the broccoli onto a large baking tray, drizzle with the oil and season. Pop under the grill and cook for 5–6 minutes until charred.

To serve, spread the tahini dressing all over a platter, top with the broccoli and then sprinkle over the sesame and pomegranate seeds, the herbs and spring onions. Finish with a drizzle of olive oil.

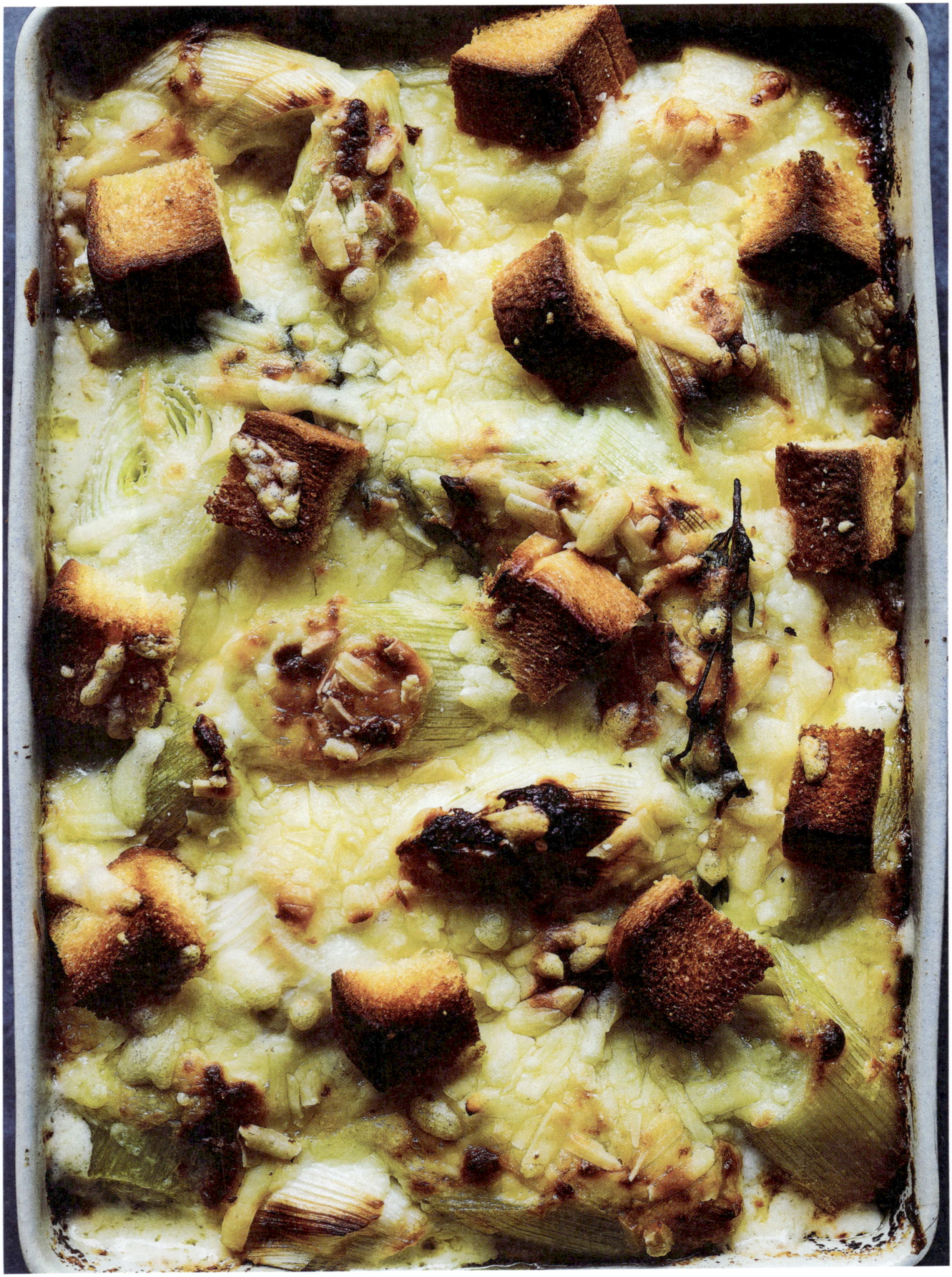

CHEESY BRIOCHE LEEKS
\
SERVES 6

600g leeks, sliced
200ml double cream
100g butter
a few sprigs of thyme, leaves picked
250g Cheddar, grated
200g fresh brioche, cubed
sea salt and freshly ground black pepper

A great cheesy side dish to have up your sleeve, with the Cheddar providing a delicious tang to the golden sauce. You could try mixing things up with a different hard cheese – Comté, Gruyère or Manchego would all be good here. Serve alongside salmon or chicken dishes.

Preheat the oven to 200°C (180°C fan)/400°F/gas 6.

Set a pan over a medium heat and cook the leeks in the cream, butter and thyme for 2–3 minutes until soft. Stir in half the cheese and season well. Cook until the cheese has melted, then remove from the heat.

Put the brioche in a 20 x 15cm ovenproof dish and toast in the oven until golden. Remove from the oven and take out half the brioche. Top the brioche in the dish with the leek mixture, the remaining cheese and then the rest of the brioche. Roast for 10 minutes.

POMMES ALIGOT
\
SERVES 4

1kg Yukon Gold potatoes, or other floury potatoes, such as Maris Piper or King Edward, peeled and diced
2 garlic cloves, minced
100g butter
100ml double cream
500g Tomme d'Auvergne or Tomme de l'Aubrac, or 250g mozzarella and 250g Gruyère, rind removed and diced

This French classic is the best cheesy mash you will ever have! Fact. It's a good idea to search for the right cheese, however, as this will ensure that you get that iconic stretchy consistency, as will the Yukon Gold potatoes. Aligot is delicious served with lamb.

Cook the potatoes in lots of boiling salted water until you can pierce them easily. Drain.

Pass the cooked potatoes through a ricer. Return to the pan and beat in the garlic, butter and cream, then half the cheese. Beat until fully mixed, then add the rest of the cheese and beat again.

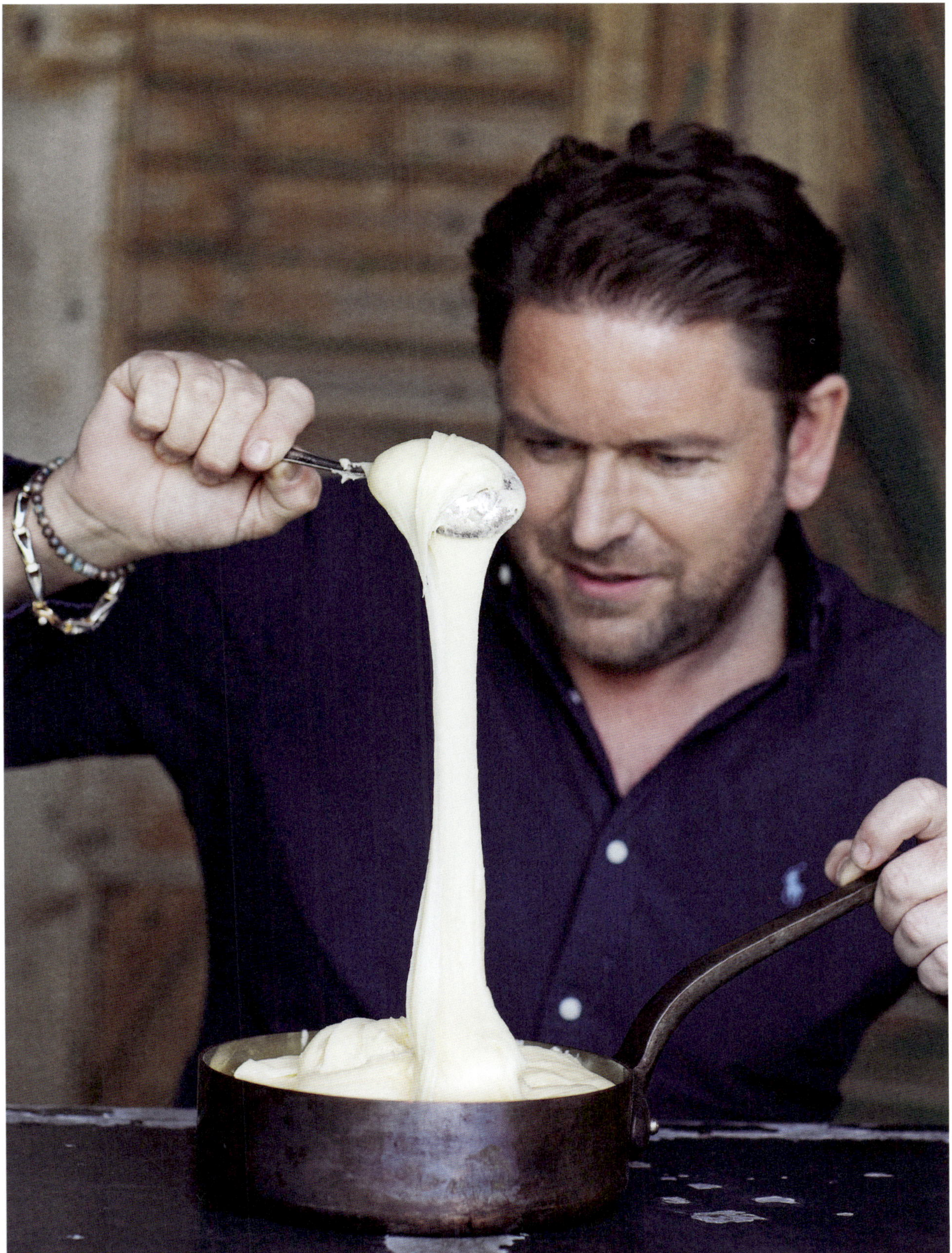

PARMESAN ROASTIES
\
SERVES 8

2kg King Edward potatoes, peeled
100g beef dripping
50ml olive oil
50g butter
100g Parmesan, grated
sea salt

What could be better than a crispy, golden roast potato? Well, the answer is one covered with a dusting of grated Parmesan to provide another layer of flavour and cheesy deliciousness. These are perfect served as part of a roast dinner.

Preheat the oven to 200C (180°C fan)/400°F/gas 6.

Cut the larger potatoes in half, then pop them all into a pan of boiling salted water. Bring back to the boil and cook for 3–4 minutes. Drain and shake in the colander.

Place a roasting tray in the oven with the beef dripping, oil and butter and when hot and sizzling, tip in the potatoes. Roast for 40–45 minutes. Remove from the oven, top with the Parmesan and slightly crush the potatoes with the back of a spoon. Return to the oven for a further 10 minutes until crisp and golden.

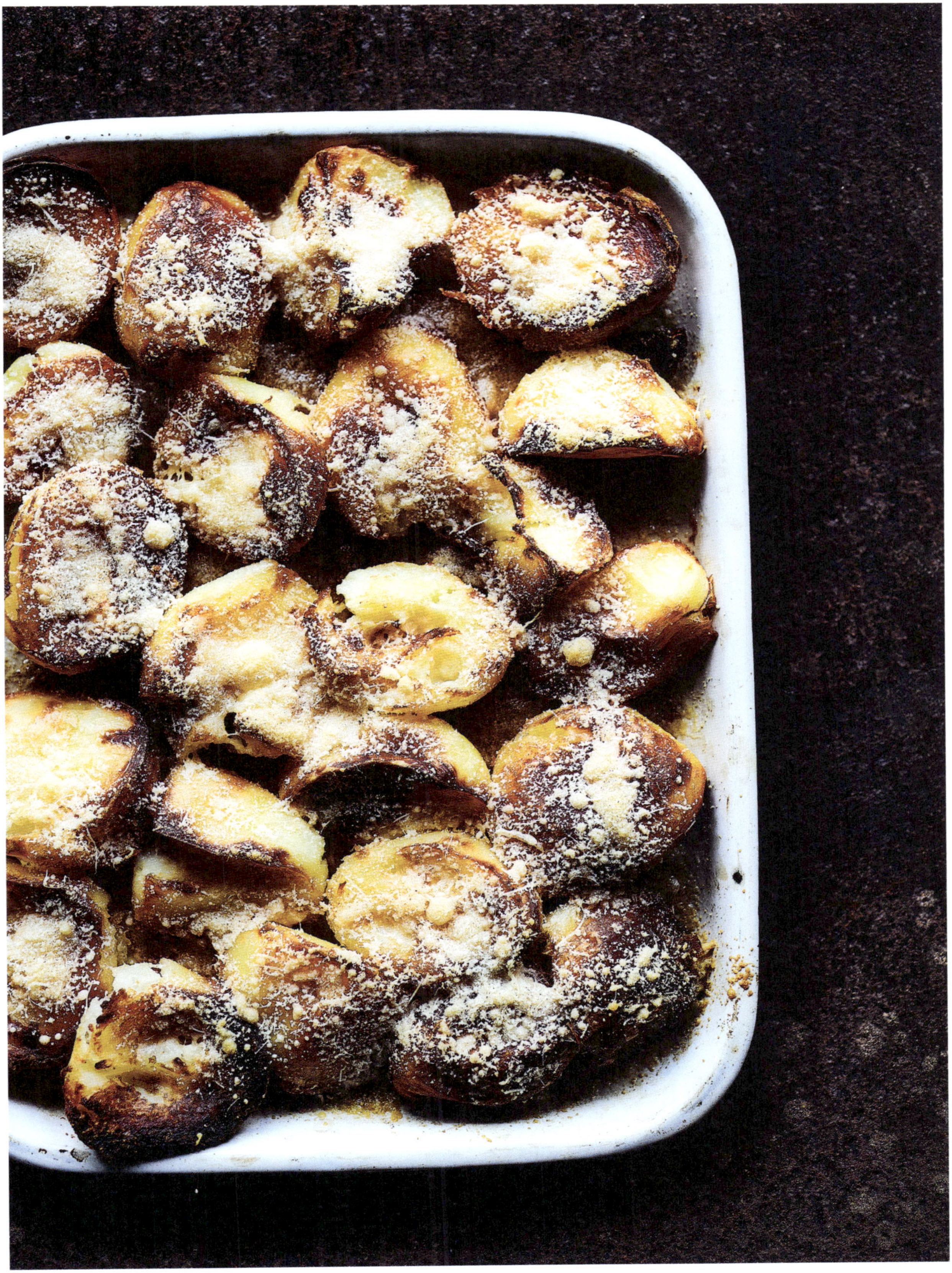

SWEET

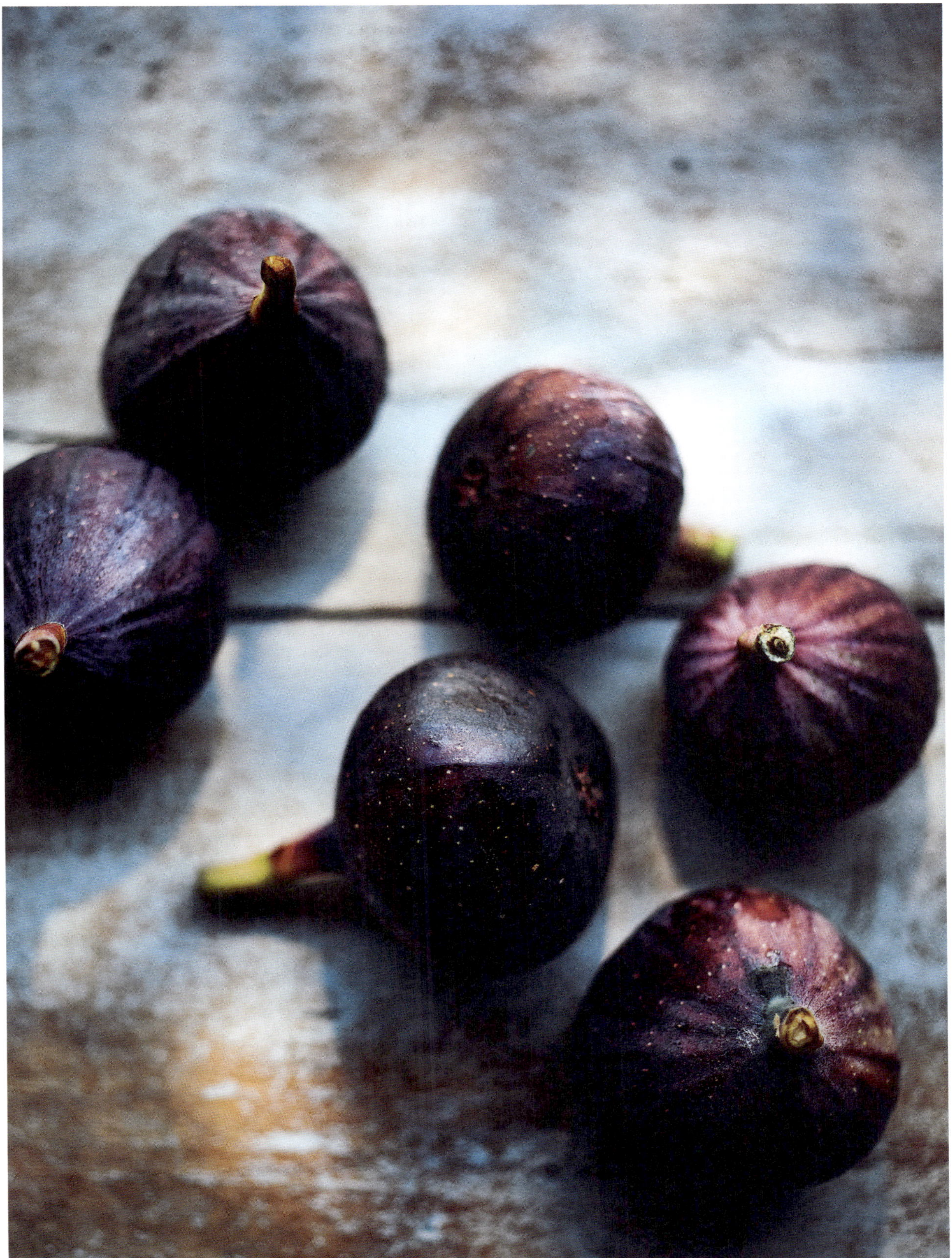

APPLE TARTE TATIN
\
SERVES 6–8

250g caster sugar
125g butter
50ml Drambuie
14 Pink Lady apples, peeled, cored and halved
plain flour, for dusting
200g all-butter puff pastry

TO SERVE
Sharpham Rushmore
cider

Here I've paired the classic French tart with a good chunk of a mixed cow's and goat's milk cheese and a glass of refreshing cider to pick up on the apple flavour. Sharpham Rushmore is rich and creamy with a subtle sweetness, so if you can't get your hands on some, then try to find a cheese similar in texture and flavour.

Preheat the oven to 200°C (180°C fan)/400°F/gas 6.

Melt the sugar, butter and Drambuie in a large ovenproof pan over a high heat. Pack the apples in tightly and cook for 15 minutes, basting the apples with the liquid during cooking. Remove from the heat.

On a floured work surface, roll out the puff pastry into a circle the same diameter as your pan. Lay the pastry on top of the apples and tuck the edges in. Bake in the oven for 30 minutes.

To serve, place a plate on top of the pan, flip and invert the tart, so that the apples are on top. Slice and serve with a slice of cheese and a glass of cider.

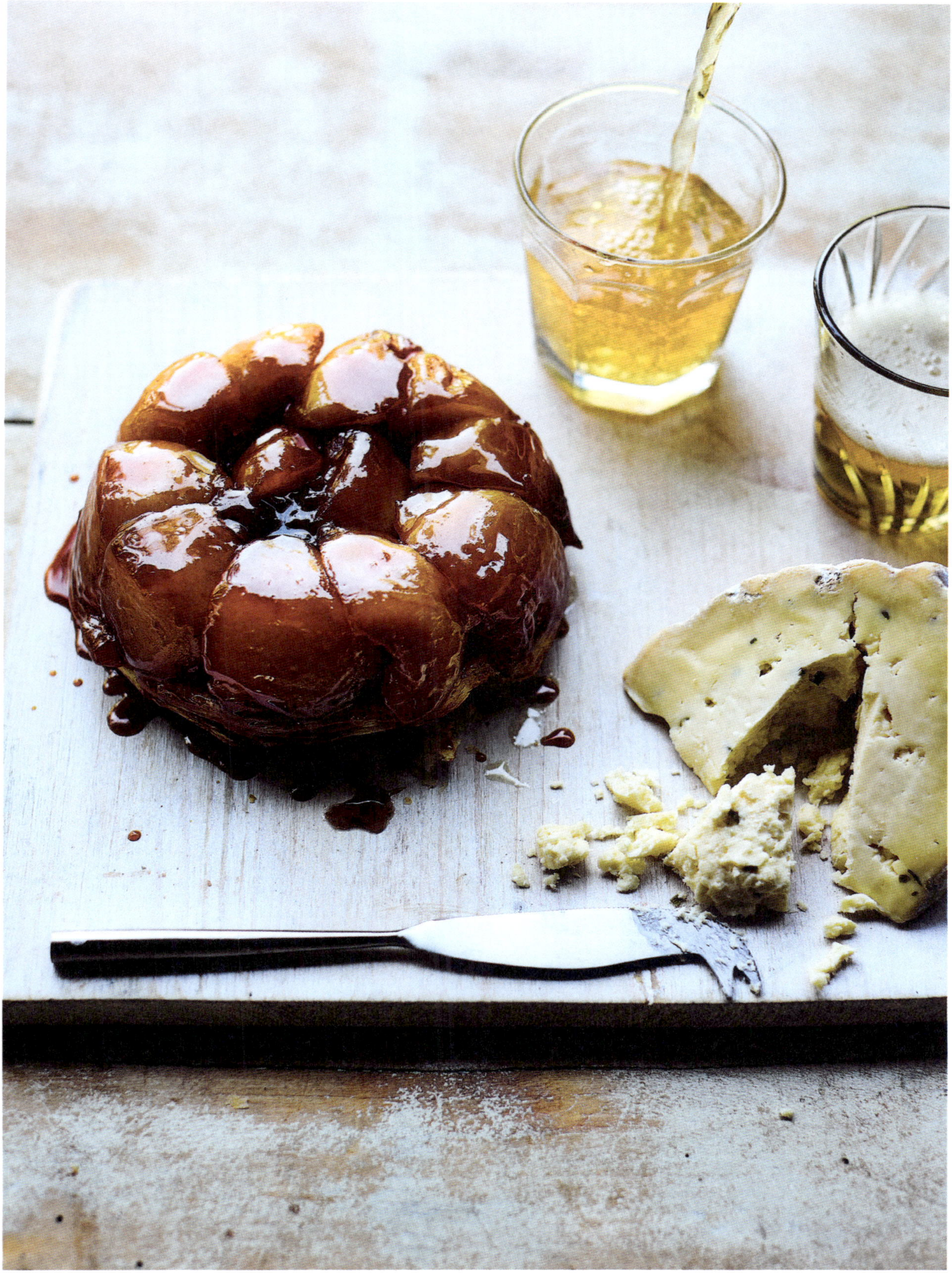

COCONUT AND GINGER CHEESECAKE
\
MAKES 4

100g ginger cake, thinly sliced
200g full-fat cream cheese
200ml full-fat crème fraîche
300ml double cream, whipped
25g caster sugar
1 tablespoon dark rum
1 tsp vanilla bean paste
50g desiccated coconut, toasted

TO SERVE
pineapple, cut into chunks
papaya, cut into chunks
cape gooseberries
coconut shavings
a couple of sprigs of mint

The luxurious creaminess of this coconut and ginger cheesecake comes from a holy trinity of dairy products – cream cheese, crème fraîche and double cream. As always, make sure you use full-fat versions to ensure the best flavour and texture.

Preheat the oven to 110°C (90°C fan)/225°F/gas ¼.

Place the ginger cake on a lined baking tray and put into the oven to dry out for 4 hours.

Put the ginger cake in a food processor and blitz to a fine crumb. Divide most of the ginger crumb evenly between four 10cm ring moulds and flatten with the back of the spoon.

Whisk together the cream cheese, crème fraîche, cream, sugar, rum, vanilla and coconut, then spoon into the moulds. Smooth the top of the mixture, top with the remaining ginger crumb, then place the cheesecakes into the centre of four serving plates. Heat the outside of the rings with a kitchen blowtorch to remove them.

Decorate with a selection of fruit, coconut shavings and mint sprigs.

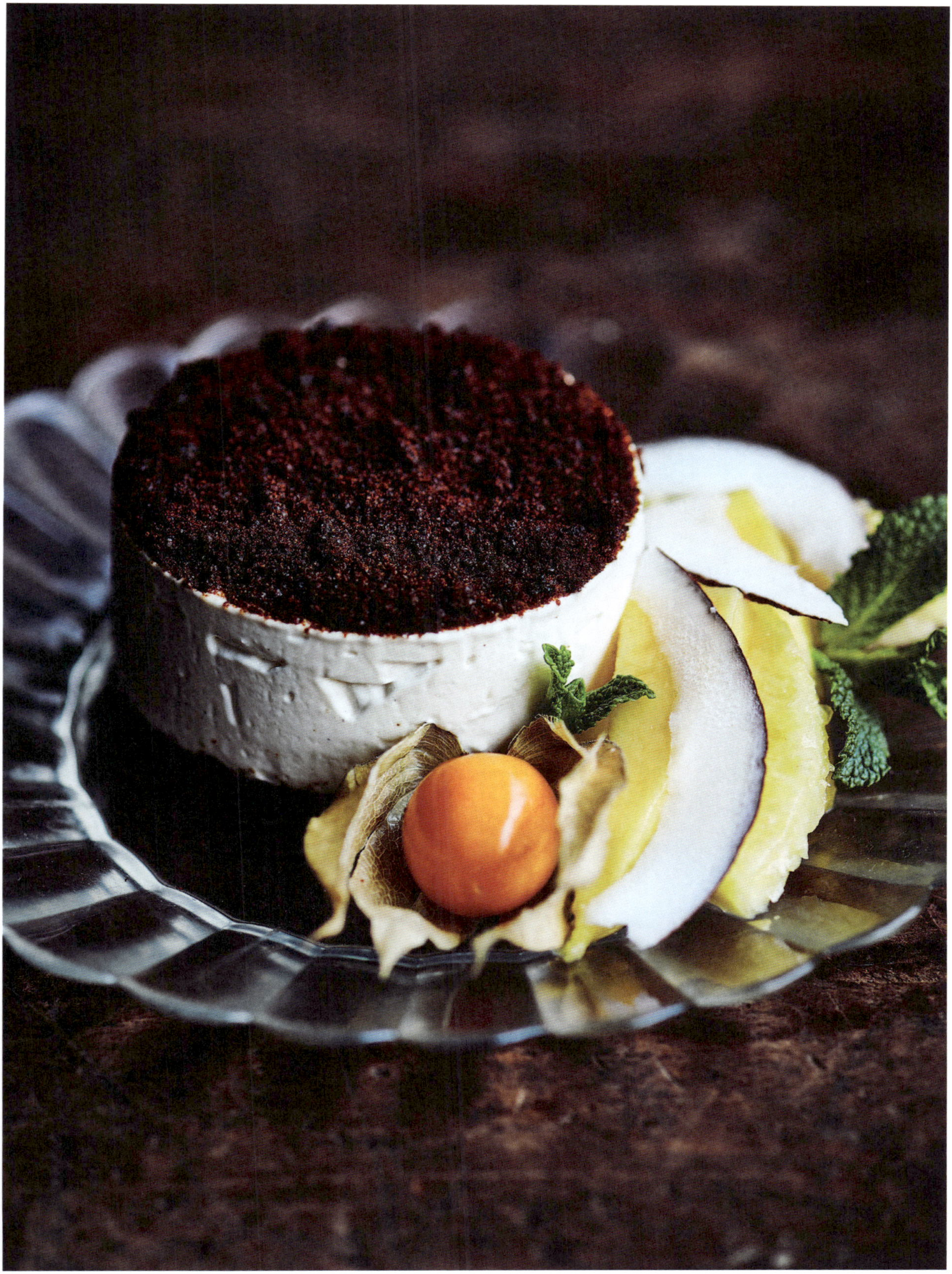

NEW YORK BAKED RASPBERRY CHEESECAKE
\
SERVES 8

160g digestive biscuits or graham crackers
85g butter, melted, plus extra for greasing
1 tablespoon caster sugar

FOR THE TOPPING
1 teaspoon vanilla bean paste
zest and juice of 1 unwaxed lemon
200g caster sugar
50g cornflour
850g full-fat cream cheese
4 large eggs
175ml soured cream
400g raspberries
icing sugar, for dusting

I've changed up the classic New York cheesecake here by adding raspberries to bring a fruity flavour to the distinctive rich, creamy filling. The perfect dessert to finish off a summer dinner or BBQ.

Preheat the oven to 160°C (140°C fan)/325°F/gas 3. Grease and line a 23cm springform cake tin with baking parchment.

Put the biscuits in a food processor and blitz to a fine crumb. Transfer to a bowl and mix together with the melted butter and sugar. Place the mixture in the bottom of the prepared cake tin and press down lightly.

Put the vanilla, lemon zest and juice, sugar, cornflour and cream cheese into a bowl and whisk together. Add the eggs, one at a time, beating well between each addition. Add the soured cream and whisk until the mixture is smooth.

Pour the mixture into the cake tin and tap it lightly on the work surface to settle. Top with the raspberries. Bake for 1¼ hours until the top is golden and the cheesecake just set. Remove from the oven and allow to cool in the tin.

Remove from the tin and place on a serving plate, then dust with icing sugar to serve. Store in the fridge for up to 2 days.

BANANA CAKE
\
SERVES 8

200g butter
200g caster sugar
100g pecans, chopped
2 bananas, sliced
3 eggs
200g self-raising flour

FOR THE TOPPING
200g full-fat cream cheese or mascarpone
2 tablespoons honey

TO DECORATE
100g honeycomb, broken into pieces
12 pecans

My banana cake is taken to the next level by combining pecans with the bananas for the loaf and is finished off with a creamy topping, sweetened with honey. You can use any soft cheese for the topping – so switch the cream cheese for mascarpone or ricotta if you have some in the fridge.

Preheat the oven to 180°C (160°C fan)/350°F/gas 4. Line a 900g loaf tin with baking parchment.

Using a stand mixer or handheld mixer, beat the butter and sugar until creamy. Add the pecans and bananas and beat until smooth. Then add the eggs and beat until completely incorporated. Fold in the flour by hand.

Spoon into the prepared loaf tin and bake for 45 minutes. Remove from the tin onto a wire rack and allow to cool completely.

Beat together the cream cheese and honey, then spoon over the cake and level out.

Decorate with the honeycomb and pecans. Store in the fridge for up to 2 days.

TIRAMISU
\
SERVES 8

350g egg yolks (about 12 egg yolks)
140g icing sugar
500g mascarpone, softened
120ml Marsala
300ml coffee (ideally made in a moka pot)
cocoa powder, for dusting

FOR THE SAVOIARDI
6 large eggs
200g caster sugar
1 teaspoon vanilla extract
a pinch of salt
240g plain flour
60g cornflour
icing sugar, for dusting

Perhaps the most famous Italian dessert, tiramisu relies on a good helping of mascarpone to make the creamy filling which contrasts so well with the coffee and dusting of cocoa.

Preheat the oven to 190°C (170°C fan)/375°F/gas 5. Line a baking tray with baking parchment.

First make the savoiardi. Separate the egg yolks from the whites and whisk the yolks, in a bowl, with half the sugar and the vanilla until firm. In another bowl, and with a thoroughly cleaned and dried whisk, whisk the egg whites with the remaining sugar and the salt until stiff peaks form. Fold into the yolk mixture. Sift the flour and cornflour together and gently fold them into the egg mixture.

Transfer the mixture to a piping bag and snip the end off. Pipe 10cm long fingers onto the prepared baking tray. Bake for about 15 minutes until they are golden and firm to the touch.

Leave to cool, then sprinkle with icing sugar.

Put the egg yolks and icing sugar in a large mixing bowl. Whisk until firm and then fold in the mascarpone.

Pour the Marsala and the coffee into a shallow bowl, then dip in the savoiardi biscuits to soak for few seconds. Form a single layer of soaked savoiardi in a deep serving dish, and cover with a layer of the mascarpone. Repeat the layers, finishing with mascarpone.

Keep refrigerated and generously sprinkle with cocoa powder before serving. Any leftovers will keep in the fridge for up to 2 days.

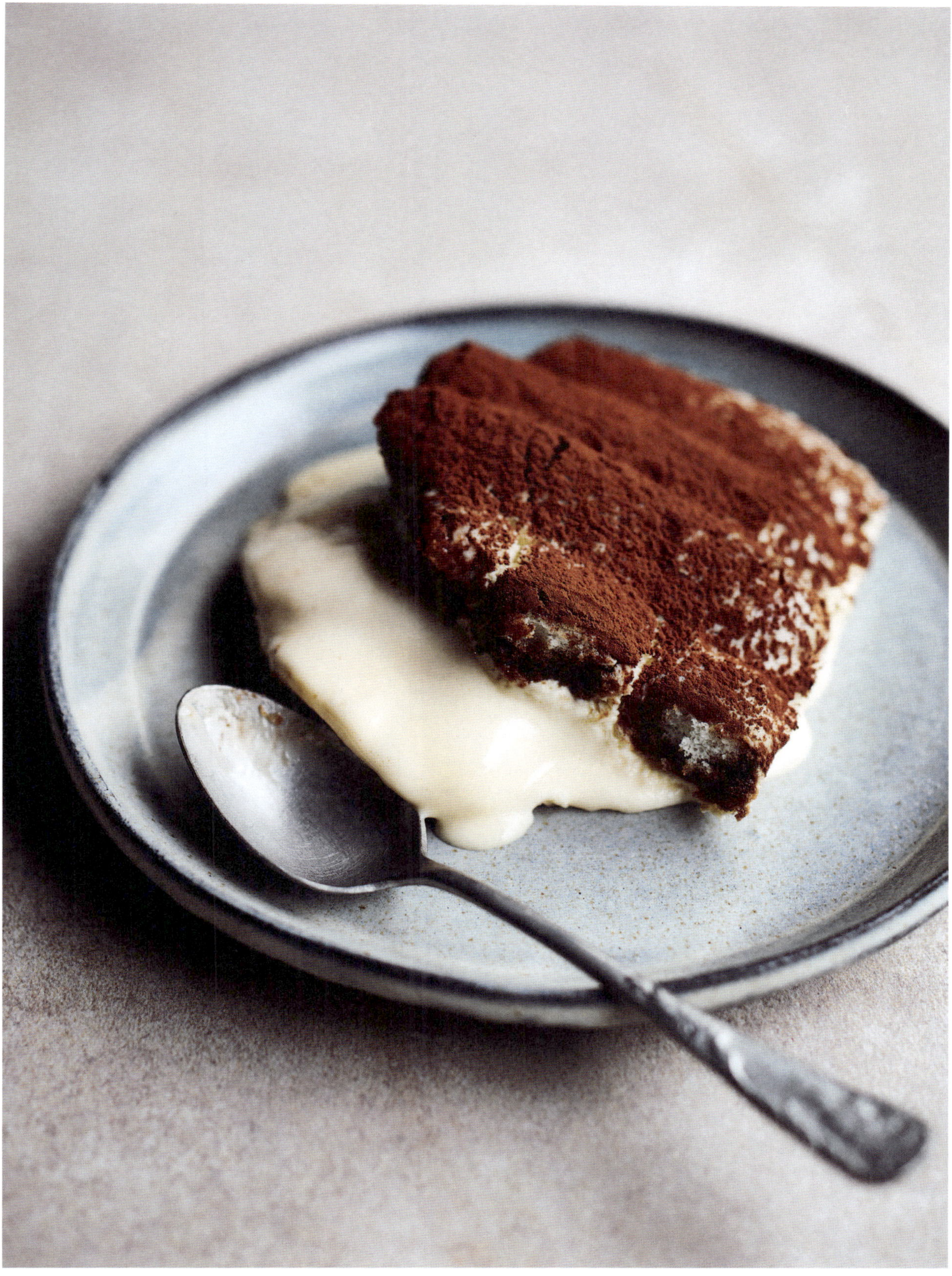

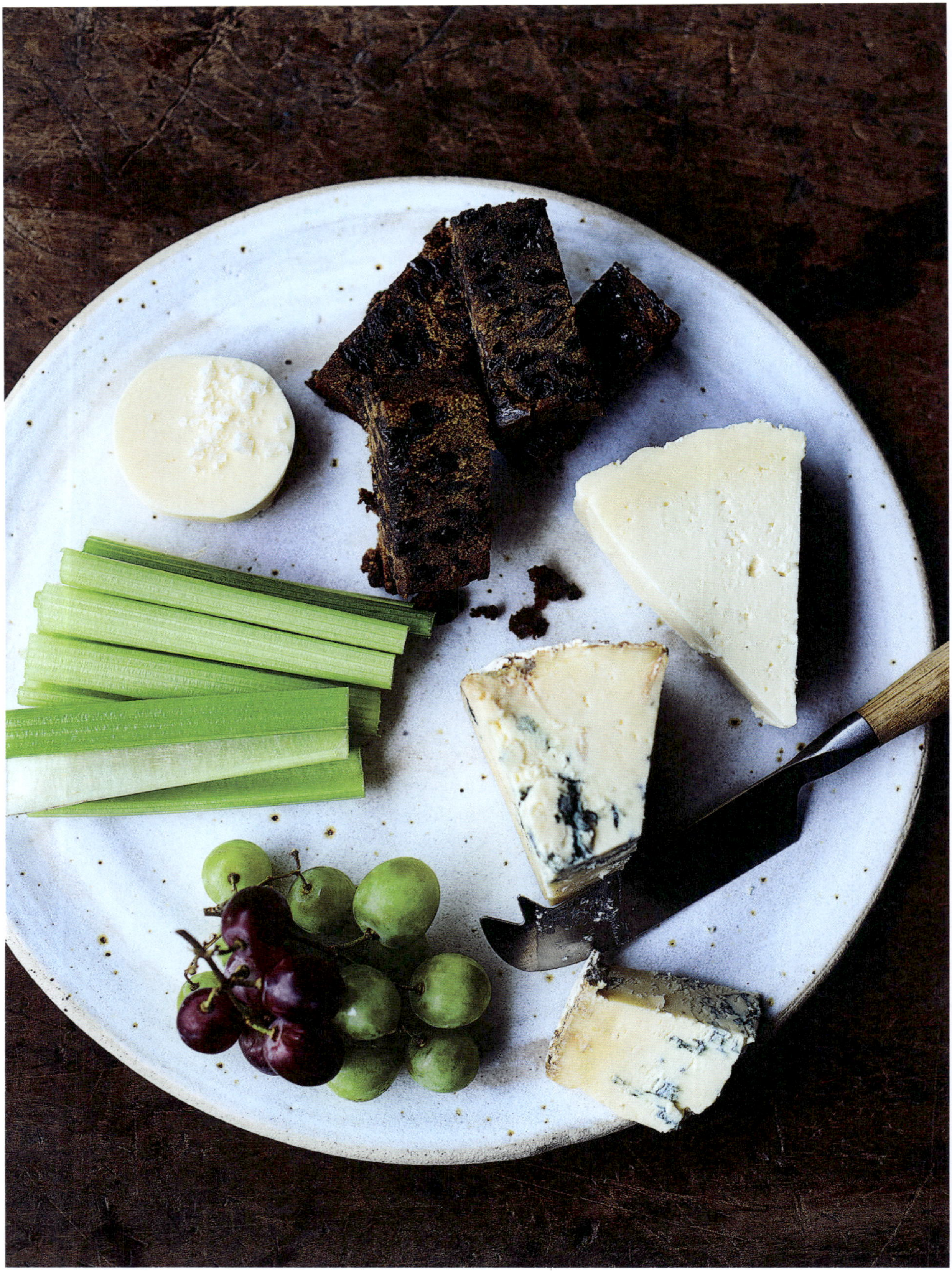

YORKSHIRE BRACK
\
SERVES 6

butter, for greasing
200g raisins
100g glacé cherries, chopped
150g mixed peel
300ml hot, strong Yorkshire tea
200g dark soft brown sugar
225g self-raising flour
1 teaspoon mixed spice
½ teaspoon baking powder
1 egg

TO SERVE
butter
Stilton
Cheddar
grapes
celery

A classic British bake, this brack is a tea loaf made from dried fruits soaked in good old Yorkshire tea. As a celebration of great British produce, serve it alongside hunks of two of our most famous cheeses – Cheddar and Stilton.

Preheat the oven to 170°C (150°C fan)/340°F/gas 3½. Grease a 900g loaf tin.

Put the raisins, glacé cherries and mixed peel in a heatproof bowl and pour over the hot tea. Leave to soak for 30 minutes.

Mix in the remaining ingredients until smooth, then spoon into the prepared tin.

Bake for 1 hour, then remove from the oven and leave in the tin to cool completely.

Slice, spread with butter and serve with Stilton, Cheddar, grapes and celery. Store in an airtight container for up to 4 days.

CARROT CAKE
\
SERVES 8

12 baby carrots
75g caster sugar

FOR THE CAKE
4 eggs
230ml vegetable oil
400g carrots, peeled and grated
150g sultanas or raisins
345g dark soft brown sugar
345g self-raising flour
1 teaspoon baking powder
1 teaspoon ground ginger
1 tablespoon ground cinnamon
1 teaspoon mixed spice

FOR THE ICING
150g butter, softened
300g full-fat cream cheese
150g icing sugar
1 teaspoon vanilla bean paste

A deliciously moist carrot cake, finished with the iconic cream cheese icing and taken up a gear with candied baby carrots for decoration. As good with an afternoon cup of tea as it is as dessert to round off a meal.

Preheat the oven to 160°C (140°C fan)/325°F/gas 3. Line a 28cm round cake tin with baking parchment.

Blanch the baby carrots in a splash of water and the caster sugar until soft. Leave to cool completely.

To make the cake, in a large bowl, beat together the eggs, oil, grated carrots and sultanas. Then beat in the sugar and fold in the flour, baking powder and spices.

Spoon into the prepared tin and bake for 1 hour. Remove from the oven and leave in the tin to cool completely.

Whisk together all the icing ingredients, then spread over the top of the cake in an even layer. Decorate with the candied baby carrots. Store in the fridge for up to 3 days.

BAKED CHEESECAKE
\
SERVES 8

23cm sponge flan
1 teaspoon vanilla bean paste
zest and juice of 1 unwaxed lemon
200g caster sugar
50g cornflour
850g full-fat cream cheese
4 large eggs
175ml double cream

TO SERVE
vanilla ice cream
mixed berries

This is a cheesecake with a difference. Instead of the usual biscuit base made from crumbled biscuits and melted butter, it uses a slab of soft sponge to provide a totally different texture to complement the creamy cheesecake topping.

Preheat the oven to 160°C (140°C fan)/325°F/gas 3.

Slice the sponge in half horizontally to form a 5mm-thick disc and place it in the bottom of a 23cm springform cake tin.

Put the vanilla, lemon zest and juice, sugar, cornflour and cream cheese into a bowl and whisk together. Add the eggs, one at a time, whisking well between each addition. Add the double cream, whisking until the mixture is smooth.

Pour the mixture into the cake tin and tap it lightly on the work surface to settle. Put the cake tin into a roasting tray, then pour hot water into the tray to a depth of 2cm to create a bain-marie. Bake for 1¼–1½ hours until the top is golden and the cheesecake just set. Remove from the oven and allow to cool in the tin.

Transfer to a serving plate. To serve, slice and top with ice cream and mixed berries. Store in the fridge for up to 2 days.

SUMMER BERRY CAKE
\
SERVES 8

FOR THE CAKE
250g caster sugar
250g butter, softened
5 eggs
1 teaspoon vanilla bean paste
250g self-raising flour

FOR THE ICING
400g full-fat cream cheese
100g icing sugar

TO DECORATE
a selection of summer berries
sprigs of mint

The ultimate summer sweet, this berry cake showcases the best of the season's produce to provide a colourful contrast to the pale icing. Simple to throw together but impressive enough to roll out for guests and special occasions.

Preheat the oven to 180°C (160°C fan)/350°F/gas 4. Line a deep 25cm cake tin with greaseproof paper.

Using a stand mixer or handheld mixer, beat the sugar and butter until pale and fluffy. Then beat in the eggs and vanilla and fold in the flour.

Pour the cake mixture into the prepared tin and bake for 1 hour. Leave in the tin to cool completely.

To make the icing, in a bowl, gently beat together the cream cheese and icing sugar.

Top the cake with the icing, then decorate with berries and mint. Store in an airtight container for up to 2 days.

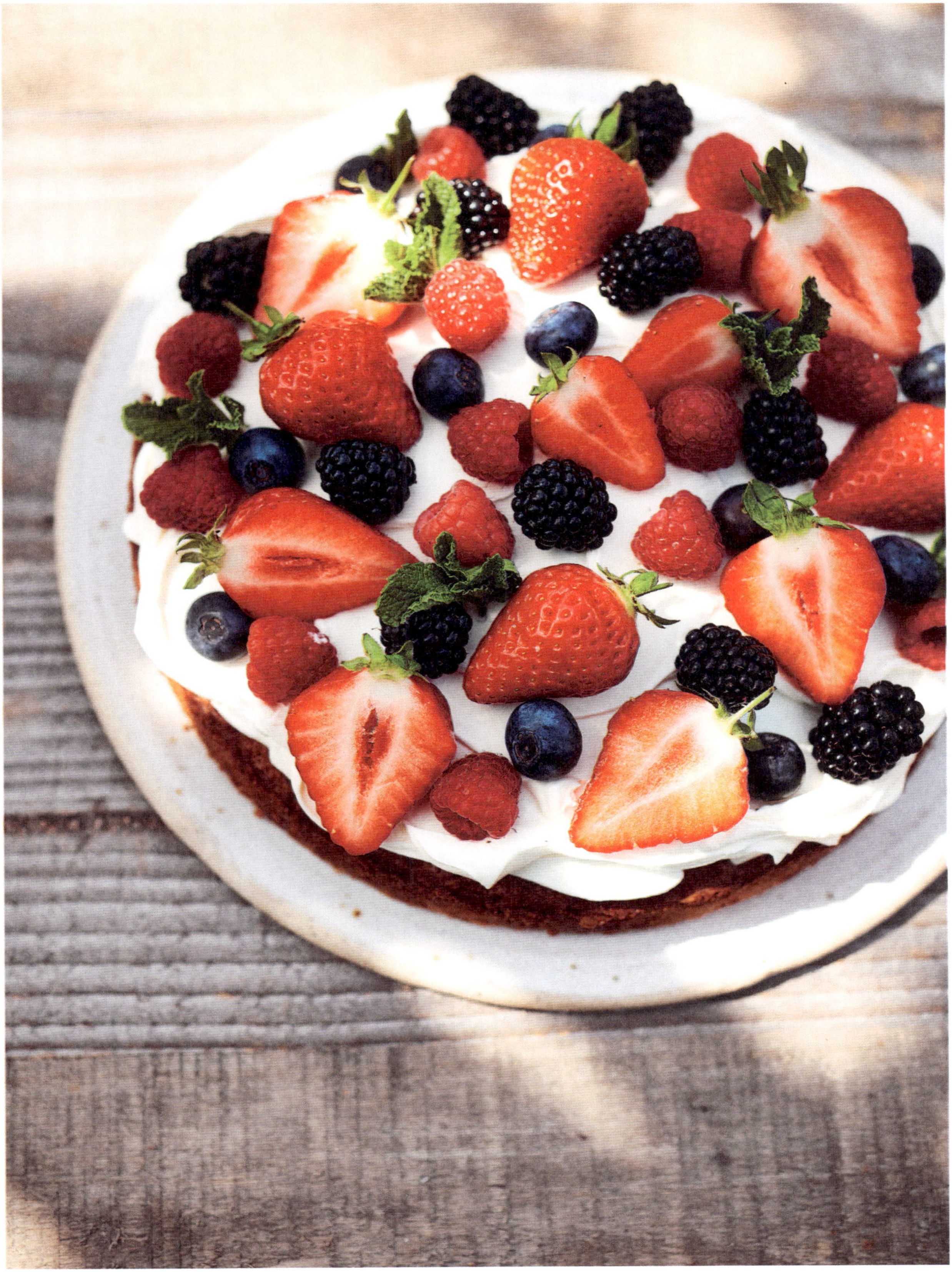

DOLCELATTE AND POACHED PEARS
\
SERVES 4

4 English pears, peeled, halved and cored
1 vanilla pod
50g caster sugar
300ml water
100ml port
250ml red wine
5 juniper berries
5 cloves
2 cinnamon sticks
rind of 1 unwaxed orange
rind of 1 unwaxed lemon

FOR THE DRESSING
100g dolcelatte
100ml crème fraîche
1 teaspoon white wine vinegar
sea salt and freshly ground black pepper

TO SERVE
olive oil, for drizzling
a few chives flowers

This dessert illustrates just how versatile cheese can be when it comes to sweet dishes. Pairing the rich wine-poached pears with a blue cheese dressing offers the most wonderful combination of flavours and contrasting colours to produce a dessert that's as pleasing on the eye as it is on the taste buds.

To poach the pears, place them in a pan with all the remaining ingredients. Bring to the boil, then reduce the heat and simmer for 10 minutes. Transfer to a large, clean jar, cover in the poaching liquid and leave to cool. Seal tight. You can do this up to a month in advance and store the pears in the jar until ready to serve.

To make the dressing, put all the ingredients in a food processor or blender and blitz together.

To serve, spoon the dressing onto plates and sit two pear halves on top of each one. Drizzle with olive oil and sprinkle over some chive flowers.

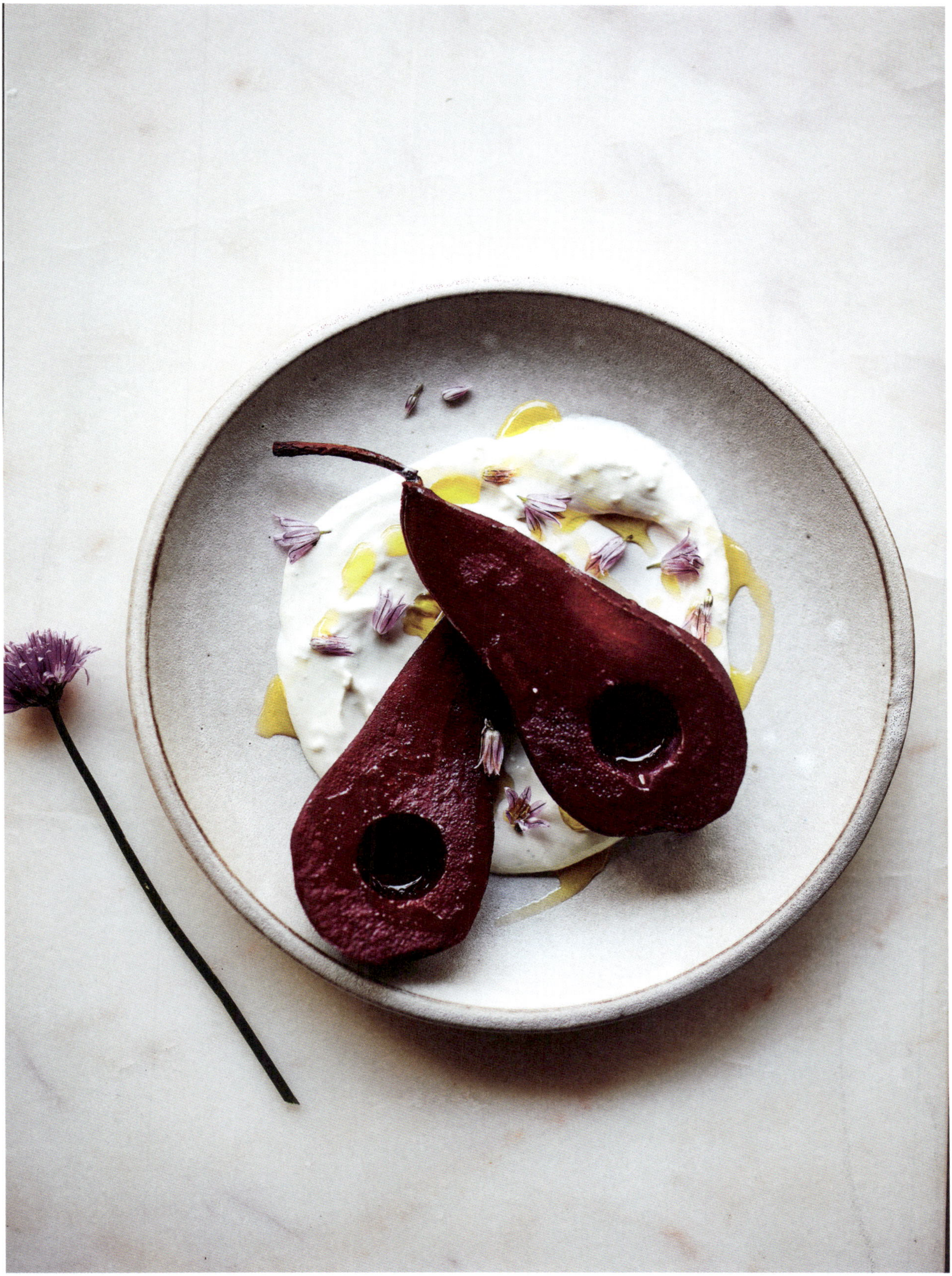

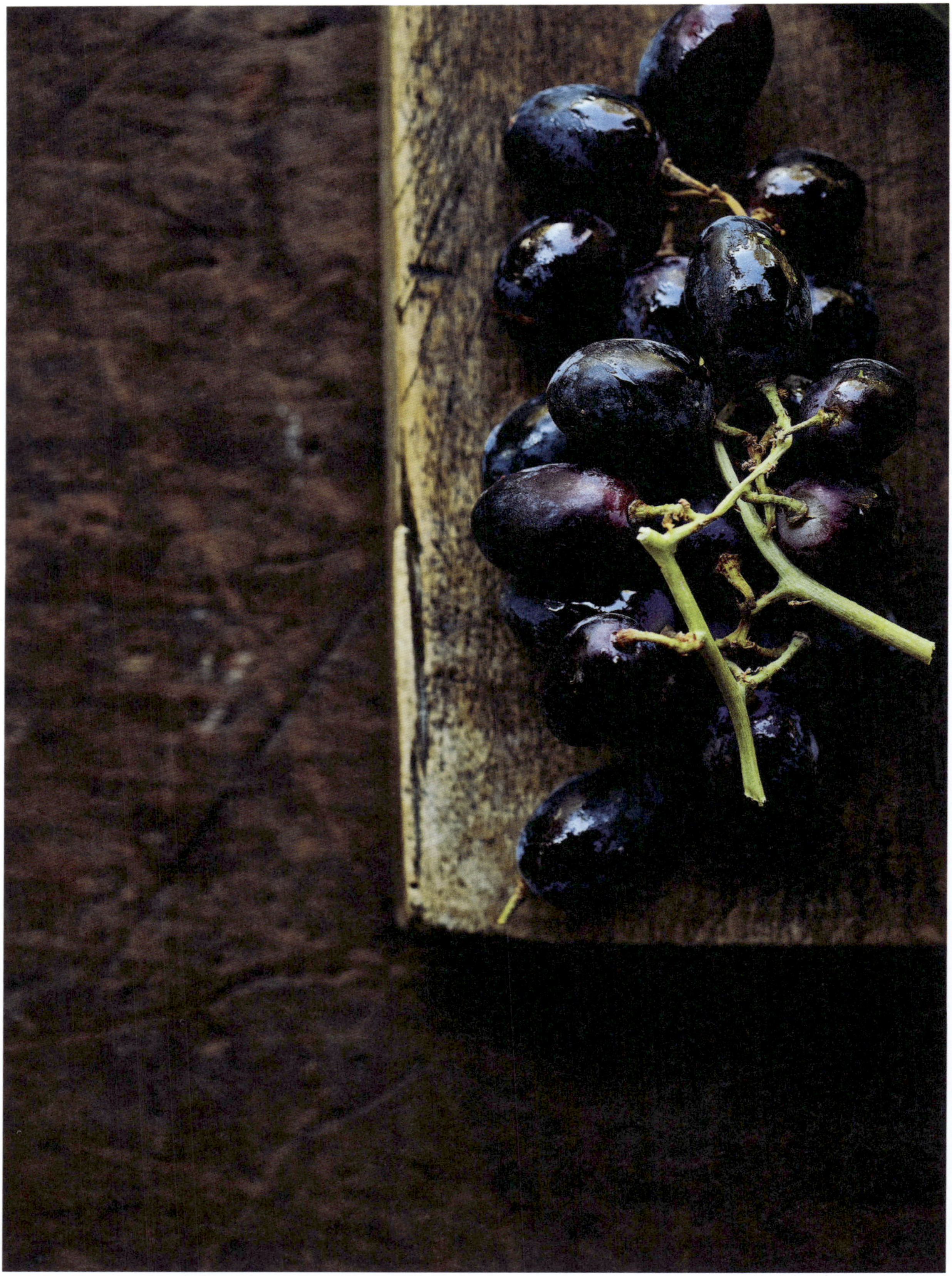

INDEX

4-cheese sarnie 43–5

A
almonds: candied almonds 78
  lamb chops with green olive tapenade, artichokes, almonds and goat's cheese 135
apple tarte tatin 200
Arbroath smokie omelette 114
arrabbiata sauce, mozzarella sandwiches with 83
artichokes: lamb chops with green olive tapenade, artichokes, almonds and goat's cheese 135
asparagus: asparagus and Wensleydale tart 108
  rack of lamb with asparagus and sheep's cheese 155

B
bacon: baked Camembert with bacon, pear chutney and walnut salad 16
  Brie and bacon croissant butter pudding 42
  leek and potato soup with crispy bacon and blue cheese toasts 80
  loaded fries 187
  tartiflette with Tomme 176
banana cake 205
basil pesto 116
beef: best-ever cheeseburger 109
  cottage pie 104
  fillet steak with lobster mac and cheese 128
  fillet steak with Taleggio potatoes and leeks 112
  lasagne 138
  pasta ragout 152
  stroganoff steak with blue cheese 170
  wild garlic barley risotto with fillet steak and pickled kohlrabi 118
beetroot: goat's cheese and beetroot with hazelnut breadcrumbs 66
berries: summer berry cake 212
biscuits, Parmesan and rosemary 84
brack, Yorkshire 209
bread: 4-cheese sarnie 43–5
  blue cheese toasts 80
  cheese and onion bread with pickles 65
  cheese, ham and tomato sandwich 34
  cheesy cob croute-style 46
  crab rarebit toasts 52
  flatbread with ricotta, figs, Parma ham and walnuts 69
  focaccia with Parmesan, Taleggio and rosemary 188
  French onion soup with cheese lids 49
  large cheese, pancetta and ham toastie 26
  mozzarella sandwiches with arrabbiata sauce 83
  muffaletta with slaw 72
  pecan soda bread 23
  smoked haddock Welsh rarebit 86
  warm cheese fondue with nibbles 60
Brie 13
  Brie and bacon croissant butter pudding 42
  cheese, ham and tomato sandwich 34
  hazelnut-fried Brie with rhubarb chutney 38
brioche: cheesy brioche leeks 193
  French toast sandwich 64
  tart brioche with smoked haddock and Tunworth 106
broad beans: Spanish salad 98
broccoli, quiche 124
buffalo chicken wings with crumbled blue cheese 30
bulgur wheat: warm bulgur wheat salad with feta 92
burgers: best-ever cheeseburger 109
burrata 13
  burrata-filled lamb meatballs with tomato sauce and basil pesto 116
  nectarine and burrata salad 78
  strawberries and mozzarella with mint pesto 32
butter paneer curry 120

C
Caesar salad, warm pasta 119
cakes: banana cake 205
  carrot cake 210
  summer berry cake 212
Camembert 13
  baked Camembert with bacon, pear chutney and walnut salad 16
  cheese and onion bread with pickles 65
  Parmesan and rosemary biscuits with baked Camembert, figs and honey 84
cannelloni, mushroom and ricotta 139
carrot cake 210
cauliflower cheese 184
Cheddar 12
  4-cheese sarnie 43–5
  Arbroath smokie omelette 114
  cauliflower cheese 184
  cheese and pickle pies 27
  cheese and thyme straws 24
  cheesy brioche leeks 193
  cheesy cob croute-style 46
  cheesy mashed potatoes 186
  cheesy potato waffles 187
  cottage pie 104
  crab rarebit toasts 52
  double-baked cheese soufflé 50
  fillet steak with lobster mac and cheese 128
  Gouda and Cheddar cheese scones 35
  homemade crumpets with cheese and Marmite 57
  homemade nachos with cheese sauce 70
  large cheese, pancetta and ham toastie 26
  loaded fries 187
  smoked haddock Welsh rarebit 86
  warm cheese fondue with nibbles 60
  Welsh rarebit toastie 100
cheese, varieties 12–13
cheese straws: cheese and thyme straws 24
cheeseboard, best-ever 18–19
cheeseburger, best-ever 109
cheesecake: baked cheesecake 211
  coconut and ginger cheesecake 202
  New York baked raspberry cheesecake 204
cheesy brioche leeks 193
cheesy cob croute-style 46
cheesy mashed potatoes 186
cheesy potato waffles 187
chicken: buffalo chicken wings with crumbled blue cheese 30
  chicken schnitzel with halloumi 122
  chicken stuffed with herbs and ricotta 127
  loaded potato skins with fried chicken 147
  roast chicken with Parmesan baby leeks 162
chicory: chicory, feta and pomegranate salad 101
  Italian sausage gnocchi with frisée 132
chillies: chilli jam 75
  chilli sauce 69
chorizo: warm cheese fondue with nibbles 60
chutney 18
  pear chutney 16
  rhubarb chutney 38
coconut and ginger cheesecake 202
coffee: tiramisu 206
Comté 12
  Comté soufflé 40
  French onion soup with cheese lids 49
  Tenderstem broccoli quiche 124

INDEX \ **217**

wild mushroom tart 178
coquilles St Jacques 125
cottage pie 104
courgette flowers: deep-fried courgette flowers with sauce vierge 53
crab rarebit toasts 52
cream cheese 13
   baked cheesecake 211
   banana cake 205
   carrot cake 210
   coconut and ginger cheesecake 202
   mackerel pâté with melba toast 74
   New York baked raspberry cheesecake 204
   salmon mousse 88
   summer berry cake 212
   tahini dressing 191
croissant butter pudding, Brie and bacon 42
croquetas with Ibérico ham and Manchego 56
crumpets: homemade crumpets with cheese and Marmite 57
Cuddy's Cave: best-ever cheeseburger 109
curry, butter paneer 120

D

Dauphinoise potatoes 186
deep-fried courgette flowers with sauce vierge 53
digestive biscuits: New York baked raspberry cheesecake 204
Dolcelatte 13
   Dolcelatte with poached pears 214
   duck confit salad 58
   tomato tart with Dolcelatte 179
double-baked cheese soufflé 50
dressing, tahini 191
dried fruit: Yorkshire brack 209
duck confit salad 58

E

eggs: Arbroath smokie omelette 114
   Comté soufflé 40
   double-baked cheese soufflé 50
   Tenderstem broccoli quiche 124
   tiramisu 206

F

feta 13
   chicory, feta and pomegranate salad 101
   lamb fillets, fig and feta salad 142
   spanakopita 154
   warm bulgur wheat salad with feta 92
figs: flatbread with ricotta, figs, Parma ham and pecans 69
   lamb fillets, fig and feta salad 142
   Parmesan and rosemary biscuits with baked Camembert, figs and honey 84
   ricotta with figs and pecan soda bread 23
filo pastry: spanakopita 154
fish: Arbroath smokie omelette 114
   mackerel pâté with melba toast 74
   salmon mousse 88
   smoked haddock Welsh rarebit 86
   tart brioche with smoked haddock and Tunworth 106
flatbread with ricotta, figs, Parma ham and pecans 69
focaccia with Parmesan, Taleggio and rosemary 188
fondue, warm cheese 60
French toast sandwich 64
fries: halloumi fries with chilli sauce 63
   loaded fries 187

G

ginger: coconut and ginger cheesecake 202
gnocchi: Italian sausage gnocchi with frisée 132
   lamb with Stilton gnocchi 144
goat's cheese: goat's cheese and red onion tart 115
   goat's cheese and beetroot with hazelnut breadcrumbs 66
   lamb chops with green olive tapenade, artichokes, almonds and goat's cheese 135
   summer vegetable tarts 174
   warm lentil salad with whipped goat's cheese butter 96
gooseberries: chutney 18
Gorgonzola 13
   flatbread with ricotta, figs, Parma ham and pecans 69
   pork chops with Gorgonzola maître d'hôtel butter 148
Gouda 12
   Gouda and Cheddar cheese scones 35
   warm cheese fondue with nibbles 60
gougères, cheese 37
Gruyère 12
   cheese gougères 37
   cheese, ham and tomato sandwich 34
   cheesy cob croute-style 46
   coquilles St Jacques 125
   Dauphinoise potatoes 186
   French toast sandwich 64
   grilled lobster thermidor 169
   pommes aligot 194

H

haddock: smoked haddock Welsh rarebit 86
   tart brioche with smoked haddock and Tunworth 106

halloumi 13
   best-ever cheeseboard 18–19
   chicken schnitzel with halloumi 122
   halloumi fries with chilli sauce 63
   halloumi with chilli jam 75
ham: cheese, ham and tomato sandwich 34
   croquetas with Ibérico ham and Manchego 56
   flatbread with ricotta, figs, Parma ham and pecans 69
   large cheese, pancetta and ham toastie 26
   loaded potato skins with fried chicken 147
   muffaletta with slaw 72
   Spanish salad 98
hazelnuts: goat's cheese and beetroot with hazelnut breadcrumbs 66
   hazelnut-fried Brie with rhubarb chutney 38
   polenta with sautéed mushrooms and hazelnuts 161
herbs: chicken stuffed with herbs and ricotta 127
   herbed lamb rack with ratatouille 131
honey, Parmesan and rosemary biscuits with baked Camembert, figs and 84

I

Ibérico ham: croquetas with Ibérico ham and Manchego 56
Italian sausage gnocchi with frisée 132

J

jam, chilli 75

K

kohlrabi, pickled 118

L

lamb: burrata-filled lamb meatballs with tomato sauce and basil pesto 116
   herbed lamb rack with ratatouille 131
   lamb chops with green olive tapenade, artichokes, almonds and goat's cheese 135
   lamb fillets, fig and feta salad 142
   lamb with Stilton gnocchi 144
   rack of lamb with asparagus and sheep's cheese 155
   stuffed tomatoes 89
lasagne 138
leeks: cheesy brioche leeks 193
   fillet steak with Taleggio potatoes and leeks 112
   leek and potato soup with crispy bacon and blue cheese toasts 80
   roast chicken with Parmesan baby leeks 162

lentils: warm lentil salad with whipped goat's cheese butter 96
lettuce: duck confit salad 58
warm pasta Caesar salad 119
loaded fries 187
loaded potato skins with fried chicken 147
lobster: fillet steak with lobster mac and cheese 128
grilled lobster thermidor 169

M
mac and cheese, fillet steak with lobster 128
mackerel pâté with melba toast 74
Manchego 13
croquetas with Ibérico ham and Manchego 56
Spanish salad 98
Margherita pizza 150
Marmite: 4-cheese sarnie 43–5
homemade crumpets with cheese and Marmite 57
mascarpone 12
pea risotto 158
pumpkin ravioli 164
summer vegetable tarts 174
tiramisu 206
meatballs: burrata-filled lamb meatballs with tomato sauce and basil pesto 116
melba toast, mackerel pâté with 74
mint pesto 32
mortadella: 4-cheese sarnie 43–5
mousse, salmon 88
mozzarella 12–13
4-cheese sarnie 43–5
baked potatoes with sausages and sloppy Joe sauce 134
cheese and pickle pies 27
cheesy mashed potatoes 186
lasagne 138
Margherita pizza 150
mozzarella sandwiches with arrabbiata sauce 83
muffaletta with slaw 72
strawberries and mozzarella with mint pesto 32
stuffed tomatoes 89
muffaletta with slaw 72
mushrooms: mushroom and ricotta cannelloni 139
polenta with sautéed mushrooms and hazelnuts 161
stroganoff steak with blue cheese 170
wild mushroom tart 178

N
nachos: homemade nachos with cheese sauce 70
nectarine and burrata salad with candied almonds 78
New York baked raspberry cheesecake 204

O
olives: green olive tapenade 135
omelette, Arbroath smokie 114
onions: cheese and onion bread with pickles 65
French onion soup with cheese lids 49
goat's cheese and red onion tart 115

P
pancetta: cheese, ham and tomato sandwich 34
French toast sandwich 64
large cheese, pancetta and ham toastie 26
warm cheese fondue with nibbles 60
warm pasta Caesar salad 119
paneer 13
butter paneer curry 120
Parma ham: flatbread with ricotta, figs, Parma ham and pecans 69
Parmesan 12
4-cheese sarnie 43–5
cheese and thyme straws 24
focaccia with Parmesan, Taleggio and rosemary 188
herbed lamb rack with ratatouille 131
Italian sausage gnocchi with frisée 132
Parmesan and rosemary biscuits 84
Parmesan roasties 196
polenta with sautéed mushrooms and hazelnuts 161
roast chicken with Parmesan baby leeks 162
warm pasta Caesar salad 119
pasta: lasagne 138
mushroom and ricotta cannelloni 139
pasta ragout 152
pumpkin ravioli 164
warm pasta Caesar salad 119
pâté: mackerel pâté with melba toast 74
pearl barley: wild garlic barley risotto with fillet steak and pickled kohlrabi 118
pears: dolcelatte with poached pears 214
pear chutney 16
peas: pea risotto 158
Spanish salad 98
pecans: candied pecans 63
duck confit salad 58
flatbread with ricotta, figs, Parma ham and pecans 69
pecan soda bread 23
Pecorino 13
flatbread with ricotta, figs, Parma ham and pecans 69

Margherita pizza 150
pesto: basil pesto 116
mint pesto 32
pickle: cheese and onion bread with pickles 65
cheese and pickle pies 27
pickled kohlrabi 118
pies: cheese and pickle pies 27
cottage pie 104
pizza, Margherita 150
polenta with sautéed mushrooms and hazelnuts 161
pomegranate: chicory, feta and pomegranate salad 101
pommes aligot 194
pork: baked potatoes with sausages and sloppy Joe sauce 134
pasta ragout 152
pork chops with Gorgonzola maître d'hôtel butter 148
potatoes: baked potatoes with sausages and sloppy Joe sauce 134
cheesy mashed potatoes 186
cheesy potato waffles 187
coquilles St Jacques 125
cottage pie 104
Dauphinoise potatoes 186
fillet steak with Taleggio potatoes and leeks 112
Italian sausage gnocchi with frisée 132
lamb with Stilton gnocchi 144
leek and potato soup with crispy bacon and blue cheese toasts 80
loaded fries 187
loaded potato skins with fried chicken 147
Parmesan roasties 196
pommes aligot 194
tartiflette with Tomme 176
warm cheese fondue with nibbles 60
prawns: coquilles St Jacques 125
Provolone 12
muffaletta with slaw 72
puff pastry: apple tarte tatin 200
goat's cheese and red onion tart 115
tomato tart with Dolcelatte 179
pumpkin ravioli 164
purple sprouting broccoli with tahini dressing 191

Q
quiche, Tenderstem broccoli 124

R
ragout, pasta 152
rarebit: crab rarebit toasts 52
smoked haddock Welsh rarebit 86
Welsh rarebit toastie 100
raspberries: baked cheesecake 211

INDEX \ 219

New York baked raspberry cheesecake 204
ratatouille, herbed lamb rack with 131
ravioli, pumpkin 164
Red Leicester 12
  4-cheese sarnie 43–5
  homemade nachos with cheese sauce 70
rhubarb chutney 38
rice: pea risotto 158
ricotta 12
  chicken stuffed with herbs and ricotta 127
  deep-fried courgette flowers with sauce vierge 53
  flatbread with ricotta, figs, Parma ham and pecans 69
  mushroom and ricotta cannelloni 139
  ricotta with figs and pecan soda bread 23
risotto: pea risotto 158
  wild garlic barley risotto with fillet steak and pickled kohlrabi 118
rosemary: focaccia with Parmesan, Taleggio and rosemary 188
  Parmesan and rosemary biscuits 84

S

salads: baked Camembert with bacon, pear chutney and walnut salad 16
  chicory, feta and pomegranate salad 101
  duck confit salad 58
  lamb fillets, fig and feta salad 142
  nectarine and burrata salad with candied almonds 78
  slaw 72
  Spanish salad 98
  warm bulgur wheat salad with feta 92
  warm lentil salad with whipped goat's cheese butter 96
  warm pasta Caesar salad 119
salami: 4-cheese sarnie 43–5
  muffaletta with slaw 72
salmon mousse 88
sandwiches: 4-cheese sarnie 43–5
  cheese, ham and tomato sandwich 34
  French toast sandwich 64
  mozzarella sandwiches with arrabbiata sauce 83
sauce, chilli 69
sauce vierge, deep-fried courgette flowers with 53
sausages: baked potatoes with sausages and sloppy Joe sauce 134
  Italian sausage gnocchi with frisée pasta ragout 152
savoiardi: tiramisu 206
scallops: coquilles St Jacques 125
schnitzels: chicken schnitzel with halloumi 122

scones, Gouda and Cheddar cheese 35
shallot tarte tatin with sheep's curd 166
Sharpham Elmhirst: best-ever cheeseboard 18–19
Sharpham Rushmore: apple tarte tatin 200
Sharpham Savour: best-ever cheeseboard 18–19
sheep's cheese, rack of lamb with asparagus and 155
sheep's curd, shallot tarte tatin with 166
slaw, muffaletta with 72
sloppy Joe sauce, baked potatoes with sausages and 134
smoked haddock: smoked haddock Welsh rarebit 86
  tart brioche with smoked haddock and Tunworth 106
smoked salmon mousse 88
soda bread, pecan 23
soufflé: Comté soufflé 40
  double-baked cheese soufflé 50
soups: French onion soup with cheese lids 49
  leek and potato soup with crispy bacon and blue cheese toasts 80
spanakopita 154
Spanish salad 98
spinach: spanakopita 154
sriracha sauce: buffalo chicken wings with crumbled blue cheese 30
  homemade nachos with cheese sauce 70
Stilton 13
  blue cheese toasts 80
  buffalo chicken wings with crumbled blue cheese 30
  lamb with Stilton gnocchi 144
  stroganoff steak with blue cheese 170
  Yorkshire brack 209
strawberries and mozzarella with mint pesto 32
stroganoff steak with blue cheese 170
stuffed tomatoes 89
summer berry cake 212
summer vegetable tarts 174

T

tahini dressing, purple sprouting broccoli with 191
Taleggio 13
  fillet steak with Taleggio potatoes and leeks 112
  focaccia with Parmesan, Taleggio and rosemary 188
  loaded potato skins with fried chicken 147
tapenade, green olive 135
tart brioche with smoked haddock and Tunworth 106
tartiflette with Tomme 176
tarts: apple tarte tatin 200
  asparagus and Wensleydale tart 108
  goat's cheese and red onion tart 115
  shallot tarte tatin with sheep's curd 166
  summer vegetable tarts 174
  tomato tart with Dolcelatte 179
  wild mushroom tart 178
tea loaf: Yorkshire brack 209
tiramisu 206
toasties: large cheese, pancetta and ham toastie 26
  Welsh rarebit toastie 100
tomatoes: arrabbiata sauce 83
  burrata-filled lamb meatballs with tomato sauce and basil pesto 116
  cheese, ham and tomato sandwich 34
  crab rarebit toasts 52
  Margherita pizza 150
  stuffed tomatoes 89
  tomato tart with Dolcelatte 179
Tomme d'Auvergne 12
  pommes aligot 194
  tartiflette with Tomme 176
tortillas: homemade nachos with cheese sauce 70
Tunworth 13
  best-ever cheeseboard 18–19
  tart brioche with smoked haddock and Tunworth 106

V

vegetables: summer vegetable tarts 174

W

waffles, cheesy potato 187
walnuts: baked Camembert with bacon, pear chutney and walnut salad 16
warm cheese fondue with nibbles 60
Welsh rarebit: smoked haddock Welsh rarebit 86
  Welsh rarebit toastie 100
Wensleydale 12
  asparagus and Wensleydale tart 108
  wild garlic barley risotto with fillet steak and pickled kohlrabi 118

Y

Yorkshire brack 209

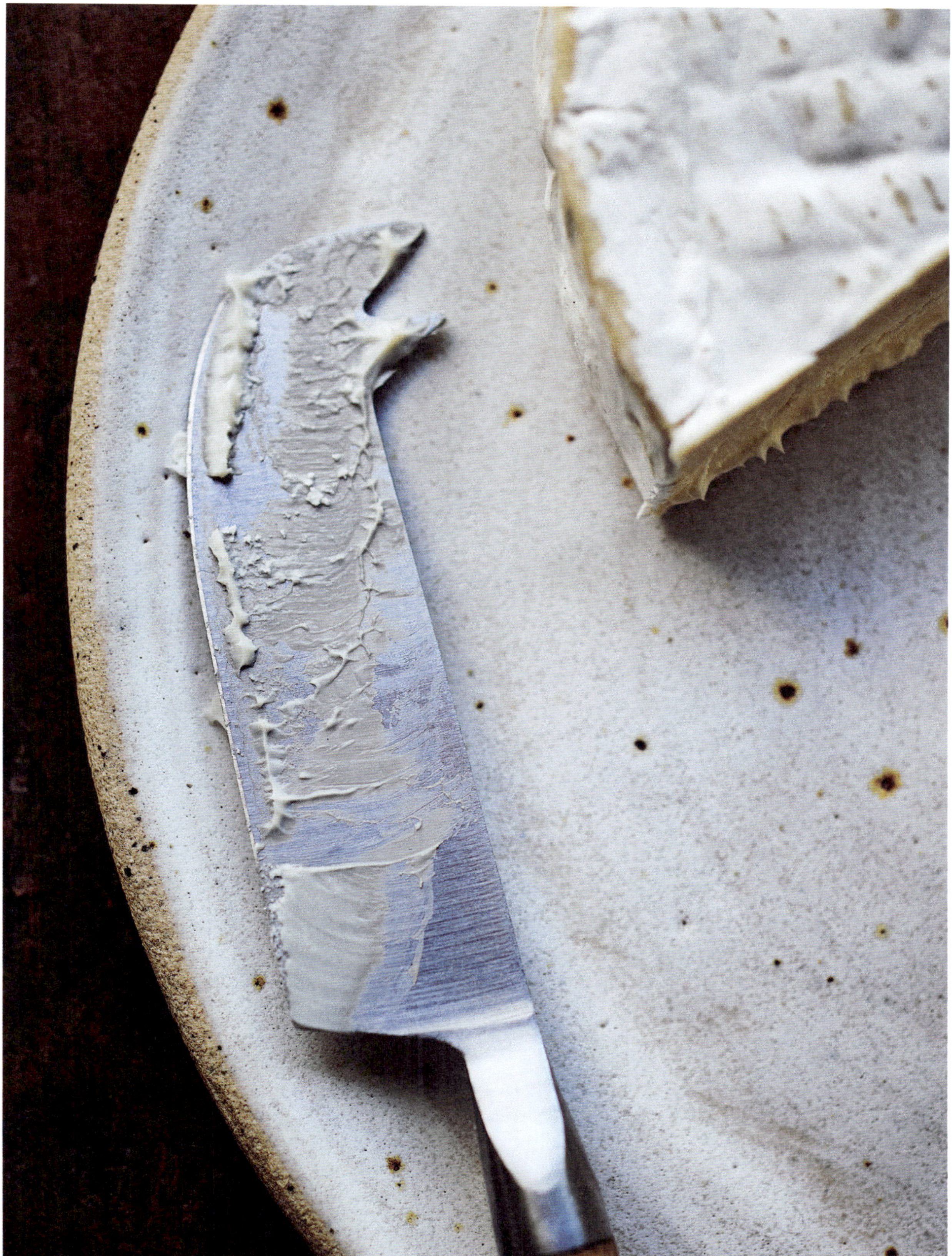

ACKNOWLEDGEMENTS
\

I would like to thank all the team at Quadrille for another great cookbook. Your help and constant phone calls help us all get it done on time. Along with the help of a super team who make it happen – from Dan the Man, who is becoming a bit of a legend behind the camera, to Sam Head and Alan Thatcher with another sterling effort. Thanks to all the team back at the head office at Limelight for keeping my diary still busy after 30 odd years.

But, most importantly, and lastly, thank you to all the producers, not just in the UK, but all over the place, who work tirelessly to produce the cheese that we all know and love. May that continue with gusto well after I am gone. Thank you.

DEDICATION
\

I dedicate this book to several chefs we have lost recently – Dave Myers, Alastair Little and Bill Granger, to name just a few.

MANAGING DIRECTOR Sarah Lavelle
EDITORIAL DIRECTOR Sophie Allen
PROJECT EDITOR Vicky Orchard
SENIOR DESIGNER Gemma Hayden
PHOTOGRAPHER Dan Jones
PHOTOGRAPHER'S ASSISTANT Rosie Alsop
HOME ECONOMIST AND FOOD STYLIST Sam Head
FOOD STYLIST Alan Thatcher
PROP STYLIST Faye Wears
HAIR AND MAKE UP Alice Theobald
PRODUCTION DIRECTOR Stephen Lang
PRODUCTION MANAGER Sabeena Atchia

Quadrille, Penguin Random House UK, One Embassy Gardens, 8 Viaduct Gardens, London SW11 7BW

Quadrille Publishing Limited is part of the Penguin Random House group of companies whose addresses can be found at global.penguinrandomhouse.com

Penguin Random House UK

Text © James Martin 2024
Photography © Dan Jones 2024
Design © Quadrille 2024
The images on pages 24, 40, 61, 94, 140, 141 and the endpapers were taken at La Fromagerie, Marylebone, London.

James Martin has asserted his right to be identified as the author of this Work in accordance with the Copyright, Designs and Patents Act 1988.

No part of this book may be used or reproduced in any manner for the purpose of training artificial intelligence technologies or systems. In accordance with Article 4(3) of the DSM Directive 2019/790, Penguin Random House expressly reserves this work from the text and data mining exception.

Published by Quadrille in 2024.
www.penguin.co.uk

A CIP catalogue record for this book is available from the British Library.

ISBN 978 1837831 30 2
10 9 8 7 6 5 4 3 2

Printed and bound in Germany by Mohn Media.

The authorised representative in the EEA is Penguin Random House Ireland, Morrison Chambers, 32 Nassau Street, Dublin D02 YH68.

Penguin Random House is committed to a sustainable future for our business, our readers and our planet. This book is made from Forest Stewardship Council® certified paper.

MIX
Paper | Supporting responsible forestry
FSC® C018179